THE OSBORNE/McGRAW-HILL

MS-DOS®
USER'S GUIDE

Paul Hoffman
Tamara Nicoloff

Osborne/McGraw-Hill
Berkeley, California

Published by
Osborne/McGraw-Hill
2600 Tenth Street
Berkeley, California 94710
U.S.A.

For information on translations and book
distributors outside of the U.S.A., please write to
Osborne/McGraw-Hill at the above address.

A list of trademarks referenced in this book appears on page 313.

The tables in this book are available on disk from Proper Software,
2000 Center Street, Suite 1024, Berkeley, CA 94704. The disk costs $10
(which includes tax, shipping, and handling) and also contains public
domain programs that can be run on an IBM PC.

MS-DOS® User's Guide

4567890 DODO 8987

ISBN 0-07-881131-7

Karen Hanson, Acquisitions Editor
Jean Stein, Technical Editor
Ralph Baumgartner, Erick Schmitt, Technical Reviewers
Ted Gartner, Copy Editor
Jan Benes, Text Design
Yashi Okita, Cover Design

TABLE OF CONTENTS

ACKNOWLEDGMENTS

Pam Edstrom, Chris Larson, and Amy Powers at Microsoft Corporation helped our research into MS-DOS. Dale Gifford gave excellent technical hints. Jack Krasner supplied guidance on accounting packages. Bob Kermish from Computerland of Oakland, CA, answered many IBM questions. Bonnie Bozorg and Karen Nebelkopf helped us with word processing. We thank them all.

Paul Hoffman
Tamara Nicoloff

INTRODUCTION

This book will be useful to anyone who owns a microcomputer with the MS-DOS operating system, such as the IBM PC or PCjr. It contains information about what MS-DOS is, what you can do with it, how to give it commands, and what application programs (such as word processing and accounting packages) you can use with it.

This book answers the questions that most MS-DOS users ask: What is MS-DOS? What can it do for me? Do I need to spend a lot of time learning about MS-DOS? What software can I use with my MS-DOS computer?

Although this book is primarily written so novice users can easily understand it, it also contains a wealth of useful information for advanced users. If you have been confused by your manual, this book will help you understand many of the concepts it presents.

Some manufacturers have modified MS-DOS to suit their computers, and some have even given it a new name (such as PC-DOS for the IBM PC). However, these variations of MS-DOS are usually very minor. This book is written for all varieties of MS-DOS versions 1 and 2.

Why You Should Read This Book

Whether they are new to their computer or have been using it for years, most computer users are not familiar with all of the functions their MS-DOS operating system can perform. This book will provide a gentle but direct introduction to these functions. The book also helps you judge how relevant each MS-DOS feature is to your own needs. The book has several other important features, including:

- **A complete list of all MS-DOS commands.** All of the MS-DOS commands are presented in Chapter 3. They are organized in functional groups, so that you can quickly determine the relationship between commands. Many examples of each command are provided to show its use in a range of situations.

- **Numerous clear and comprehensive illustrations.** Each example shows practical uses of important MS-DOS concepts.

- **A chapter on how to handle emergencies.** Chapter 5 shows you what to do about "crashed" disks, power failures, and accidentally erased files; it also provides tips for avoiding disasters.

- **Detailed guides of how to find application programs, magazines, and books.** Chapters 6 and 7 provide much more than just the common sources. They also give advice on how and where to shop, and they describe easy methods for keeping up with the rapidly changing market.

- **An up-to-date description of MS-DOS.** This book tells you about versions 1 and 2 of MS-DOS. If you have version 1, which was released earlier and includes fewer commands, don't worry that you won't be able to follow instructions. The book always notes which commands or comments apply only to version 2.

- **Non-technical explanations of advanced features.** Chapter 4 on advanced MS-DOS usage will help you understand why MS-DOS is a superior operating system. To minimize confusion, advanced features are described after the more common MS-DOS commands.

This book differs in several important ways from others you may have seen on the same subject. First, it doesn't assume that the MS-DOS manual that came with your computer is a sufficient guide to the individual MS-DOS commands. It fills in any gaps in the manual, providing complete explanations. Nor does this book insist that MS-DOS users need to learn how to program in BASIC. Instead, it tells you how to buy already existing programs that can do almost anything.

Third, this book doesn't suggest that you need to understand all of the MS-DOS features and commands. On the contrary, you will probably only use about ten commands regularly during the life of your computer. If some features won't benefit you, the book clearly states that.

And finally, this book doesn't assume that you own an IBM PC. Whatever MS-DOS computer you have, this book will be valuable to you. Although the IBM PC's version of MS-DOS is explained in depth, most popular MS-DOS computers have very similar features in their versions of MS-DOS.

How This Book Is Organized

The authors remember vividly how hard it is to learn about computers and how frustrating first experiences can be without a good guide. This book is full of practical advice, not just descriptions of the operating system. The book's style and organization permit a quick and easy understanding so that you can use the MS-DOS commands as soon as possible.

The first two chapters present the background you need to get started with MS-DOS; the rest of the book gives you the specific methods to work with MS-DOS. To get the most out of this book, you should read the beginning three chapters and at least skim the rest. More advanced users can skim over most of the first two chapters and concentrate on the commands themselves; you should at least read the beginning of each chapter to ensure that you get a feel for all of the information that is presented.

Because the descriptions are comprehensive and complete, some computer terms have been used when the common language would not suffice. However, all technical terms throughout the book are italicized and defined when they first appear and are consistently used afterward. They are also listed in the glossary. The following summarizes the contents of each chapter and appendix.

Chapter 1 presents an introduction to the MS-DOS operating system, which includes answering common questions such as, "What does an operating system do?" and, "How do I work with MS-DOS?" It also describes how MS-DOS manages the various pieces of hardware in your system. The chapter is aimed at novice users, but is also helpful if you have used other operating systems, such as CP/M, but are new to MS-DOS.

Chapter 2 illustrates how the MS-DOS commands are commonly used. It explains the basics of running MS-DOS and introduces you to using files, directories, and batch files. The sample session at the end of the chapter gives you an example of how your new knowledge might be used.

Most of your interaction with your computer will be through MS-DOS commands. Chapter 3 presents a full description of these commands. The commands are grouped by their function (for instance, a group of commands that show the contents of your files), with the most commonly used commands presented first. Beginning users only need to read the first three function groups (file maintenance, file output, and disk maintenance) to be able to use most of MS-DOS's features. Chapter 3 is also a reference which can be used as specific information is needed.

Chapter 4 presents advanced information about MS-DOS, including version 2's tree-like directory structure. The chapter is useful to advanced MS-DOS users, as well as novices with hard disk systems. However, beginning users do not need to read this chapter before using MS-DOS.

When you have used your computer for a few weeks, you will probably need to read Chapter 5, which discusses emergencies, how to handle them, and how to prevent them. It also lists some programs and application packages that are available to help you recover from disasters or to prevent disasters from happening (such as programs which make copies of copy-protected diskettes).

Chapter 6 looks at many popular application programs and discusses how to buy them. As you use your computer more, you will probably want to purchase software that is tailored for your particular needs. The chapter describes the types of programs available, lists hundreds of products in all major fields of software, and tells you how to shop for them.

Chapter 7 discusses magazines and books that will tell you more about MS-DOS, MS-DOS products, and computers in general. The chapter covers several popular magazines and books; it also suggests ways to save time and money while obtaining a reference collection.

Appendix A contains a short alphabetical guide to the MS-DOS commands. Appendix B describes the differences between the MS-DOS versions. Appendix C describes how to determine if a computer is IBM PC compatible or not. Appendix D tells you what you should look for when purchasing a computer; it also provides comparative information on more than 20 MS-DOS computers. Appendix E lists names and addresses of the hardware and software manufacturers mentioned throughout the book.

Finally, Appendix F is a complete glossary. You can use it as a quick reference for unfamiliar words or phrases, although most terms are defined in the chapters when they are first used.

A User's Guide and a Reference Manual

As mentioned earlier, this book is designed to be used as an MS-DOS introduction and a reference manual. If you are using this book as a reference, Appendix A gives an alphabetical summary of the commands, their syntax, and the section in which they are discussed in Chapter 3.

Throughout the book, you will find subjects that are important to beginners as well as to advanced users. The beginning of each section tells you for whom the information is intended, so that you can determine what material is important to you.

While you read this book, remember that MS-DOS provides you with a way to communicate with your computer. Although it has a large number of features, you only need to know a few of them to use it effectively.

We hope that your experiences with MS-DOS and this book are successful.

PH
TN
1984

1

INTRODUCING MS-DOS

What MS-DOS Does
How MS-DOS Uses
   Disks and Files
A Brief History of MS-DOS
What MS-DOS Can't Do

Why learn about MS-DOS? If you are like most people, the main reason you own a computer is because you want to run *application programs,* such as word processing and accounting programs, that are tailored to solve specific problems or perform certain tasks.

Application programs are valuable, and this book devotes a lot of attention to them in Chapter 6. However, application programs can't do everything. Many of these application programs assume that you already know how to use MS-DOS's commands, so they will not include instructions about all of the functions that are necessary to support the program. Therefore, you may find that some tasks you want to perform (for example, formatting a new disk to prepare it for use) are not covered by your application programs. They can only be done with your operating system, MS-DOS.

Formatting disks is only one small part of MS-DOS's role. The MS-DOS operating system is a program that manages your computer's *hardware* including its disk drives, keyboard, monitor, and printer) and allows you to run other programs. In fact, you can't do much on your computer without an operating system.

WHAT MS-DOS DOES

You might think of MS-DOS as similar to the cockpit of an airplane. Without it, there is plenty of potential, but you cannot fly the airplane. The operating system allows you (the pilot) to control your computer by telling it "where to go" and what to do. Like the controls in an airplane's cockpit, the operating system coordinates the parts of the computer and gives you an easy method for controlling them. In this chapter, you will begin to learn how MS-DOS performs this role.

MS-DOS is an acronym for *MicroSoft Disk Operating System*; it is a generic name for the operating system that is licensed by Microsoft Corporation for use on several microcomputers made by different manufacturers. (Some of these computer manufacturers have altered MS-DOS for their computers and given it a new name, such as *PC-DOS* or *Z-DOS*.)

From the name *disk operating system* (or *DOS*), you might think that all MS-DOS does is manage your disks. The term DOS has remained in the technological vocabulary because many years ago operating systems did little more than control disks. MS-DOS does much more than this, however. It provides a way to tell the computer which program or command you want to run, where it will find the program or command, and what it should do with it. For instance, it might send information to the display screen, to a printer, or to a communications port to be sent to another system. The operating system can be thought of as working on two levels.

The first level is that of a hardware management system: MS-DOS coordinates your computer's *central processing unit* (*CPU*) (which is the microprocessor chip that acts as the "brains" of your computer) with the rest of your computer's hardware. In this capacity MS-DOS takes the character you type on your computer's keyboard, codes it into a form that the CPU can understand, and then displays it on your monitor in a form that you can understand. For instance, if you are using a spreadsheet or word processing program, MS-DOS acts as the go-between that converts the electronic signals your keyboard generates into control codes that your application program can use. MS-DOS also performs small tasks that are related to using programs, such as formatting a disk or telling you what files are on a disk.

The second level on which MS-DOS operates is the utility function. In this capacity, MS-DOS executes *commands,* which let you interact directly with your computer. These commands perform such functions as naming files on the disk or copying files from one disk to another.

MS-DOS treats its own commands just like application programs. These commands, however, are more limited than are most application programs. They do not perform tasks like word processing or accounting; instead, they are used for maintaining and housekeeping your computer. Each command has a name that is usually easy to remember. For example, to copy information from one disk to another, you use the COPY command. All of these commands are discussed in Chapter 3.

Most of this book is about this second utility level of MS-DOS. In Chapters 2 through 5, you learn to use the MS-DOS commands for day-to-day upkeep of your files and disks. This chapter, however, looks more closely at the first level, the one in which MS-DOS works to coordinate all of the parts of your computer system. Two major elements of this coordinator role are communicating between hardware components and running application programs.

Communicating With Your Hardware

The CPU in your computer can't function well without an operating system. It needs a master traffic manager to coordinate all of the information that it gets from the keyboard, the disk drives, and other hardware in your computer. MS-DOS coordinates the hardware, and it lets the CPU communicate with almost any other part of your computer. For example, without the operating system, the CPU has no way to find data and programs on the disks.

After you load the operating system (usually when you first turn on your computer), it is kept in the computer's random-access memory (*RAM*). RAM is like a huge scratchpad filled with numbers and instructions; as a program runs, it reads some of the contents of RAM and changes some of the information in it. RAM memory is temporary; that is, it is only maintained by the electric power in your computer. When you turn off your computer, all of the information in RAM is forgotten (which is why a power failure can be so disastrous when you are using your computer). Any information in RAM is lost as soon as power is cut, even if it is off for just an instant. A few of the MS-DOS computers have a battery backup, which prevents RAM from losing data during power failures.

Although the CPU does not need help from the operating system to communicate with RAM, it is important to know a bit about RAM since that is where all of your programs stay while they are being run. You can imagine RAM as being like a set of many boxes called bytes. Each *byte* is equal to the amount of memory needed to store a single keyboard character (like a Q or a @). The amount of RAM that you have in your computer is measured in *K*, or *kilobytes.* A kilobyte equals 1024 bytes.

Returning to the analogy of RAM as a set of boxes, you can imagine each byte, or box, to be divided into eight compartments, called *bits,* which are either full or empty (see Figure 1-1). As you can see, each box has a number, known as its *address,* which tells its position in RAM. The CPU constantly uses these addresses to access the contents of the boxes. The CPU also receives data from outside sources (such as the disk or the keyboard) and places it in RAM. The contents of RAM are altered as it performs tasks like calculations and comparisons of numbers.

The process of putting data into RAM from sources like the keyboard, and alternately taking information from RAM and sending it to a different hardware device like the display screen, is called *I/O*, or *input/output*. Every time that you "read" information from some hardware device like a disk drive, or "write" information to a hardware device like a printer, MS-DOS performs I/O.

A *device* is simply a piece of hardware that uses I/O. For instance, a printer is a common device that you probably own; other common devices are disk drives and monitors. Most MS-DOS computers have plugs (called *ports*) to

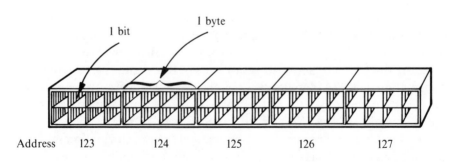

Figure 1-1.   Example of bits and bytes

connect them to other hardware devices. The two common types of ports are *serial* and *parallel*. The difference is based on internal methods that the device connected to the port uses to communicate with the computer. This difference between the two methods does not affect the performance of the device, but it does mean that you have to be careful in selecting the proper type of device for the ports on your computer. You cannot connect a serial printer to a parallel printer port or vice versa; nothing will happen. (Generally, only printers are attached to parallel ports; most other external devices, such as modems, are attached to serial ports.)

When the CPU needs to communicate with other hardware, it simply calls on the portion of the operating system that knows about your hardware. All of these processes happen in a matter of microseconds — so quickly that you often don't value the importance of what is being accomplished. For instance, if you run a word processing program, the program will ask MS-DOS for each character you type on the keyboard. In this case, the program tells MS-DOS, "I'm ready for a keyboard character; has the user typed one? If not, I'll wait until it is typed."

Running Application Programs

You may have noticed that the last example described a process of communication, not just between hardware devices, but between hardware and a software application program. The second important part of MS-DOS's traffic manager role is to help your programs run smoothly. Any program that you run can ask the operating system for help in communicating with your hardware. For example, a word processing program may need to know how many disk drives you have in your computer. Instead of having to know all of the computer commands to figure this out, it can just ask the operating system.

In its role as the intermediary between the CPU and an application program, MS-DOS performs two important tasks for you: it gets the program you want to run and places it in RAM, and it helps the program perform I/O. For instance, when you tell MS-DOS that you want to do word processing, you are really instructing it to get the word processing program off the disk, load it into RAM, and tell the CPU where in the program to start.

The operating system also translates an application program's requests into a standard language so that the same program can be used on different computers. This is why you can use some programs on computers made by many different manufacturers. For instance, a program can say to the operating system, "Print these characters on the screen," without having to know anything about what that particular computer requires for its display. Thus, even though computers that run MS-DOS may be quite different, a program can run on any of them since MS-DOS helps it communicate with the hardware in a standard way.

Most people who use MS-DOS as their operating system do so because there are so many application programs for it. As you will see in Chapter 6, there are thousands of application programs that run with MS-DOS (that is, they require the MS-DOS operating system in order to run at all). However, since some software is written for other operating systems (such as CP/M, which is discussed later in this chapter), not every application program will run on your computer. You must be sure that the program you buy runs with MS-DOS as its operating system or you will not be able to use it on your MS-DOS computer. Since some programs require certain hardware, such as a specific printer or a certain amount of RAM, you should be sure that you have the correct hardware necessary before buying any software.

You have seen how MS-DOS takes information from one device and transfers it to another. This process occurs so commonly in the day-to-day transfer of information to and from disk files that it is worthwhile to look more closely at what files are and how they are stored on disks.

HOW MS-DOS USES DISKS AND FILES

When you save data on a disk, the information is stored in a file. Storing information in files is like organizing data into file folders in a filing cabinet. A *file* is a collection of information identified with a unique name that you assign. Files are basic to using your computer; without them, your work would be lost when your computer was turned off.

The information in a file may consist of text (such as a memo), data (such as a mailing list), or a program (such as word processing). The file can be any length, limited only by the space available on the disk on which it is stored. When you want a program to work on a file (either to get information out of the file or to add information to the file), you simply use the command to access a file and tell the program the file's name.

Files are stored on disks or diskettes. A *disk* is a round piece of rigid material covered with magnetic media; a *diskette* (or floppy disk) is a flexible version of a disk. Most of this book's discussions refer to diskettes, but almost all MS-DOS commands work exactly the same with either disks or diskettes. This book will use the term diskette to refer specifically to flexible diskettes and the term disk for broader references that apply both to disks and diskettes.

What happens when MS-DOS retrieves stored files from a disk for you?

The disk spins at a high speed while the disk head moves in and out (a disk head is similar to the heads on a tape recorder). The movement is similar to selecting a song on a record player. When you ask to look at a file, the head first moves to the *directory,* a special area on the disk that holds information about each file. It finds the location of the file you want and then moves to that file on the disk.

You may wonder how the disk head finds the file. There are entries in the directory that contain two numbers for each file: the *track* and the *sector.* MS-DOS uses this information to pinpoint the location of each file on the disk. The number of bytes in each sector is constant on a disk, but different disk drives on your computer may have different numbers of bytes per sector and different numbers of sectors per track. Fortunately, MS-DOS keeps all of this straight for you.

Figure 1-2 illustrates tracks and sectors on a diskette. The track number is essentially a measure of how far the file is from the edge of the disk. Tracks are

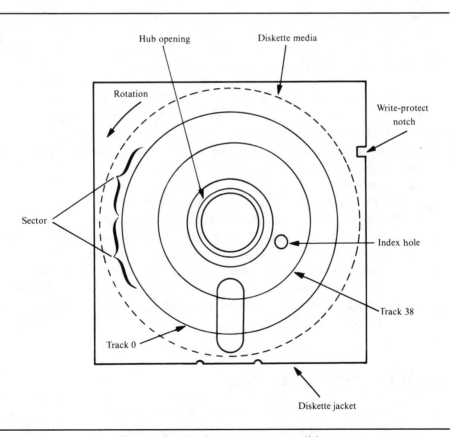

Figure 1-2. Tracks and sectors on a disk

concentric rings on the disk. Since each track can contain a great deal of information, tracks are divided into sectors. Continuing the record analogy, tracks are like grooves, and sectors are like portions of one groove. Sectors are measured from a fixed point counterclockwise all the way around and back to the beginning point on the disk.

Thus, the directory entry tells the disk head how far out on the disk to look and how long to wait during a rotation before it should start reading information. Finding a particular track is similar to selecting a song on a record. Selecting the sector is like looking for one or two bars of music within a track.

The *disk drive* is the mechanism that holds the disk. Almost every MS-DOS computer has at least one disk drive. The two main types of disk drives are distinguished by the types of disks they use: floppy or hard disks. There are two main differences between floppy and hard disks: hard disks hold much more data than floppy diskettes, and they can access their data about ten times faster. A floppy diskette usually holds between 150 and 750K; a hard disk often holds between 5000 and 20,000K, about 25 times as much. (Hard disk capacity is often measured in *megabytes*. A megabyte is 1000K; a 5M hard disk holds 5000K.) Of course, hard disks cost much more than floppy diskettes (a floppy disk drive costs between $200 and $400; a 10M hard disk drive is about $1500 to $2500).

You may have heard of another form of "disk drive" called a *RAM disk*. It is really not a disk drive at all, but a way of making MS-DOS think that part of the RAM in your computer is a disk drive. Since reading and writing to RAM is about five to ten times as fast as reading and writing to a hard disk (and incredibly faster than a floppy diskette), programs that use a lot of disk accesses (such as word processing and accounting) run much faster when a RAM disk is used.

If you have at least 128K of extra RAM in your computer, you can run a RAM disk program that will separate that RAM from the rest of the system. After it is separated, the program will make MS-DOS think that the information stored in this RAM is information stored on another disk drive. This means that you can now copy to and from the RAM with the same commands you use to copy to and from disks. Since the information in RAM is lost when you turn off your computer, you must copy all files from the RAM disk to another disk in order to save them.

LOOKING INSIDE MS-DOS

Many people run their MS-DOS computers for years without knowing anything about what MS-DOS is doing for them. But a little understanding of how MS-DOS works can help you use your operating system effectively. It can also help you determine the limits of what you can expect MS-DOS to do.

If you could look inside MS-DOS, you would see a very complicated mass of computer instructions. These instructions are written in *machine language*, which is a special language that your CPU knows how to read (many application programs are also written in machine language). Fortunately, you do not need to know machine language in order to use MS-DOS. Nor do you need to know how MS-DOS does its job. However, the process by which MS-DOS runs programs is not hard to understand, and it is helpful to know something about it, especially when you are giving commands directly to MS-DOS.

How MS-DOS Runs Commands

The processes discussed in this section relate to the utilities function of MS-DOS, and you will be learning to put these functions to use in the next five chapters. MS-DOS is like a program that is always working. When you first turn on your computer, MS-DOS is read from disk into RAM and begins running (a complete description of this is provided in Chapter 2). When MS-DOS is ready for you to give it a command or run a program, it displays a *prompt* on the screen and waits for you to tell it what to do. A prompt is simply a signal indicating that a program (in this case, MS-DOS) is waiting for you to type something.

The MS-DOS prompt, usually A> or B>, tells you that the MS-DOS *command interpreter* is waiting for you to tell it what to do next. The job of the command interpreter is to read commands that you give to MS-DOS, find the program or command you want to run, and start it running. (In the rest of this section, the word "command" will be used, but the process applies equally to any program that MS-DOS will run.)

To run a command, you simply type its name on the keyboard. MS-DOS displays the characters on the screen as you type them. Then you press the RETURN key, which is usually in the middle row of the right column of the alphabetic keys. It may also be marked with a symbol such as an arrow pointing down and to the left. On some computers, this key may be labeled ENTER.

After you tell MS-DOS the command name, the operating system must find the command program. It has two choices of where to find it. A command can be in either internal or external storage. *Internal* commands are built right into MS-DOS itself. This means that MS-DOS does not have to look on a disk for them since they are loaded into RAM with the rest of

MS-DOS. Other commands are *external*. Whenever you run these commands, MS-DOS must read them from the disk before it can execute them. (About half of MS-DOS's commands are external.) A *batch file* is a special type of external command made up of a set of MS-DOS commands (discussed further in Chapter 2). Figure 1-3 shows the steps the operating system follows when you tell it to run a command.

There is no difference in the way in which you tell MS-DOS to run external or internal commands. Therefore, you often don't have to know what type of

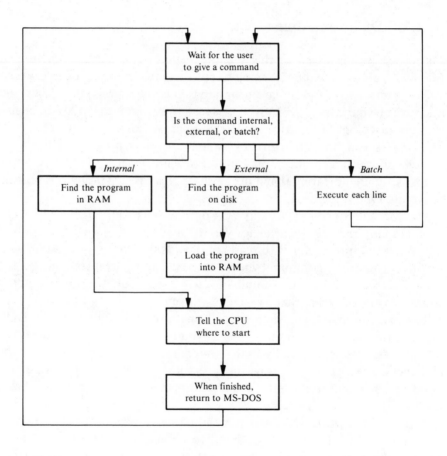

Figure 1-3. How MS-DOS runs a program

command you are asking MS-DOS to run. You can ignore the differences for now, but later you will see why you need to know if a command is external or internal.

When you run an external command, you must be sure that the disk that has the command on it is in the disk drive. If it is not in the drive (or if you have misspelled the command name), MS-DOS will give the *error message* "Bad command or file name." Error messages, as you might guess from their name, are simply communications by which MS-DOS lets you know that there is something wrong. Chapter 5 will discuss how to avoid error messages and how to interpret them.

Remember that MS-DOS is always kept in RAM, even when you tell it to run a command or an application program. When you run a command, MS-DOS loads it into the memory adjacent to the operating system, as is shown in Figure 1-4. If the command wants to do something that the CPU can't handle by itself (such as printing a character on the screen), it "calls" on a subprogram, which is like a small part of the operating system, to perform the function. Refer to Figure 1-5. In this illustration each box in the operation system represents a subprogram. Each box in the application program represents a program step. When you finish with the command, the operating system remains in RAM ready for the next set of instructions.

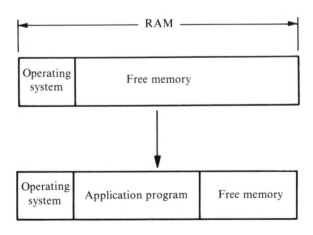

Figure 1-4.   The operating system loading a program into memory

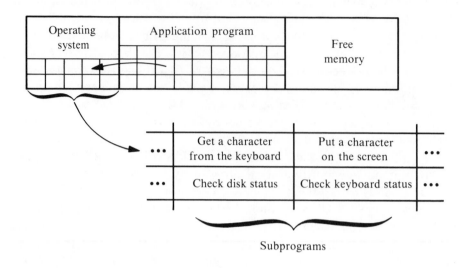

Figure 1-5. Calling a subprogram of the operating system

A BRIEF HISTORY OF MS-DOS

The story of how MS-DOS was created illustrates the unpredictable course of events in the computer industry. It is also tied to developments in micro-processor chips. Almost all MS-DOS computers use either an 8086 or an 8088 chip as their CPU. Both these chips are designed by Intel Corporation, and they both use the same set of computer instructions. Therefore, a command does not need to know which CPU chip it is being run on.

The numbering system used for these chips is somewhat obscure: a higher number on a chip does not mean that it is newer or faster than one with a lower number. In fact, the 8086 chip is the faster of the two since it reads and writes data from and to your computer's RAM 16 bits (or two bytes) at a time, while the 8088 reads data 8 bits (or one byte) at a time. Since both chips handle data in 16-bit chunks, the 8088 must read two 8-bit chunks before it can process the same information.

The 8086 processor is important to the story of MS-DOS, since MS-DOS was originally designed by Tim Paterson and Seattle Computer Products in

1980 to be the operating system for their newly designed CPU board with an 8086 processor. When the Seattle Computer CPU board first appeared on the market in mid-1979, MS-DOS was not even on the drawing boards. Digital Research had announced that the CP/M-86 operating system would soon be ready to run the 8086 system, and so expectations were that no other operating system would be needed. (Digital Research's CP/M operating system was at that time the most popular operating system for computers that used the 8080 or Z80 microprocessor chip.)

The arrival of CP/M-86 was delayed, however, and after waiting almost a year, Seattle Computer decided to write its own operating system called QDOS. Four months later, in August 1980, QDOS was ready for sale to Seattle's customers. Shortly after its release, another Seattle-based firm called Microsoft decided to buy QDOS and market it as its own operating system under the name MS-DOS. Microsoft had become famous for its version of BASIC, but had never before sold an operating system. A few months after MS-DOS was released, CP/M-86 appeared.

Microsoft has released new versions of MS-DOS as it has made improvements on the program. Each subsequent release of MS-DOS is called a nev version; these versions are numbered, such as "version 1" and "version 2. The first release of MS-DOS was called 1.0; as improvements were made, Microsoft released versions 1.1 and 1.2. These new, higher-numbered revisions did not contain any new commands or features. Version 2.0, however, released in early 1983, had many new features. Version 2.1, released in late 1983, fixed the few bugs in version 2.0. This book will use integers (1 and 2) as it refers to the major versions of MS-DOS.

You may be familiar with other operating systems, such as CP/M-80. If you have used CP/M, you may wonder how much MS-DOS has in common with it. Since CP/M was the most popular operating system at the time MS-DOS was being designed, there are many similarities. Most of the basic MS-DOS concepts are either the same as those in CP/M or simple extensions of them. For instance, both operating systems take commands in the same fashion: the operating system gives a prompt (in fact, both use A>), and the user types in a command. The command structure is the same: a command name followed by more specific instructions called *arguments*. Both operating systems have internal and external commands.

The command arguments in MS-DOS are usually much easier to remember and use than those in CP/M. The names of the MS-DOS commands are also easier to remember. For instance, the MS-DOS command to copy files is called COPY; in CP/M, it is called PIP. Many of the MS-DOS commands provide much more information than similar CP/M commands. MS-DOS has a number of other useful features that CP/M lacks. If you are accustomed to using CP/M, it will probably take you very little time to learn MS-DOS.

WHAT MS-DOS CAN'T DO

Of course, MS-DOS is not the "ultimate" operating system since it does not include every possible feature that an operating system can have. As Microsoft improves MS-DOS, it adds new features. In the previous discussion of operating systems, you learned what a bare-bones operating system can do: help the CPU interact with hardware and run programs. However, some other operating systems can do much more than this. Consider the following two situations.

What do you do if you have a job that involves using two separate programs? For instance, you may want to include some of your accounting data in a report or memo that you are writing. With versions 1 or 2 of MS-DOS, you can run only one program at a time: you would first run your accounting program to get the results, and then you would run your word processing program to write the memo. Future versions of MS-DOS may allow both programs to run at the same time. Other sophisticated operating systems also allow this capability. The ability to run several programs simultaneously is called *multitasking,* or *concurrency.*

Here is a second situation. What do you do if you work in an office with many people wanting to use one computer? MS-DOS is a *single-user* operating system. Therefore, when you run MS-DOS, you are the only person who can give it commands. A *multiuser* operating system allows many users at different terminals to run programs at the same time, thus sharing all of the computer's resources. (Some operating systems, such as UNIX, are both multiuser and multitasking.) Since Microsoft releases new versions of MS-DOS regularly, a multiuser version may be available soon. In fact, Microsoft already sells XENIX, its version of UNIX, and has said that the two operating systems will merge sometime in the future.

Now that you know what MS-DOS is and why MS-DOS is important to running your computer, you are ready to learn how to use it. Of course, using MS-DOS is much more interesting than learning about it. The next chapter will let you do this. It also presents the basic information you will need to start using MS-DOS.

2

USING MS-DOS: INTRODUCING COMMANDS AND FILES

Most people find that MS-DOS is fairly easy to learn once they understand a few concepts. This chapter will explain how to

- Start your computer
- Use MS-DOS commands and run application programs
- Use files
- Write batch files.

In addition, this chapter introduces several MS-DOS commands and shows you how to use them to perform some common tasks. It does not attempt to present all the MS-DOS commands or even all of the different ways you can use the commands that are discussed here. For that information, refer to Chapter 3, "The MS-DOS Commands." Chapter 3 discusses all of the MS-DOS commands in depth, including both their common and their uncommon uses. You can use it as a reference for finding out about any command.

Most of the commands introduced in this chapter are accompanied by examples. Try the commands in the examples on your computer. The most elementary commands will be presented first. Since most MS-DOS commands have names closely related to the actions they perform, the use of each command should be easy to remember. If you need to refer to them later, they are also explained in detail in Chapter 3.

STARTING UP MS-DOS

There is no standard method for loading MS-DOS into a computer; each brand of computer has its own method. You normally load the operating system by inserting the operating system disk into one of the disk drives before the computer is turned on. If your system loads (or *boots*) MS-DOS off a diskette, you generally use the same diskette (called the *system disk*) each time you start the system. The historical derivation for the term "boot" is the saying about "pulling yourself up by your own bootstraps." Different computers take different amounts of time to boot up.

A few computers use different start-up methods to load MS-DOS into memory. For instance, many computers that have hard disks read the operating system off the hard disk, and no system disk is required. If you have a hard disk system and want to boot MS-DOS directly, you may need to copy the operating system onto the hard disk. You should consult the manual that came with your computer for the exact instructions.

After MS-DOS is loaded, the first thing you will probably see is a prompt to "Enter new date:". This will happen unless your system disk contains a special file called an *AUTOEXEC.BAT* file, which is a series of commands written into a special file that automatically executes when you boot the system. AUTOEXEC.BAT files are discussed in full at the end of this chapter.

The date prompt looks something like this:

```
Current date is Tue 1-01-1980
Enter new date:
```

The shaded block that appears to the right of the date prompt is called the
cursor. The cursor is a block or underline on your screen that shows where the
next character that you type will appear. Notice that the cursor is waiting after
the colon on the second line.

Type in the date as three numbers separated by either hyphens (-) or slashes
(/). Valid formats for September 14, 1984, are shown here. Notice that you
must always put the month first, then the day, and then the year.

```
9-14-84
9/14/84
09/14/84
```

If you make a mistake while you are typing, press the BACKSPACE key
(sometimes labeled with an arrow pointing to the left ←) to back over the
incorrect characters. When you are finished, press the RETURN key.

Why does MS-DOS want to know the date? When it saves files on disk, it
records both the date and time so you will know when you created the file. It
isn't mandatory to record the date and time, however. If you don't want to
bother typing in the correct date, simply press the RETURN key and MS-DOS
will assume that the date is January 1, 1980 (or whatever date it displayed).
MS-DOS now prompts you for the time.

```
Current time is 0:00:12.83
Enter new time:
```

As with the date prompt, MS-DOS expects you to respond using a specific
format. The only format acceptable is in hours, minutes, and seconds separated by colons (:). The hours are kept in the 24-hour format. For instance,
2 P.M. is called 14, and the hour before midnight is 23.

Since you rarely need to know such exact time, you do not have to include
the seconds. If you do include them, you can also include hundredths of
seconds by following the seconds with a period and the number. Here are
some examples of valid times:

```
10:11:12
15:45
0:0:0.5
```

The first example shows 12 seconds after 10:11 A.M.; the second shows 3:45
P.M.; and the third shows half a second past midnight.

You use the BACKSPACE key to correct mistakes, and you can press the
RETURN key without typing anything if you don't want to record the correct

time. Don't worry if you enter the wrong date or time; there are commands (appropriately called DATE and TIME) to change them easily.

After you enter the date and time, you will see a start-up message that identifies your version of DOS. The A> prompt will appear after the start-up message.

```
The IBM Personal Computer DOS
Version 2.00 (C)Copyright IBM Corp 1981, 1982, 1983

A>
```

A few computers use a colon (:) instead of a greater than sign (>) after the A in the prompt.

The standard prompt, A>, is what you will see after you have given MS-DOS the date and time. A> is how MS-DOS tells you it is waiting for you to give it a command. When you see A>, you know that no other program is running.

WHAT TO DO WHEN YOU SEE
THE A > PROMPT

Now that the A> prompt is on your display, the next step is to give MS-DOS a command. In general, to give a command or run a program, you type the name of the command or program and press the RETURN key. (There are other things you can type after the name of a command; these are covered later in this chapter.) The first command you may want to give is the DIR command, which displays a list of all the files that are on your disk. The following example shows you how to do this. (In this book examples are separated from the rest of the text in brackets. They will be used throughout the book to illustrate the commands or procedures discussed in the text.)

When you see the A> prompt, type DIR. (You may type it in either upper- or lowercase letters.) Your entry should look something like this on the screen:

```
A>DIR
```

Notice that what you type is underscored in the illustration. Throughout this book, what you type is underscored so it will be easily distinguished from the messages generated by MS-DOS.

Next press the RETURN key. The DIR command runs and types a list of all the files on the A: drive. You have just given your first MS-DOS command.

The DIR command is an internal command. Remember from Chapter 1 that internal commands are always in memory and that MS-DOS does not look for them on your disks.

As you type in commands, you can use some of the special keys on the keyboard to help you. You can press the BACKSPACE key to erase a wrong character (as you did with the date and time prompts). If you want to get rid of an entire line, press the key marked ESC or ESCAPE.

If MS-DOS gives you an error message such as "Bad command or file name" when you attempt to run a command, you should not worry. This indicates the most common error: simply typing the program's name incorrectly. Some of the common MS-DOS error messages are discussed in Chapter 5.

The Default Drive and External Commands

As you have seen, the MS-DOS prompt tells you that the operating system is waiting for a command. The prompt also tells you something else. It tells you which disk drive MS-DOS will automatically go to when it looks for commands and files. This drive is called the *default drive*. "Default" means something that is assumed unless otherwise specified.

When MS-DOS prompts you with A>, the default drive is the A: drive. When it prompts you with B> or C>, it tells you that the default drive is B: or C: (disk letters are usually followed by colons to distinguish them from file names).

You may wonder where the letters A: and B: came from. Your computer may have many disk drives, or it may have just one. The arrangement of the disk drives is usually top to bottom or left to right. The disks are lettered starting with A:, which is the first disk on your computer; B:, the second, and so on. Your computer manual should explain how the disks are lettered. If you have a hard disk, MS-DOS may treat it as if it were split into smaller disks, each with its own letter. Figure 2-1 shows some possible computer setups.

It is not important to know which drive holds the MS-DOS system disk when you give an internal command like DIR. However, this does make a difference when you give an external command since MS-DOS must read external commands from the system disk before it can perform them. MS-DOS will normally look on the default drive as it tries to read the command.

Setup #1:

Disks:	Floppy 1	Floppy 2
Letter:	A:	B:

Setup #2

Disks:	Floppy 1	Hard Disk 1
Letter:	A:	C:

Setup #3

Disks:	Floppy 1	Floppy 2	Hard Disk 1	Hard Disk 2
Letter:	A:	B:	C:	D:

Setup #4

Disks:	Floppy 1	Hard Disk 1	Hard Disk 2	RAM Disk
Letter:	A:	B:	C:	D:

Figure 2-1. Possible disk lettering systems

For instance, when you listed the directory of your system disk, you probably saw a file called BASIC.COM. The BASIC command is an external command that lets you write BASIC programs. To run an external command, you simply type in its name just as you do to run internal commands.

For example, to start BASIC, give the command

```
A>BASIC
```

(Remember that when you give commands to MS-DOS, you must press the RETURN key after typing the command.) You can hear the disk drive whir as it reads BASIC from the disk. MS-DOS loads the BASIC program and starts running it.

To get out of the BASIC program, type the word SYSTEM and press the RETURN key. You will then see the A> prompt again.

When you tell MS-DOS to run an external command, it will look only on the disk in the default drive unless you tell it otherwise. If the commands you want to run are on the B: disk, you may want to change the default drive from A: to B:. You can change the default drive by giving another letter followed by a colon and pressing the RETURN key.

For instance, to change the default drive from A: to B:, give the command

```
A>B:
B>
```

The B> prompt shows that the default drive has been changed to B:.

If the program is not on the default drive and you did not tell it which disk to look on, MS-DOS will print "Bad command or file name" on the screen.

Changing the default drive is one way to run a command from a different disk, but doing so often would be a nuisance. Fortunately, there is an easier way to tell MS-DOS where to look for something. Simply give the disk drive name before the program.

For example, if the default drive is B:, and BASIC.COM is on A:, give the command

```
B>A:BASIC
```

This tells MS-DOS not to look on the default drive at all, but to look only on A:. This is easier than changing the default drive as you would do in the following:

```
B>A:
A>BASIC
```

GIVING ARGUMENTS IN COMMANDS

The MS-DOS commands you have used so far have been quite simple ones. It is possible to give more information to MS-DOS when you give commands so MS-DOS will perform more complicated tasks.

You give MS-DOS more information in commands by using modifiers called *arguments*. Almost every MS-DOS command has required or optional arguments. Knowing how to use arguments allows you to use your computer more effectively.

You use arguments to modify both internal and external commands. Their function is very similar to that of modifiers in common speech. For example, instead of telling someone to "buy," you might say, "buy a newspaper at the store." The argument does not alter the job that is being performed by the command; it just gives the command more information with which to work.

In the same way, you may also provide specific instructions about what you want when you give MS-DOS a command. You do this by giving the command name first and then adding arguments to modify the command. This is similar to writing short sentences in English, except that every sentence begins with the verb (as in "copy these files from this disk to that one" or "print this file").

For instance, you already saw how the DIR command displays the list of files on your disk:

```
A>DIR
```

The DIR command with no arguments lists the files on the default drive, which is A: in this case. You can give the command an optional argument that further defines which drive you want to see the directory of. For example:

```
A>DIR B:
```

Here B: is an argument that instructs the DIR command to display the files on B:, not the default drive.

The DIR command takes an *optional argument* since it can work with or without an argument. Some commands, however, have *required arguments* because they need to know what they are intended to work on.

For instance, the TYPE command, which "types" the contents of a file on the screen, requires that you tell it the name of the file you want typed out. Suppose you wanted to see the text in a file called ACCNTS.RPT. You would give the command

```
A>TYPE ACCNTS.RPT
```

The contents of ACCTS.RPT would be displayed on the screen. If you simply entered the command TYPE with no argument, MS-DOS would respond with an "Invalid number of parameters" error message.

Not all files can be displayed in readable form by using the TYPE command. If you try to type a file that is not written in the standard character set, called the American Standard Code for Information Interchange (ASCII), your computer will beep and display unreadable characters on the screen.

There are many types of arguments you can give to commands; the most common are either names of disk drives or files. In the two previous examples, the DIR command took a drive name (B:), while the TYPE command took a file name (ACCNTS.RPT). The other types of arguments are explained in Chapter 3.

SOME SIMPLE COMMANDS:
FORMAT AND COPY

Now that you have seen how to start MS-DOS and give it commands, you are ready to start putting your computer to more practical uses. The first task that you need to learn is how to prepare and copy your disks. You will use some more of the MS-DOS commands in this section.

Preparing Disks for Use
With the FORMAT Command

Most disks are not ready to use when you buy them. They first need to be *formatted*. The formatting process involves putting electronic marks on the disk so that MS-DOS will know how to find the correct places to put data on the disk. Note, however, that anything that is on a disk before you format it is always lost in the formatting process.

Formatting a disk is similar to painting white lines in a parking lot. Just as the lines indicate where to park cars, the format pattern on a disk tells MS-DOS where it can put data. If the parking lot is new, there will be no previous lines; however, if there are old lines, you must first paint the entire lot black so that your new lines are obvious. By painting the lot black, or formatting the disk, all of the old "information" is lost.

When you format a used disk, all of the information that was on the disk is erased. Therefore, when you use the FORMAT command, you must be especially careful not to use a disk that contains information you may need in the future. Check the contents of a used disk with the DIR command before formatting it. Hard disks usually come already formatted; it is very unlikely that you will ever need to format a hard disk.

The FORMAT command takes the name of the drive that you want to format as its argument.

For example, to format a diskette in drive B:, insert a new, blank diskette and give the command

```
A>FORMAT B:
```

This will format the diskette in the B: drive.

You will learn another of the FORMAT command's arguments shortly.

Copying Files With the COPY Command

The COPY command lets you copy files from one disk to another. It takes at least two arguments: the name of the file you want to copy and the name of the drive you want to copy it to. (Actually, the COPY command can do much more than this, and its other functions are described in Chapter 3.)

For instance, if you give the command

```
A>COPY BASIC.COM B:
```

MS-DOS will copy the file BASIC.COM from the A: disk to the B: disk.

Using FORMAT and COPY to Back Up
Your System Diskette

Now that you know how to use both the FORMAT and COPY commands, you can put them to good use. In this section, you will make a backup copy of your MS-DOS system diskette (the diskette that you use to boot up MS-DOS).

Why make a copy of your system diskette? It is never wise to rely on a single diskette for day-to-day needs. Too many things can happen. An accidental erasure, a spilled cup of coffee, even a power failure as you are reading from or writing to a disk can damage either the diskette or the important files it contains.

To prevent an unforeseen catastrophe, you should make a copy of this diskette and then you should use the copy instead of the original. If something does happen to the copy, you can make another copy of the original. The FORMAT and COPY commands allow you to make copies of your MS-DOS system diskette.

To copy the system diskette, you first need to format a diskette using the FORMAT command with a special argument called the /S argument. The /S argument causes the FORMAT command to create an area called the *boot tracks* on the diskette and to place special files called *system files* (also called *hidden files* because they are not listed when you give the DIR command). Boot tracks and system files are not needed on the diskettes you use for data files, but they are needed on a system diskette because they contain essential parts of the MS-DOS operating system.

Once the new diskette has been formatted with the /S argument, the next step is to copy all of the files from the system diskette to the new diskette.

For example, if you have a computer with two disks, first put the system diskette in the A: drive and a new, blank diskette in the B: drive. Then give the command

```
A>FORMAT B: /S

Formatting ... format complete
```

The diskette in the B: drive is now bootable (that is, you can start up your computer with it). It does not yet contain the many MS-DOS files shown in your directory listing, however. To copy these files, give the command

```
A>COPY A:*.* B:
```

(The *.* used in the COPY command is described later. It tells MS-DOS to copy all of the files that are on A:, regardless of their names.)

Another way to make a complete copy of the system diskette is with the DISKCOPY command. This command is also described in Chapter 3.

Making a Partial Backup
Of Your System Diskette

You will probably find that for day-to-day use not all of the commands included on your MS-DOS system diskette are necessary. If you want to make a second backup diskette with only these common commands on it, you will have more space for other files.

To determine which commands you want to have on the disk, consult Table 2-1. This table lists MS-DOS's external commands, gives their approximate

Table 2-1. MS-DOS External Commands

Command	Size (in K)	Commonly Used	IBM-Specific
ASSIGN	1		
BACKUP	4	*	*
BASICA	26	*	
CHKDSK	6	*	
COMP	3		
DEBUG	12		
DISKCOMP	3		*
DISKCOPY	2	*	*
EDLIN	5		
EXE2BIN	2		
FDISK	6		*
FIND	6		
FORMAT	6	*	
GRAPHICS	1		*
LINK	40		
MODE	3	*	*
MORE	1		
PRINT	5	*	
RECOVER	2		
RESTORE	4	*	*
SORT	1		
SYS	1		
TREE	2		*

size on disk (in K), and tells whether the commands are common enough to be put on your system disk. The size is listed so you can determine what percent of your system disk will be taken up by these files. Table 2-1 also indicates which commands are IBM-specific. (Other manufacturers often have the same commands, but sometimes with different names.) Since most of the commonly used external commands are quite short, you can place all of them on one diskette with some room to spare. If you have many different application programs, you can put each one on a different diskette.

To make a partial backup of your system diskette, simply follow the FORMAT /S instructions and then copy the commonly used commands listed in the table.

Write-Protecting Your System Diskette

Now that you have a backup copy of your MS-DOS system diskette you should protect it against accidental erasure or unwanted changes. You can do this by *write-protecting* it.

If your computer uses 5 1/4-inch diskettes, you may have noticed the notch on the right side of the diskette about an inch from the top. This is the *write-protect notch* (shown in Figure 2-2). When you cover this notch with

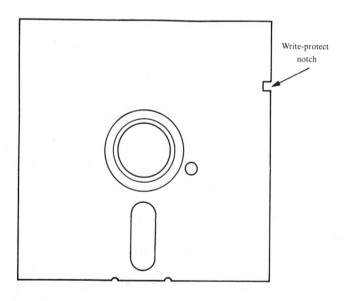

Write-protect
notch

Figure 2-2. Write-protect notch on a diskette

tape or sticky tabs (usually included in boxes of diskettes), MS-DOS will protect the diskette by not allowing you to write on it. MS-DOS will, however, still be able to read from the diskette.

It is a good practice to write-protect diskettes that you do not want to write on: the disks that came with your computer as well as your copies of the system diskette. Of course, you can peel the tab off and write information on the disk if you need to. The basic idea behind write-protecting a diskette is to reduce the chance of accidentally destroying important information.

USING FILES IN COMMANDS AND PROGRAMS

The most common use of the MS-DOS commands will probably be to help you create, maintain, and move files on the computer. There is, of course, much more to know about commands. However, to use MS-DOS effectively, you only need to know how to use a few common commands. The following discussion briefly presents some of them. Since this section is about files, not commands, not all of the uses of these commands are presented.

Creating Files

Files are always created by programs. You might instruct a program to create a file (such as a piece of text created by a word processing program), or a program might create files that it uses itself. This section describes the general method for creating files without going into all of the specific commands.

One way to create files is with a *text editor*. (Text editors are also used to revise the contents of text files.) The EDLIN command, which is included with MS-DOS, is one example of a text editor. Editing a file with EDLIN is slow and tedious because it only lets you see a small part of your file at one time; most other editors let you see much more. Detailed instructions for using EDLIN are beyond the scope of this book, but if you wish to try it, refer to the instructions in your computer's manual. If you have a word processing program, you can use this to create and edit files. In Chapter 6 you will see that many other better text editors and word processors are available (some are free).

Most of your application programs will also create files. For instance, an accounting program will create files to hold your figures, and a spreadsheet program will create files to hold your financial models. In addition, if you use a programming language, it will allow you to save your programs in files on disk.

Naming Files

In order to store a file on disk, you must give it a name. Each file is referred to with a unique name called the *file specifier*. The file specifier is split into two parts: the *file name* and the *extension*. Each file must have a name, but the extension is optional. The file name and extension are used to describe the contents of the file. The combination of the file name and extension must be unique on the disk; that is, one disk cannot have two files with identical file specifiers. The rule to remember when naming your file is that the file name can be eight characters long and the extension three characters long.

The file name and the extension are always separated by a dot (.). For instance, PHONES.DAT is a file specifier: PHONES is the file name and DAT is the extension. Other examples of file specifiers are ACCTS.BAS, DENTAL12.COM, and TIMEPRNT (it is permissible to have a file name without an extension, as in the last example). When you ask MS-DOS to read or write a file, you must give both the file name and the extension, if there is one.

The term "file name" is often used in computer manuals instead of "file specifier." If you read "file name," remember it almost always refers to the whole file specifier, including the extension. The file extension is often called the *file type*.

You have a fair amount of freedom in naming files, but keep the following guidelines in mind as you choose file names and extensions:

- Not all characters you see on your keyboard are legal in file names. Many are used in other parts of MS-DOS, and they could be confused if they appeared in a file name. The characters you can and can't use to name your files are shown in Figure 2-3.

LEGAL

All of the letters (uppercase only):

  A B C D E F G H I J K L M N O P Q R S T U V W X Y Z

The numerals:

  0 1 2 3 4 5 6 7 8 9

Many of the punctuation symbols, specifically:

  ! @ # $ % ^ & ( ) { } - _ ' ` ~

ILLEGAL

You cannot use the following characters:

  , . / \ ¦ ? * " : ; [ ] + =

Figure 2-3. Legal and illegal file name characters

- Select a file name that is pertinent to the contents of the file. For instance, a letter to someone named Holly might be called HOLLYLET.TXT, or your taxes database for 1984 might be called TAX-84.DAT. Appropriate file names make it easier to know the file's contents immediately without having to look at the file on the screen.

- MS-DOS does not allow you to have file names that are the same as the device names it uses. (Device names are names for specific hardware devices like the printer.) The names that you can't use are AUX, COM1, COM2, CON, LST, LST1, LST2, LST3, PRN, and NUL. When you know more about devices, you will see why MS-DOS would get very confused if you used these as file names.

- Include an extension in your file specifiers even though it is not required. A more detailed name gives you more information when you see the list of files later. The extension also adds information to the file name that could become important later. For example, when you write a letter to the Edsel Corporation, instead of naming the file EDSEL, you could name it EDSEL.LET or EDSEL.TXT. If you create another file later with Edsel calculations, you might name it EDSEL.DAT. The extension lets you easily differentiate it from the other EDSEL file.

- Name files relating to the same subject with similar names. This makes it much easier to search through your disk for a file or a group of files. Thus, you might name your memos to Ms. Wong WONG1.MEM, WONG2.MEM, and so forth.

- Use standard file extensions when possible. Table 2-2 lists some of the conventional extensions used in the microcomputer industry. Of course, you can ignore these conventions and name your own files whatever you please. However, some programs will assume that your files will have certain extensions and will not be able to find them if they don't.

- Avoid using some of the extensions that have special meanings to MS-DOS (such as COM and EXE and BAT). If you use these letters, MS-DOS may assume these files are commands and try to execute them. This could cause disastrous results. (By the way, you can tell which files on a disk are commands, programs, and batch files by looking at the extensions. Commands all have either COM or EXE extensions, and batch files have BAT extensions.)

- Even though you can use many of the punctuation symbols, most people use only a few of them. In general, using the dollar sign ($), the hyphen (-), and the underscore (_) should give you enough characters to define a name. Figure 2-4 lists some valid and invalid file specifiers.

Table 2-2. Common File Extensions

Extension	Meaning
ASM	Assembly language source program
BAK	Backup copy of another file
BAS	BASIC program
BAT	Batch file
BIN	Binary file used by a program
C	C source program
COB	Cobol source program
COM	Program
DAT	Data file
EXE	Program
OBJ	Object file from a compiler
OVR	Supplemental file for an application program
PAS	Pascal source program
SYS	Special system program
TEX	Text file
TXT	Text file

Valid:

MODEMS.DOC
CHAP-3A.TXT
PHONES.DAT
10IDEAS

Valid, But Not Recommended:

XX'`^ ^ XX
!!!!!!!!.@@@

Invalid:

COMPUTERS.DOC
CHAP-3A.TEXT
PHONES.NAMES.DAT
10IDEAS?

Reason:

File name more than 8 characters long
Extension more than 3 characters long
Two extensions
Invalid character (?)

Figure 2-4. Examples of valid and invalid file specifiers

Using Wild-Card Characters
For Groups of Files

You can use some MS-DOS commands to work on a group of files with similar names or extensions. Grouping files together when using a command can save you a great deal of typing. Using a common name for a group of files is like using the last name for a family of people. Instead of saying, "I want to meet Bob Patterson, Jennifer Patterson, Duane Patterson, and Randy Patterson," you could say, "I want to meet the Patterson family." Similarly, you could use first names to meet a group of people: "I want to meet everyone here whose name is Sally."

Using one name for a group of files can save a great deal of time and effort. For instance, you may want to transfer copies of all 40 of your BASIC programs from A: to B:. You would need to give the COPY command 40 separate times:

```
A>COPY PROG1.BAS B:

A>COPY PROG2.BAS B:
```

and so forth.

To save you from this huge job, MS-DOS has two special characters you can use in the file name when you want to specify more than one file: the question mark (?) and the asterisk (*). These characters are used in file specifiers when you want MS-DOS to act on a group of files instead of an individual file. Instead of matching the file names letter for letter, these characters make MS-DOS look for files that have any character in the part of the file name that has the ? or *. Just as wild cards in poker can be used to represent any card, these two characters can be used to represent any keyboard character. They are called, appropriately, *wild-card characters*.

The ? is used to match any one character at the position at which it appears in the file name.

For example, if you want to copy all files whose names are five letters long, the first four of which are PROG, and have BAS extensions, you would give the command

```
A>COPY PROG?.BAS B:
```

The command would copy PROG*1*.BAS, PROG*2*.BAS, PROG*A*.BAS, PROG*B*.BAS, and so forth from drive A: to drive B:. It would not copy either

PROG10.BAS or PROGRAM.BAS, since their names have more letters than PROG?.BAS and the question mark only matches one character. Another example is

```
A>COPY TAX?83.DAT B:
```

This command would copy TAX*A*83.DAT, TAX*1*83.DAT, TAX-83.DAT, and so forth, but it would not copy TAXAB83.DAT or TAXA.DAT.

A second wild-card character, the * character, will match any number of characters at the position at which it appears in the file name. This means that the number of letters you are matching is unimportant. It also means that you can match files with different letters in the location that you specify with the * character.

For example, to copy any file whose name begins with the letters PROG and whose extension is BAS, give the command

```
A>COPY PROG*.BAS B:
```

This matches PROG1.BAS, PROG1A.BAS, PROG9999.BAS, and PROG2B2B.BAS.

As you can see by comparing this example with the previous one, using the asterisk (sometimes called a star) always matches at least as many files as using a question mark.

You can use more than one wild-card character in a file specification. For example, B???E.* matches the files named BLARE.COM, B000E.123, B-D-E.TXT, and BRAKE.

Using a wild-card character makes the earlier problem (how to copy all of the BASIC programs from A: to B:) much easier to solve. To copy any file that has the extension BAS, regardless of the number of letters in the name, you would replace the file name with an asterisk after the COPY command:

```
A>COPY *.BAS B:
```

If, instead, you want to copy every file to B:, regardless of the name or extension, you would give the command

```
A>COPY *.* B:
```

This is the same procedure you used earlier in this chapter to make a copy of your system diskette.

Using Device Names in Commands

As you have seen, you can use the COPY command to copy files to or from a disk. You can also use the COPY command to move information to or from a device. MS-DOS gives you an extremely easy way to communicate with devices like the printer, the communications port, and the keyboard and screen.

It is highly unlikely that you will need to use device names with the COPY command because most programs that use devices have internal commands that automatically communicate with the devices. In case you do need to know the names, they are listed and defined in Table 2-3. All of the device names are three characters long (sometimes followed by a number) with a colon (:) after them. Some of the devices are synonyms of each other, such as AUX: and COM1:, or LPT1: and PRN:.

Table 2-3.   Device Names Used by MS-DOS

Name and Synonym	Device
CON:	Console. This is actually the combination of the keyboard and screen. Input is taken from the keyboard, and output is displayed on the screen.
AUX: and COM1:	The first communications (serial) port. This is also referred to as the Asynchronous Communications Adapter Port or the RS-232 Port. Not all computers have this port. The second and third communications ports (if your computer has them) are called COM2: and COM3:.
LPT1: and PRN:	The parallel printer port. This is sometimes referred to as the Centronics Port or the Parallel Port. Not all computers have this port. Since many printers use a serial port, you may have to redirect I/O to this port with the MODE command or a similar command supplied by your manufacturer. The second and third parallel ports (if your computer has them) are called LPT2: and LPT3:.
NUL:	A nonexistent device, used only for testing application programs.

Instead of using the name of a file in the COPY command, you use the name of the device. Just like a file, any device can be used for input (reading) or output (writing). In fact, since communicating with these devices is similar to copying data to and from files, you should find learning about the device names to be a continuation of learning about file names. The only command that you use device names with is the COPY command.

For example, you may want to send a file to a computer that is connected by a cable to your communications port. To do this, give the command

```
A>COPY MYFILE.TXT COM1:
```

This causes the file MYFILE.TXT to be copied from the diskette in the A: drive to your communications port.

As another example, to send the file to a printer that is attached to the parallel port, you would give the command

```
A>COPY MYFILE.TXT PRN:
```

USING BATCH FILES
TO COMBINE MS-DOS COMMANDS

Now that you have learned a number of MS-DOS commands and are familiar with the general method for using commands, you are ready to learn to execute a group of them one after the other. If you have several commands to execute, you can save a lot of time by combining them into one text file called a *batch file*. When you run a batch file, it executes those commands for you just as if you were typing them in at that moment.

Writing a batch file is like writing a very simple program that gives MS-DOS a list of commands to perform. It is far simpler than programming, however. When you are ready to execute the commands, you give MS-DOS the batch file name instead of the name of each one of the commands.

You can use any commands or programs in a batch file that you would normally run from the A> prompt. You can see how combining the commands like this saves a lot of time in typing.

For example, suppose you use an accounting program called ACCT that creates a file called SALES.DAT. You run the program every day, and every time you run ACCT, you also use the COPY command to copy the file SALES.DAT to the file SALESNEW.DAT. In addition, your ACCT program requires you to give on the command line the name of the two other files that it works with, MAINACCT.DAT and NEWREPT.TXT. Without using a batch file, you would normally give the commands

```
A>ACCT SALES.DAT MAINACCT.DAT NEWREPT.TXT

A>COPY SALES.DAT SALESNEW.DAT

A>
```

Since you always type all three file names and the second command, you can greatly reduce your typing by using a batch file. To create a batch file, you use a text editor. Suppose you named the batch file DAILY.BAT:

```
DAILY.BAT

    ACCT SALES.DAT MAINACCT.DAT NEWREPT.TXT
    COPY SALES.DAT SALESNEW.DAT
```

Any time you see a file folder like this, it indicates the contents are an MS-DOS file. Now when you want to run your batch file, you can give one simple command, DAILY, to MS-DOS (you don't need to type in the extension BAT). When MS-DOS finds the batch file called DAILY.BAT, it will begin to execute the commands in it:

```
A>DAILY

A>ACCT SALES.DAT MAINACCT.DAT NEWREPT.TXT

A>COPY SALES.DAT SALESNEW.DAT

A>
```

Notice how MS-DOS first found your batch file (DAILY.BAT) and then executed each line in it.

As MS-DOS executes each line, it types the line on the screen for you.

Rules for Naming Batch Files

There are a few rules you should follow when you name your batch files:

- A batch file name must include the extension BAT so that when you give the command MS-DOS will recognize it as a batch file.
- Do not name a batch file with the same file name as a command. If you do, MS-DOS will run the command, not your batch file. When you give MS-DOS a command, it first checks if it is an internal command; if not, it looks for the name with a COM extension, then an EXE extension, and then the BAT extension.
- Since batch files are just like other files, the same rules apply for which characters you can and cannot use.

You can put any MS-DOS commands into a batch file, and you can make your batch file any length. Each command must be on a separate line since MS-DOS reads the commands from the batch file just as you would have typed them in response to the MS-DOS prompt.

MS-DOS also gives you special commands for use only in batch files to make batch processing even easier. They let you change disks between commands, check whether a particular file exists, and perform other useful tasks. These batch file commands are described in "Batch File Commands" in Chapter 3.

Using Arguments Inside Batch Files

The previous examples show how to use batch files when you always run the same set of commands with the same arguments. But what do you do if you want to give a command in your batch file a different argument each time you run it? MS-DOS permits you to use *argument substitution* to change arguments when you run the batch file. These new arguments are then used in the commands that are in the batch file. Incidentally, MS-DOS does not care what kind of argument you give; it can be a file name, a drive name, or anything you wish.

To substitute an argument on the command line of a batch file, you use a percent sign and the number of the argument in the batch file. (For instance, the first argument would be called %1.) The *percent sign* tells MS-DOS to replace the %1 in the batch file with the first argument from the command line, to replace %2 in the batch file with the second argument from the command line, and so on. The following is an example of where argument substitution can be useful.

Suppose you need to copy a group of report files from your A: disk to either your B: or your C: disk. You could make two different batch files, one that copies the files to B: and the other that copies them to C:. However, to save even more time you can write one batch file that uses argument substitution. The RPTCOPY.BAT batch file could be

```
RPTCOPY.BAT

   COPY *.RPT %1
```

Notice that in this batch file the second argument after the COPY command is %1. Whenever you use this batch file, you must give as an argument the disk name you want to copy the files to. MS-DOS will then substitute into the COPY command in your batch file the device name that you tell it.

To run the RPTCOPY batch file with C: as the argument, type

```
A>RPTCOPY C:

A>COPY *.RPT C:
        5 File(s) copied

A>
```

When MS-DOS sees the %1 in your RPTCOPY batch file, it replaces it with C: because that is the first argument on your command line. You can use the same batch file to copy to the B: disk.

```
A>RPTCOPY B:

A>COPY *.RPT B:
        5 File(s) copied

A>
```

If you have several commands that use the same argument each time you run your batch file, you can use a percent sign argument more than once.

For example, suppose that you always run the CALC-BEG command together with the CALC-END command. Each command takes the same argument, a data file name. You can write a CALCBOTH.BAT file to run the CALC-BEG and the CALC-END programs with the same argument.

CALCBOTH.BAT

```
CALC-BEG %1
CALC-END %1
```

When you run this file with FY1982.DAT as the argument, you see the following:

```
A>CALCBOTH FY1982.DAT

A>CALC-BEG FY1982.DAT

A>CALC-END FY1982.DAT

A>
```

If you want to substitute several arguments into a command, you can use more percent signs: %2, %3, %4, and so forth. In fact, MS-DOS permits you to give as many as nine arguments to your batch file. Just as before, if you use a second argument, MS-DOS will replace every %2 in your batch file with the second argument, will replace each %3 with the third argument, and so on.

MS-DOS's ability to include many arguments in your batch file is a valuable tool. With it, you can create batch files that perform complex tasks.

Suppose you need to give a unique name to the second and third files in the accounting program in the DAILY.BAT file example used earlier. You would begin by rewriting that file so that it includes two arguments to be substituted:

```
DAILY.BAT

ACCT SALES.DAT %1 %2
COPY SALES.DAT SALESNEW.DAT
```

You then give the DAILY command and the two file names:

```
A>DAILY RECEIVE.DAT RCVREPT.TXT

A>ACCT SALES.DAT RECEIVE.DAT RCVREPT.TXT

A>COPY SALES.DAT SALESNEW.DAT

A>
```

Now that you are familiar with batch file substitution arguments, you can see why you should avoid using percent signs in file names (as noted in Figure 2-3). If you do have a file specifier in your batch program that contains a percent sign (such as N%X.DAT), you must remember to give it another percent sign (N%%X.DAT). This second percent sign tells MS-DOS that the first percent sign was meant as a part of the file name.

The AUTOEXEC.BAT File

There is one type of batch file that hasn't been discussed yet. This batch file automatically runs (or "auto executes") every time you start up the computer, and it is called the AUTOEXEC.BAT file. The AUTOEXEC.BAT file can be written to run certain programs automatically or to print out the results from programs you ran the day before as soon as you boot up your computer.

To write an AUTOEXEC.BAT file, you simply create a batch file (like the ones already shown) and give it the file name AUTOEXEC.BAT. You can write an AUTOEXEC.BAT file with whatever commands you want. Then each time you boot MS-DOS, it will search for the file AUTOEXEC.BAT and, if it finds it, automatically execute the commands. Incidentally, this is the special file mentioned at the beginning of the chapter that prevents MS-DOS from asking you for the date and the time.

Commands that set system settings (such as the date and the time) are commonly put in the AUTOEXEC.BAT file. You can also include some software packages, which are meant to be loaded into memory immediately after the system is turned on. An example of a typical AUTOEXEC.BAT file is given at the end of the "Batch File Commands" section in Chapter 3.

Linking Batch Files

You can include the name of one batch file within another batch file as long as you put it at the end of the file. This means that batch files can be linked together. For instance, you can write a batch file that first runs your inventory programs and then links with another batch file that prints the output. (The advantage of separating the printing commands into a second batch file is that you can then use this second batch file by itself.)

Remember, however, that you can only link programs together with the last line of your batch file. MS-DOS is unable to return to one batch file once you have linked to another, with one exception. This problem and its solution are explained fully under "The COMMAND Command" in Chapter 3.

A SAMPLE SESSION WITH MS-DOS

You now know almost everything you need to start using MS-DOS like a pro. This section will present an example of a typical computer session that you might have with MS-DOS.

Suppose that your tasks for the day are to run a report-generating package that is part of your inventory control system and to write a memo about the results of the report. You will also print the memo and make a copy on a diskette of both the memo and the report. These tasks will be presented step by step.

Step 1: Using a Batch File to Run the Program

You want to run the inventory report program first. Running the program is easy because you have already written a batch file (called INVRPT) to handle the three different commands you usually give. The file INVRPT.BAT contains

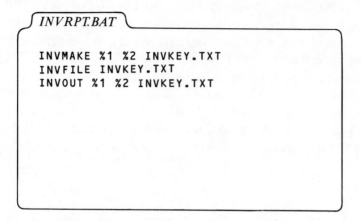

```
INVRPT.BAT

INVMAKE %1 %2 INVKEY.TXT
INVFILE INVKEY.TXT
INVOUT %1 %2 INVKEY.TXT
```

All you need to do is tell the batch file what the beginning and end dates for the report are.

```
A>INVRPT 8/1/84 8/15/84

A>INVMAKE 8/1/84 8/15/84 INVKEY.TXT

A>INVFILE INVKEY.TXT

A>INVOUT 8/1/84 8/15/84 INVKEY.TXT
The report is saved in file INVRPT93.TXT

A>
```

The last message ("The report is saved...") is printed by the INVOUT program. This hypothetical program tells you the name of the file that it produced and saved on disk (in this case, INVRPT93.TXT). When the program is finished, the A> prompt returns.

Step 2: Analyzing the Report

The next step is to analyze the report you just produced. You can either look at it on the screen or print it on the printer. To display the report on the screen, use the TYPE command.

```
A>TYPE INVRPT93.TXT

                Inventory Report for 8/1/84 to 8/15/84

Parts that need to be reordered by 8/20/84:

Item            On hand         Reorder level        Price
------------------------------------------------------------
CF3499             8                 12               14.50
CF5000            52                 60                1.19
   .               .                  .                 .
   .               .                  .                 .
   .               .                  .                 .
```

If the report turns out to be longer than you expected, you can print it with the
PRINT command. The PRINT command is like the TYPE command, except
that it prints the file on the printer instead of the screen.

```
A>PRINT INVRPT93.TXT

             A:INVRPT93.TXT is currently being printed

A>
```

Step 3: Writing the Memo

After evaluating the report, you use your word processing program to write a
memo detailing your findings. Since each word processor is different, this
book will not attempt to explain how to write the memo.

Suppose you are running a word processing program called TEXTP and
you want to edit the file INVRPT93.TXT. You would give the command

```
A>TEXTP INVRPT93.TXT
```

You add text to the report that was produced and possibly rearrange the
results. After you finish the memo, you want to print it on the printer. Many
word processing programs will print the memo if you ask them to, but others
won't. In this case, TEXTP doesn't, so you must return to MS-DOS. You save
the memo under the name NEWINV.MEM, use a TEXTP command to
return to MS-DOS, and then give the MS-DOS PRINT command.

```
A>PRINT NEWINV.MEM

             A:NEWINV .MEM is currently being printed

A>
```

Step 4: Copying the Memo and Report Files

Remember that for this job, you wanted a copy of the memo and report on disk. To do this, you put a formatted disk into the second drive (B:) and make sure it is blank by using the DIR command.

```
A>DIR B:

 Volume in Drive B has no label
 Directory of B:\

 File not found

 A>
```

The message before "File not found" will vary according to the particular version of MS-DOS you are running (this one comes from version 2). However, it really doesn't matter because you found what you wanted to know: there is nothing on the disk.

Now you copy your report and memo files:

```
A>COPY INVRPT93.TXT B:
        1 File(s) copied

A>COPY NEWINV.MEM B:
        1 File(s) copied

 A>█
```

Remember that the COPY command takes two arguments: the source of data and the destination for the data. In these cases, the source is the file in A:, the default drive, and the destination is drive B:. To be sure that you copied everything correctly, you check the contents of B: with the DIR command:

```
A>DIR B:

 Volume in Drive B has no label
 Directory of B:\

 INVRPT93 TXT      8110      8-20-84   10:42p
 NEWINV   MEM       631      8-20-84   11:20p
         2 File(s)        151515 bytes free

 A>█
```

The DIR command gives you the file name, file extension, number of bytes in the file, and the date and time it was created. It also tells you how many files are on the disk and the amount of space you have left ("bytes free") before the disk is full.

You are now finished with your tasks. You should feel comfortable giving MS-DOS commands and answering the questions that the program asks. You are ready to learn the many other MS-DOS commands described in the next chapter.

3

MS-DOS COMMANDS

This chapter describes the MS-DOS commands included with your system and tells you how to use them. Most of the command descriptions include examples that show how the commands can be entered. These examples are hypothetical; for instance, most contain file names that are not present on your disks. You should use them as general prototypes for using a certain command for a certain purpose.

In addition to the standard MS-DOS commands, this chapter also covers many commands that IBM has added to PC-DOS. Many of these IBM-specific commands have been copied by other computer manufacturers, so you may find them on non-IBM computers.

Although some versions of MS-DOS have slightly different commands, they only vary within major version releases. Therefore, the commands in version 1.0 will perform the same function as those in the next major release, version 1.1, but they may be different in version 2. This chapter lists the commands used in both versions; new commands that are included only in version 2 are noted at the top of each command. Appendix B provides more information on the differences between the commands in versions 1 and 2.

Your computer may have come with both MS-DOS and application programs such as a word processing or spreadsheet program. Since MS-DOS does not include application programs, they are not explained here. The instruction manuals for these programs should be included with them. If you find program disks without any documentation (that is, a manual that explains how to use the program), ask your computer dealer. Application programs that run under MS-DOS are discussed in Chapter 6.

HOW THIS CHAPTER IS ORGANIZED

All of the MS-DOS commands in this chapter are presented in general functional groups. For example, you will find that all of the commands used to maintain files (such as copying and erasing) are grouped together under the heading "File Maintenance Commands." Figure 3-1 shows all of these functional groups, the commands in each group, and the page on which each command is described.

If you are interested in using this chapter as a reference, you will find Appendix A valuable. Appendix A provides an alphabetical list of all of the commands, their syntax, and the functional group within which they are described in this chapter.

Each command description includes the following information:

- *The command profile box.* This includes any shortened names for the same command. It also tells you whether the command was introduced in version 2 of MS-DOS, whether the command is internal or external, and whether the command is IBM-specific.
- *Common Uses.* This section shows how to use the command and all of its arguments in different ways. Most of the examples for each command are contained here. A few commands also contain a section called "Other Uses" that describes less practical uses of the command.
- *Rules.* Some commands have definite rules about when you can or cannot use them. You will find these rules in this section.

MS-DOS Commands		Page Where Command Can Be Found
File Maintenance Commands		
ERASE	Removes files from a disk	52
RENAME	Gives files new names	54
COPY	Makes copies of files	57
COMP	Compares files	63
EDLIN	Edits text files	65
File Output Commands		
TYPE	Displays a file on the screen	67
PRINT	Prints a file on the printer	68
MORE	Displays a file on the screen with pauses	72
Disk Maintenance Commands		
DIR	Displays the list of files on a disk	74
FORMAT	Prepares a disk for MS-DOS	78
SYS	Puts the system files and boot tracks on a diskette	82
CHKDSK	Examines and repairs disks	84
RECOVER	Repairs files with bad sectors	89
DISKCOPY	Copies an entire diskette	91
DISKCOMP	Compares two diskettes	94
FDISK	Performs maintenance on the IBM PC/XT	96
BACKUP	Makes backup copies of the hard disk	97
RESTORE	Makes copies of backup files	97
System Settings		
DATE	Sets the date	99
TIME	Sets the time	100
VERIFY	Tells MS-DOS to double-check when it writes on disks	101
MODE	Changes communication parameters	103
VER	Displays the MS-DOS version number	108
VOL	Displays the label of a disk	109
PROMPT	Changes the MS-DOS prompt	110
BREAK	Causes MS-DOS to check for user interrupts more often	112
ASSIGN	Changes the letters assigned to disks	114
CTTY	Changes the console to a serial port	116
SET	Changes environment strings	117

Figure 3-1. Command groupings in this chapter

MS-DOS Commands		**Page Where Command Can Be Found**
Path Maintenance Commands		
MKDIR	Adds sub-directories to a disk	120
CHDIR	Changes default sub-directory	122
RMDIR	Removes sub-directories from a disk	124
TREE	Prints out list of sub-directories	126
PATH	Changes the command search list	128
Batch File Commands		
ECHO	Prints message on the screen	132
PAUSE	Waits for a key to be pressed	133
IF	Executes commands based on a decision	135
FOR	Repeats a command for many choices	139
GOTO	Jumps to a different part of a batch file	142
REM	Puts a note in a batch file	145
SHIFT	Moves the command line arguments	146
COMMAND	Runs another program	147
Other Commands		
FIND	Searches for text in a file	150
SORT	Sorts a text file	153
CLS	Clears the screen	155
GRAPHICS	Allows you to print graphics screens	155
Programming Tools		
LINK	Combines object files	156
DEBUG	Examines and changes binary files	158
EXE2BIN	Converts EXE files to COM files	158

Figure 3-1. Command groupings in this chapter *(continued)*

- *Warnings and common errors.* This section lists any problems that are common to specific commands; it also provides warnings that can help you avoid big problems. (Chapter 5, "Handling Emergencies," explains how to recover from the negative results of some disasters.)
- *Syntax.* The *syntax* is an ordered arrangement of the command's arguments that you give on the command line. This section lists the complete syntax for using each command. The syntax section usually contains much more information than you immediately need to use the command, but this information is helpful for understanding exactly how to give the command. General syntaxes are provided in the "Common Uses" section.

HOW TO READ A COMMAND SYNTAX

To give a command, you must learn to write a little of MS-DOS's language. For MS-DOS to be able to read your command, you need to arrange the command name and its arguments in the command's syntax. The syntax can be short and simple or long and complex. It specifies everything that the command needs to perform its work. By carefully reading the syntax and supplying all of the information in arguments, you can be sure the command will run smoothly.

The following three concepts are important in understanding how to interpret the command syntax notations in this book.

- *Special symbols.* This book uses special symbols to indicate different types of arguments. These symbols are listed in Table 3-1. Any argument that does not have special symbols around it is required for that command. As you will see, most arguments are optional. You should familiarize yourself with these special symbols since they are used in this book and in many other computer books as well.
- *Italicized arguments.* These arguments, also known as *generic arguments*, are used to indicate that the argument can take many values. For example, in the syntax "TYPE *filespec*", *filespec* indicates that any file name, or file specification, can be used. The *filespec* argument is an invented word used to signal where a file name should be. Some of the generic arguments used throughout this chapter are shown in Table 3-2; other command-specific arguments are described as they occur in the individual command syntax.
- *Single-letter arguments.* Many commands have single-letter arguments preceded by a slash (for example, / V). It is important to realize that these

Table 3-1. Symbols Used in Command Syntaxes

Symbol	Description
[ ]	Square brackets indicate that everything inside them is optional.
{ }	Curly braces indicate that you must choose exactly one of the choices inside the braces. Each choice is separated by a vertical bar (|).
. . .	Ellipses indicate that you can repeat the last set of arguments again.

Table 3-2. Generic Arguments in Command Syntaxes

Generic Argument	Description
d:	Disk descriptor, such as A: or B:.
path	The path name associated with the file.
filename	The name of a file (or group of files), excluding the file extension. You can use wild-card file names unless the command description says otherwise.
ext	The extension of a file or group of files. You can use wild-card file names unless the command description says otherwise.
filespec	A file specifier that contains at least a filename. Thus, the syntax for a *filespec* is [*d:*][*path*]*filename*[*.ext*]
n	A number. For example, COM*n*: can mean COM1:, COM2:, and so on.
string	A group of characters. For instance, "xxyyz" is a string of five characters; "Hi there" is a string of eight characters.

arguments mean different things in different commands. This use of the same letter with different meanings can be somewhat confusing. You should always check that the single-letter argument you are using is correct for that command. (Some manuals call these single-letter arguments *options*.) When you type in these arguments, be sure that you use the forward slash (/), not the back slash (\ ).

In the following examples, you can see the importance of understanding a command's syntax.

The first example is

VERIFY [{ OFF | ON }]

The square brackets indicate that the VERIFY command can have either no arguments or only one argument; the curly braces indicate that the argument must be either ON or OFF. Thus, the command must be given as VERIFY, VERIFY OFF, or VERIFY ON.

The next example is

DIR [*d:*]

With this syntax, the DIR command can either be given by itself or with a disk descriptor like B:.

The third example is

TYPE *filespec*

The *filespec*, which is usually just the name of a file, is required in this command. Remember that the *filespec* can also include the name of the disk or the sub-directory (sub-directories are explained in Chapter 4).

STOPPING A COMMAND

After you start running a command, you may decide that you want to stop it. This might happen if you discover that the command is typing out information you don't need. You can usually do this by holding down the CONTROL key and pressing the C key. This tells MS-DOS that you want to stop the command. After you press CONTROL-C, the screen should display the A> prompt.

Pressing CONTROL-C works most of the time, but unfortunately, not all the time. Some computers use the *BREAK key* instead of CONTROL-C. Some other computers, such as the IBM PC, require you to hold down the CONTROL key and the BREAK key at the same time.

If you need to stop a command and the method just described doesn't work, some computers have a *reset button* you can push as a last resort. Other machines use a series of keys. For instance, on the IBM PC you reset the machine by holding down the ALT, CONTROL, and DELETE keys at the same time. Pushing the reset button tells the machine to stop what it is doing, no matter what the consequences are.

Using the reset button is an effective way to stop a command, but it is *not* recommended. You can seriously damage information on your disks if the computer was writing information when you pushed the reset button. If you do need to use the reset button, you should always verify afterwards that any files on your disk are intact. You can do this with the CHKDSK command, described later in this chapter.

Sometimes you may want a program to stop only temporarily without going back to the A> prompt. If a command is printing a great deal of information on the screen, you can usually stop the process by pressing a key (or combination of keys). Since this combination will vary with the type of computer you own, you should read your computer manual to find out which key or keys halt a program. (On the IBM PC, this is the combination of the CONTROL and the NUMLOCK keys.) Pressing the RETURN key often resumes execution of the command.

FILE MAINTENANCE COMMANDS

This section discusses the following commands:

ERASE (also DEL)	*Removes files from a disk*
RENAME (also REN)	*Gives files new names*
COPY	*Makes copies of files*
COMP	*Compares files*
EDLIN	*Edits text files*

These MS-DOS commands are used for creating and manipulating files. The first three of these you will use quite often; you may find that you use the latter two commands rarely, if at all.

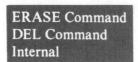

ERASE Command
DEL Command
Internal

The ERASE command removes a file or a group of files from the directory of a disk. The DEL command is identical to the ERASE command.

Common Uses

There are several reasons to use the ERASE command. If one of your programs has created a useless file, or if you have a file that you no longer need on a disk, you can remove it with the ERASE command. Since storage is limited, it is important to erase old files and free up space for new files. However, remember that once you erase a file, it is difficult or impossible to get it back. (Some utility programs on the market can recover erased files in some cases. See "Disk-Saving Utilities" in Chapter 5.)

The general syntax of the ERASE command is

ERASE *filespec*

The process of erasing a file is simple, requiring only the name of the file to be erased.

For instance, to erase a file called BOSTON88.TST on the default drive, give the command

```
A>ERASE BOSTON88.TST
```

or,

```
A>DEL BOSTON88.TST
```

The file will be removed from the disk and the directory.

You can use wild-card characters with the ERASE command. In this way, you can erase more than one file at a time.

For instance, to erase all of the files with the extension BAK (which is used for backup files), give the command:

```
A>ERASE *.BAK
```

If you ask to erase all of the files on a disk, the ERASE command will double-check with you before doing so.

```
A>ERASE *.*
Are you sure (Y/N)?Y
```

Whenever you see this message, think about the contents of the files carefully. Once you erase a file, there is no easy way to recover it; in fact, there may be no way to recover it.

Rules

You must tell the ERASE command which files you want to erase. If you forget the file name, MS-DOS will give you the message "Invalid number of parameters."

If you specify which disk the file is on and then forget the file name, MS-DOS will report "File not found." This is because, as a precaution, the ERASE command requires that when you give a disk specifier, you must also give a file name.

Warnings and Common Errors

Obviously, you must be careful not to erase important files. If other people use your computer, be cautious before you erase any files. Even though you may think that a file is unimportant or useless, someone else may need the file for an application you are not aware of.

   If you are using paths, be especially careful with the ERASE command. If you give the name of a sub-directory as the argument to the ERASE command, MS-DOS will erase all of the files from that sub-directory. This is the same as changing to the sub-directory and giving the ERASE *.* command. Paths and sub-directories are discussed in the "Path Maintenance Command" section of this chapter. They are also described in Chapter 4.

Syntax

The syntax for the ERASE command is

   ERASE   *filespec*

A *filespec* must be given with the ERASE command. The *filespec* can contain wild-card characters.

RENAME Command
REN Command
Internal

   The RENAME command changes the name of a file without changing its contents. The REN command is identical to the RENAME command.

Common Uses

There are a few reasons why you would want to change the name of a file. The contents of the file may have changed so much that the old name is no longer accurate, or you may realize that you have accidentally given two files similar names. You can now rename one of the files to avoid confusion. The common syntax for the command is

   RENAME *filespec1 filespec2*

where *filespec1* stands for the original file name and *filespec2* for the name you wish to change it to.

For example, to rename SALES.DAT to US-SALES.DAT, give the command

```
A>RENAME SALES.DAT US-SALES.DAT
```

or

```
A>REN SALES.DAT US-SALES.DAT
```

You can use the RENAME command in conjunction with the ERASE command to get rid of the current version of a file and replace it with an old version. You might want to do this if you revised a file and then decided that the original version was more appropriate.

For instance, assume you want to rename the backup program of a billing file called BILLPROG.COB. You are using a text editor that saves a backup file with the same name as the original file, but with a BAK extension. You would give the commands

```
A>ERASE BILLPROG.COB

A>RENAME BILLPROG.BAK BILLPROG.COB
```

If you simply wanted to switch the names of two files, you would need to use a temporary name since the RENAME command won't allow you to rename the two files at the same time. You may want to switch two file names if you have revised a file and then decided to use the original version instead, but you will want to have a copy of your revisions for future use.

For example, to switch the names of the files SALEPROG.COB and SALEPROG.BAK, type the following commands:

```
A>RENAME SALEPROG.COB TEMPFILE.COB

A>RENAME SALEPROG.BAK SALEPROG.COB

A>RENAME TEMPFILE.COB SALEPROG.BAK
```

In this example, TEMPFILE.COB is a temporary file name.

If you have two or more files on a disk that share either the same name or extension, you can use wild-card characters to rename these files as a group.

The first example renames all files with the file name ACCOUNTS to ACC.

```
A>RENAME ACCOUNTS.* ACC.*
```

The second example renames all files with the extension TXT to the extension TEX.

```
A>RENAME *.TXT *.TEX
```

Rules

You cannot use RENAME to change the names of a group of files that are on different disks; you must first use the COPY command to move the files onto the same disk.

You cannot rename a file with a name that already exists on the disk. If you try, MS-DOS will give you the message "Duplicate file name or file not found."

Warnings and Common Errors

The most common error is to forget the order of the two file names. RENAME requires that the old name be first and the new name be second. (Those who are familiar with the CP/M operating system will recognize that this is the opposite of CP/M's required order.)

If several people use your computer, be sure that when you rename a command or a file, everyone who uses that file knows its new name. Changing the name of a file without announcing the change is likely to cause needless confusion.

Do not change the names of any special files that are used by application programs. The WordStar program, for example, requires the overlay file WSOVLY1.OVR to be on your disk. If you change the name of the file, there is no way for WordStar to know the new name.

Syntax

Either of the following may be the syntax for the RENAME command:

RENAME *filespec1 filespec2*

or

RENAME *filespec1 filename2*[*.ext2*]

In the first form, *filespec1* is the name for the file that you are renaming, and *filespec2* is the new name for the file. In the second form, *filename2.ext2* is the new name for the file (if you do not include the extension, MS-DOS will use the same extension as in the original file name). Notice that the old name is given first.

COPY Command
Internal

The COPY command allows you to copy files from one disk to another. It also enables you to make a copy of a file on the same disk (but with a different name), copy information to and from your system's hardware devices, and combine many files into one.

Common Uses

The COPY command is one of the most frequently used commands in MS-DOS. It is most commonly used to make copies of files from one disk to another.

The first general syntax of the COPY command is

COPY *source destination*

Here, *source* is the name of the file you want to copy from, and *destination* is where you want to copy the file to.

For instance, if you wanted to copy the file OPENACCT.DAT from a disk in drive A: to a disk in drive B:, you would give the command

```
A>COPY OPENACCT.DAT B:
        1 File(s) copied
```

The file OPENACCT.DAT will be copied to drive B: with the same name.

The COPY command always tells you how many files it copied. Notice that you do not have to give the file name on the destination disk, just the drive name. This is because the COPY command assumes that you want the new file to have the same file name.

If you want to change the name of a file as MS-DOS copies it to the destination disk, simply add the new name to the COPY command.

For example:

```
A>COPY OPENACCT.DAT B:NEWACCT.DAT
      1 File(s) copied
```

Here you not only copied OPENACCT.DAT from A: to B:, but also gave the file a different name (NEWACCT.DAT) on the B: disk.

Remember that you can use the wild-card characters in the file names to copy multiple files.

For instance,

```
A>COPY *.BAT B:
```

This command copies all files with the extension BAT from the A: to the B: disk.

You can also use COPY to make a duplicate of a file on the same disk. However, the copy must have a different name since MS-DOS does not allow two files with the same name on one disk.

To make a copy of the file JUDGES.TXT:

```
A>COPY JUDGES.TXT JUDGES.NEW
      1 File(s) copied
```

As you can see, the destination disk wasn't specified, so the copy remains on the same disk. You now have a new copy of the JUDGES.TXT file (called JUDGES.NEW.) on the same disk.

If you are copying from another disk to the default disk without changing the file names, you do not need to include the name of the destination disk.

For instance, if A: is the default drive, and you want to copy the file CASHFLOW.RPT from B: to A:, give the command

```
A>COPY B:CASHFLOW.RPT
```

The COPY command will now move the file to the default drive.

You can also use the COPY command when you want MS-DOS to read from, or write to, your hardware devices. To do this, you use the device name instead of file names, and the COPY command treats the devices just like files. Device names were discussed in Chapter 2. In general, you will not use devices with the COPY command, since it is usually easier to let an application program send files to devices.

If you define the communication port (COM1:) as the destination and a file OPERWX.FOR as the source, MS-DOS will pass the data from the file to the device:

```
A>COPY OPERWX.FOR COM1:
```

This command sends the contents of OPERWX.FOR to the communications port.

If you define a device as the source, the COPY command will continue to read from the device until you enter a CONTROL-Z character followed by a RETURN (the CONTROL-Z is called the *end-of-file marker*). This method of detecting the end of a file may seem a bit arbitrary; however, when you use the COPY command with a device, it will continue to read information from the device until it sees an end-of-file marker.

If you wanted to type text directly into the SHORT.MEM file, you would use the following command:

```
A>COPY CON: SHORT.MEM
```

The device name CON: represents the keyboard and the screen. Now everything you type will be put directly into the file. You will notice that the MS-DOS prompt does not reappear. After you have typed in a few lines to finish the file, press CONTROL-Z and then the RETURN key.

When you copy from a master diskette, such as the original of your MS-DOS system disk, you may want to put a write-protect tab on it in case you accidentally give the wrong COPY command and copy information onto the diskette.

Using COPY to combine files. The second general syntax for the COPY command is

COPY *source1* + *source2 destination*

This form is used when you want to combine files end to end, or *concatenate* them. You can concatenate as many files as you want into one destination file.

For instance, if you want to make a file called STAFF.TXT, which is a copy of JANE.TXT followed by a copy of SYLVIA.TXT, give the command

```
A>COPY JANE.TXT + SYLVIA.TXT STAFF.TXT
JANE.TXT
SYLVIA.TXT
          1 File(s) copied
```

The COPY command lists each file as it adds it to the destination file, in this case on the same disk.

Using the /V argument with COPY. If MS-DOS copies your data incorrectly, disastrous consequences can arise. Although MS-DOS rarely makes an incorrect copy, most people feel that it is better to be sure. Therefore, you should always use the /V argument after each COPY command; or better yet, always set VERIFY to ON with the MS-DOS VERIFY command (described in the "System Settings" section later in this chapter).

Although this slows down the command, it makes sure that the copies you make are accurate. The assurance that your file was copied correctly is well worth the extra time it takes for MS-DOS to reread what it has written. The /V argument is put at the end of the COPY command.

For example:

```
A>COPY PURCH.ACT B: /V
          1 File(s) copied
```

This command ensures that MS-DOS copies the files PURCH.ACT accurately to the B: disk.

Other Uses

Two other arguments, the /A and /B arguments, are rarely used with the COPY command. They are quite confusing. When they are used, it is to distinguish between ASCII files and *binary files* (thus the A and B). While an ASCII file contains only normal text, such as a letter or memo, a binary file contains special nontext characters. Programs and data bases are usually binary files. The /A and /B arguments are only used when copying files that do not conform easily to these definitions. For more information on these arguments, see the MS-DOS reference manual.

Rules

You cannot copy a file on top of itself. If you try to make a copy of a file on the same disk without changing its name, MS-DOS gives the message "File cannot be copied onto itself."

Warnings and Common Errors

The most common error in using the COPY command is to reverse the order of the source and destination files. This is especially likely to happen if you are familiar with the CP/M operating system, which requires that the destination appear before the source in the command line.

If you try to copy a file that does not exist, MS-DOS will give you an error message.

For instance, if you try to copy the file TETHER.PRG and it does not exist:

```
A>COPY TETHER.PRG B:
TETHER.PRG File not found
        0 File(s) copied
```

MS-DOS will give you the error message "File not found."

Remember to give the /V option, or set VERIFY to ON, when you copy files. This will prevent errors that could occur if files are copied incorrectly.

Before you give a device as a source in the COPY command, be sure that the device is properly set up. This is especially true if the communications port is the source. Remember that the COPY command will wait forever for the data to be sent from the device. Once the data starts to come through, the COPY command will continue to read from the device until the end of the file is seen. If you accidentally give the wrong device name in a command and you cannot get your device to respond, you must reboot your computer.

Syntax

The syntax for the COPY command may seem strange at first, but it is actually very easy to use because the /A and /B arguments are rarely used. The following variations of syntax are shown on more than one line, but the COPY command (like all MS-DOS commands) is always given on one line.

Copying a file normally:

   COPY [{/A | /B}] *filespec1* [{/A | /B}] {*d:* | *filespec2*} [{/A | /B}] [/V]

Concatenating a file:

   COPY [{/A | /B}] *filespec1a* [{/A | /B}]
      [+ *filespec1b*] [{/A | /B}] ... [/V]
      {*d:* | *filespec2*} [{/A | /B}] [/V]

Copying to or from a device:

   COPY {*filespec1* | *device1*} {*filespec2* | *device2*}

In each kind of syntax, *filespec1* is the source for the copy and *filespec2* is the destination. The COPY command always copies from the first argument to the second. You can also use the wild-card characters in the file names to copy multiple files.

{/A | /B} indicates that you can use either /A or /B with any file specifier. The meaning of /A or /B depends on whether you name them as source files or destination files. The /A and /B may appear either before or after the *filespec* source.

/V causes the COPY command to verify that the data written to the destination disk is exactly what was on the source disk.

The *device* argument stands for any one of the MS-DOS device names, such as LPT1: for printer, COM1: for the communications port, and so forth. These devices and the MS-DOS device names are discussed in Chapter 2.

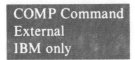

COMP Command
External
IBM only

The COMP command compares the contents of two files and reports the differences on the screen. Although this command is specific to IBM's PC-DOS, some other hardware manufacturers have similar commands.

Common Uses

You can use the COMP command to compare two files. The general syntax for the COMP command is

COMP *filespec1 filespec2*

Checking the accuracy of the new copied file with the COMP command gives you some peace of mind that the copy was successful, although the / V option of the COPY command is sufficient. You may want to use the COMP command after making a copy of a file.

For example:

```
A>COPY INVOICES.DAT B:
        1 File(s) copied

A>COMP A:INVOICES.DAT B:

A:INVOICES.DAT and B:INVOICES.DAT

Files compare ok

Compare more files (Y/N)?N
```

Notice that you do not need to repeat the name of the second file if it is identical to the first file name.

Version 2 of MS-DOS allows the COMP command to be used to check all of the files on a disk simply by telling it to compare *.* from one disk to another.

For example:

```
A>COMP *.* B:
```

Between each set of files, the COMP command asks

```
Compare more files (Y/N)?
```

Answer Y if you want to continue comparing files.

The COMP command is not recommended for comparing files if you know that one of them has been modified. You cannot compare two files of different sizes, even if the size is only different by one character. If you have only replaced characters (without altering the size), the response from the COMP command will be very difficult to read. That is because all the differences are shown with hexadecimal numbers, not letters.

To see why you do not want to use COMP to compare files that are different, suppose you compare a file named OPERA.DOC to its somewhat different backup version, OPERA.BAK. Your screen display would look something like the following:

```
A>COMP OPERA.DOC OPERA.BAK

A:OPERA    .DOC and A:OPERA     .BAK

Compare error at offset 4D
File 1 = 58
File 2 = 59

Compare error at offset 51
File 1 = 58
File 2 = 59

Compare error at offset 6A
File 1 = 53
File 2 = 56

        .
        .
        .
```

As you can see, the COMP command lets you know there are differences, but it does not make it easy to figure out what those differences are.

In comparing two diskettes, the DISKCOMP command is much faster than comparing each file. It also checks the boot tracks and directory areas of the disk. The DISKCOMP command is discussed later in this chapter in the "Disk Maintenance Commands" section.

Syntax

The syntax for the COMP command is

COMP [*filespec1 filespec2*]

The arguments *filespec1* and *filespec2* are the files to be compared. Wild-card specifications are allowed. If you forget to give any file names, or if you give only one where two are required, the COMP command will prompt you for them.

EDLIN Command
External

The EDLIN command is a line editor that can be used to create and alter the contents of text files.

Common Uses

The common form of the EDLIN command is

EDLIN *filespec*

EDLIN is a line editor, which means that you can only work with one line of your file at a time. It does not take advantage of the capabilities of the full screen of your computer. EDLIN is not recommended because it is difficult to use and is not very powerful.

This book does not describe the operation of EDLIN. To do so would require far more pages of explanation than there is space for. EDLIN is not easy to learn to use, and unless you understand it thoroughly, its use may be counterproductive. If you really want to use EDLIN, see your computer manual or one of the books listed in Chapter 7.

If your computer manufacturer did not supply a text-editing program with your computer, you should look into the many text editors available for under $100; some are even available for free. User's groups will often give away copies of text-editing programs. Chapter 6 discusses many text editors and word processors and what they can do for you; these programs are far easier to use than EDLIN.

Syntax

The syntax for the EDLIN command is

EDLIN *filespec* [/ B]

The *filespec* argument is the name of the file to be edited. If you include the / B argument, EDLIN will treat the file as a binary file and read in all of the data in every sector.

FILE OUTPUT COMMANDS

The following commands are covered in this section:

TYPE   *Displays a file on the screen*
PRINT   *Prints a file on the printer*
MORE   *Displays a file on the screen with pauses*

The previous section showed you how to move files, get rid of them, and give them new names. This section will describe another important thing you will want to do with files: look at them. The TYPE, PRINT, and MORE commands are all used to display your files on the screen or print them on paper.

These commands are *sequential commands*. This means that when you use one of these commands, you can only look at a file from beginning to end; you cannot back up and reread a portion of the file. In this sense the commands are restrictive, since people often want to move around within the file as they read and reexamine information.

To give yourself more flexibility, you can use a text editor or word processor to display the contents of a file. Almost every text editor allows you to see a text file and to move at will forward and backward through the file. Thus, you should use your word processing program to read through files, except when the files you want to see are short, or you want to keep a printed copy of the file.

You will not be able to display programs or other binary files with the commands discussed in this section. These undisplayable files usually have the extensions COM, EXE, OVR, and BIN. Undisplayable files can have as many as 256 possible character types, may appear on your screen as graphics characters, or may not appear at all. In any case, you can't use the information in these files by simply reading it. If you really want to look at the contents of these files, you can use the DEBUG command, discussed in the "Programming Tools" section of this chapter.

TYPE Command
Internal

The TYPE command displays a text file on the screen.

Common Uses

The command is very easy to use. You simply give the TYPE command followed by the file name:

TYPE *filespec*

MS-DOS will then "type" the file on your screen.

For instance, to see the file LEADSRPT.TXT on the screen, give the command

```
A>TYPE LEADSRPT.TXT

                            Sales Report

                            Tim Meyerstein


New leads generated:

        .
        .
        .
```

The TYPE command will continuously *scroll* the file (that is, show the file line by line) on the screen. Therefore, if the file is longer than the 24 or 25 lines your screen displays, you will probably find the text moving by so fast that it will be impossible to read. To read the file, you can use a special key (or combination of keys) that allows you to freeze the text on the screen. For instance, on the IBM PC, this combination is CONTROL-NUMLOCK. To stop the TYPE command, press CONTROL-C and you will return to MS-DOS.

If the file you are typing has tab characters in it (characters generated by pressing the TAB key), the TYPE command will move to the next column that is an even multiple of 8 (that is, column 8, 16, 24, and so forth) and print the text that follows the tab character. Thus, in the sample printout of the last example, the first printed characters appear in column 24 because there were three tab characters at the beginning of the line.

Warnings and Common Errors

The TYPE command does not prevent you from typing program files and binary files on the screen. If you use TYPE on these files, however, you will probably see gibberish.

Syntax

The syntax of the TYPE command is

TYPE *filespec*

The *filespec* argument is the file to be typed. You cannot use the wild-card characters in the file specification.

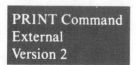

PRINT Command
External
Version 2

The PRINT command prints files on your printer and permits you to continue working with MS-DOS at the same time. It allows you to set up a queue of files to be printed one after the other.

Common Uses

The PRINT command is a sophisticated method of printing files on your printer. Other operating systems allow you to send only one file at a time to the printer, often forcing you to wait until the file is printed before you can continue giving commands. The common syntax for the PRINT command is

PRINT *filespec*

or

PRINT *filespec1 filespec2 ...*

You can queue as many as 10 files at a time for printing.

The first time you run the PRINT command after booting MS-DOS, you will be asked the name of the list device. This is the name of the device where the printed files will be sent. The device name is usually PRN or LPT (the names for the parallel printer port). When you give the device name, be sure *not* to include the colon at the end. If you have a serial printer, the device will probably be called COM1 or COM2.

If you simply press the RETURN key when the question is asked, the PRINT command will assume that you want PRN.

For instance, if you want to print the file HOSPT12.RPT and it is the first file you have printed since booting up your computer, give the command

```
A>PRINT HOSPT12.RPT
Name of list device [PRN]:COM1
Resident part of PRINT installed.

        A:HOSPT12 .RPT is currently being printed
```

The PRINT command would then print the file on your specified output device (in this case, COM1:, the serial port).

Before you give the PRINT command you should be sure that the output device is attached and turned on. Unfortunately, the PRINT command will not tell you when there is a problem with the output device, but the next time you try to give a print command, you will know because the device will refuse to print.

For example, if the printer is not turned on you will see something like this:

```
A>PRINT ACCTSRPT.TXT

        A:ACCTSRPT.TXT is currently being printed

A>PRINT MYFILE
Errors on list device indicate that it
may be off-line. Please check it.

        A:ACCTSRPT.TXT is currently being printed
        A:MYFILE  .     is in queue
```

"Off-line" is jargon for "not working as expected." The result is that neither file is printed.

Queueing files for printing. If you want to print a set of files one after another, you can list as many as 10 file names after the PRINT command. Wild-card characters can also be used to set up a queue of files. To see which files are in the print queue, give the PRINT command with no arguments.

For instance, to print the file NEWPROG.BAS and all the files that have the extension COB, give the command

```
A>PRINT NEWPROG.BAS *.COB

A>PRINT

        A:NEWPROG  .BAS is currently being printed
        A:TSTAMP   .COB is in queue
        A:TSTAMP1  .COB is in queue
        A:TSTAMP2  .COB is in queue
```

The files are now printed on the printer without any further input from you.

Using the PRINT command's arguments. If you give a PRINT command but then decide you do not want to print one of the files in the queue, you can use the /C argument of the PRINT command to cancel a particular file. Simply give the PRINT command followed by that file's name followed by /C.

For example, to cancel the file TSTAMP1.COB, give the command

```
A>PRINT TSTAMP1.COB/C

        A:NEWPROG  .BAS is currently being printed
        A:TSTAMP   .COB is in queue
        A:TSTAMP2  .COB is in queue
```

Another argument is the /T argument. You can use the /T argument to cancel all the files in the queue.

For example, give the command

```
A>PRINT /T

PRINT queue is empty.
```

All files will be deleted from the print queue.

When you cancel files with the / C or / T arguments, the PRINT command will ring the bell on the printer, print out a message on the printer, and advance the paper in the printer to the top of the next page.

The PRINT command expands tab characters, in the same fashion as the TYPE command.

Other Uses

You can use the / P argument in combination with the / C or / T arguments to queue new files. The / P argument allows you to give one command that cancels files out of the queue and allows you to add more. It is not used often.

Rules

The disk containing the file you want printed must be kept in the correct disk drive until the file has been completely printed. If you take it out, a message will be printed on the printer, and the printer will stop.

Do not alter or erase a file in the print queue before it has been printed.

Since the PRINT program remains in memory after you start it, your available RAM decreases by about 3000 bytes (3K).

Warnings and Common Errors

The most common error is not having the printer turned on when you issue the PRINT command. Fortunately, the PRINT command waits until the printer is on before attempting to print files.

Syntax

The syntax of the PRINT command is

PRINT [*filespec* ... [/ T] [/ C] [/ P] ...]

The *filespec* argument is the file to be printed. You can specify many files to be printed either with wild-cards or by listing individual file names. If you give no arguments, the PRINT command will print the list of files you put in the queue.

Using the / T argument cancels the queue of files. The / C argument allows you to cancel files in the queue. / C cancels all of the queue files until the / P argument is given. The / P argument is usually only given if you have given a / T or / C argument in the same command.

**MORE Command
External
Version 2**

The MORE command types a file on your monitor a screenful at a time and then waits for you to press any key before continuing. The MORE command uses input redirection, which is described in Chapter 4, but you do not need to know how to use input redirection to use the MORE command.

Common Uses

The MORE command is easier to use than the TYPE command for files that have more than 20 lines in them. The general syntax of the MORE command is

MORE <*filespec*

The less than sign (<) tells MS-DOS that you are using input redirection.

After displaying 23 lines of your file (if you have a 25-line screen), the program displays

```
-- More --
```

It then waits for you to press any key before continuing. When you press a key, it displays the next screen. The MORE command expands tabs just like the TYPE command.

For example, if you type the command

```
A>MORE <DATACOMM.RPT
```

the file DATACOMM.RPT will be displayed a screenful at a time.

Warnings and Common Errors

If you forget to use the < before the file name, the MORE command will simply echo each line you type. Since this is clearly not what you want, press CONTROL-C to return to MS-DOS.

Syntax

The syntax for the MORE command is

MORE <*filespec*

The less than sign (<) is required for the MORE command to work. The *filespec* argument is the file to be displayed.

DISK MAINTENANCE COMMANDS

This section discusses the following commands:

DIR	*Displays a list of files on a disk*
FORMAT	*Prepares a disk for MS-DOS*
SYS	*Puts the system files and boot tracks on a diskette*
CHKDSK	*Examines and repairs disks*
RECOVER	*Repairs files with bad sectors*
DISKCOPY	*Copies an entire diskette*
DISKCOMP	*Compares two diskettes*
FDISK	*Performs maintenance on the IBM PC/XT*
BACKUP	*Makes backup copies of the hard disk*
RESTORE	*Makes copies of backup files*

This section covers the commands that involve disks and disk directories. You can use the DIR command to find out whether certain files are on a particular disk and how large a file is. You use the FORMAT, DISKCOPY, and SYS commands to prepare floppy diskettes for use. After you have used the DISKCOPY command, the DISKCOMP command lets you compare the disks to determine if the copy was accurate.

No one plans on floppy or hard disks becoming unreadable. However, despite your best efforts, you may sometimes find that MS-DOS cannot read your disk for some reason. If you find errors on your floppy or hard disks, you should use the CHKDSK and RECOVER commands. These commands help repair unreadable disks: the CHKDSK command repairs errors in the disk directory, and the RECOVER command repairs physical errors on the disk (also known as *bad sectors*). These two commands will help you determine what is wrong and even fix it. If they don't work, be sure to read the discussion of solving emergencies in Chapter 5.

DIR Command
Internal

The DIR command lists the files on a disk and gives information about their size and when they were last updated.

Common Uses

The most common use of the DIR command is to list all of your files on the default disk. The general syntax is

DIR [*d:*]

For example, to enter the DIR command, type
```
A>DIR

 Volume in drive A is SALES
 Directory of  A:\

 CALC      EXE     25600     5-20-84    12:58p
 DRIVER    EXE     32420     1-27-84    10:35a
 SALES84   RPT      7168     8-03-84     8:04p
 MAKEFILE  BAT      1664     4-01-84    11:10p
 TOTSALES  DAT      5888     3-08-84    12:09p
 MARTY     DAT      1280     3-08-84    12:12p
 RDBMS     COM     39936     4-27-84    12:19p
 RDBMS     OVL     33120     4-27-84    12:19p
         8 File(s)      11264 bytes free
```
MS-DOS displays a listing of files like the one shown here.

The DIR listing contains several elements you may not recognize:

- The information at the top of the listing, "Volume in drive A is SALES," gives the name of the *disk label* (and the current path name, which is described in Chapter 4). The label name is set by you when you use the / V option with the FORMAT command. If you did not label your disk, this line reads "Volume in drive A has no label." If you are using version 1 of MS-DOS, you will not see this beginning information.

- The first two columns of the DIR listing contain the file name and the extension. In the DIR listing, these two parts of the file specifier are not separated by a period.

- If your disk has a system of sub-directories (which is a feature available in version 2 of MS-DOS that allows you to make many directories on one disk), there will be entries for files called . and .. (unless your current sub-directory is the root). Chapter 4 explains sub-directories in detail.

- The third column contains the size of the file in bytes. (If you are using paths, this column may contain <DIR>, which is not a file, but the name of a sub-directory.)

- The last two columns give the date and time when the file was last updated. If the file has never been updated, these columns give the date and time when it was first created. (If your computer does not have a real-time calendar and you do not routinely enter date and time when you boot up, this date and time may be incorrect.)

- The last line shows how many files are in the list and how many bytes are left on the disk for other files. If you are using version 1 of MS-DOS, this line will tell you the number of files, but not the amount of free space.

You can also view the directory of another disk by specifying the disk.

For instance,

```
A>DIR B:
```

This command makes MS-DOS list the directory of the B: disk on the screen.

Using DIR on individual files. The DIR command lets you look at individual files. You can also get a listing for a group of files by using wild-card characters in the file name.

For instance, suppose you wanted to look at the entry for MARTY.DAT. You would give the command

```
A>DIR MARTY.DAT

 Volume in drive A is SALES
 Directory of  A:\

MARTY      DAT     1280    3-08-84  12:12p
          1 File(s)         11264 bytes free
```

If you wanted to look at all of the files with DAT as their extension, you would give the command

```
A>DIR *.DAT

 Volume in drive A is SALES
 Directory of  A:\

TOTSALES DAT     5888    3-08-84  12:09p
MARTY      DAT     1280    3-08-84  12:12p
          2 File(s)         11264 bytes free
```

The use of the wild-card character (∗) for either the file name or the extension is so common that the DIR command allows you to leave it out.

For instance, the previous command (DIR ∗.DAT) could also be given as

```
A>DIR .DAT
```

The wild-card character is unnecessary. The dot preceding the extension is necessary, however, since it tells MS-DOS that the name is an extension.

Modifying the DIR listing with arguments: The DIR command may be used with two arguments, /W and /P. If the directory has a large number of files and you don't care about the size or update time information, you can use the /W argument to simplify the list.

For example, notice the change in the following two directories:

```
A>DIR C:

 Volume in drive C has no label
 Directory of  C:\

COMMAND  COM    17664    3-08-83  12:00p
ANSI       SYS     1664    3-08-83  12:00p
FORMAT   COM     6016    3-08-83  12:00p
CHKDSK   COM     6400    3-08-83  12:00p
SYS        COM     1408    3-08-83  12:00p
DISKCOPY COM     2444    3-08-83  12:00p
```

```
DISKCOMP COM      2074    3-08-83   12:00p
COMP     COM      2523    3-08-83   12:00p
EDLIN    COM      4608    3-08-83   12:00p
MODE     COM      3139    3-08-83   12:00p
FDISK    COM      6177    3-08-83   12:00p
BACKUP   COM      3687    3-08-83   12:00p
RESTORE  COM      4003    3-08-83   12:00p
PRINT    COM      4608    3-08-83   12:00p
RECOVER  COM      2304    3-08-83   12:00p
ASSIGN   COM       896    3-08-83   12:00p
TREE     COM      1513    3-08-83   12:00p
GRAPHICS COM       789    3-08-83   12:00p
SORT     EXE      1280    3-08-83   12:00p
FIND     EXE      5888    3-08-83   12:00p
MORE     COM       384    3-08-83   12:00p
BASIC    COM     16256    3-08-83   12:00p
BASICA   COM     25984    3-08-83   12:00p
        23 File(s)      31232 bytes free

A>DIR C: /W

 Volume in drive C has no label
 Directory of  C:\

COMMAND  COM     ANSI     SYS     FORMAT   COM     CHKDSK   COM     SYS      COM
DISKCOPY COM     DISKCOMP COM     COMP     COM     EDLIN    COM     MODE     COM
FDISK    COM     BACKUP   COM     RESTORE  COM     PRINT    COM     RECOVER  COM
ASSIGN   COM     TREE     COM     GRAPHICS COM     SORT     EXE     FIND     EXE
MORE     COM     BASIC    COM     BASICA   COM
        23 File(s)      31232 bytes free
```

The /P argument will make the directory listing pause at the end of each page. The message "Strike a key when ready . . ." will appear at the bottom of the screen. (This is similar to the " — More — " prompt displayed by the MORE command.) The DIR command will wait until you press a key before continuing.

Using DIR for sub-directories. If you are using paths, you can use the DIR command to get the directory of a sub-directory by simply naming it in the command.

For example:

```
A>DIR

 Volume in drive A has no label
 Directory of  A:\data

 .             <DIR>       1-19-84    6:20a
 ..            <DIR>       1-19-84    6:20a
 SHELLEY  DAT  17664       3-08-83   12:00p
 TONY     DAT   1664       3-08-83   12:00p
 PHONES        <DIR>       2-18-84   10:55p
         5 File(s)     4631232 bytes free

A>DIR PHONES

 Volume in drive A has no label
 Directory of  A:\data\phones
```

```
    .                  <DIR>        1-19-84    6:20a
    ..                 <DIR>        1-19-84    6:20a
 PHONES      DAT        9191        3-08-83   12:00p
          3 File(s)    4631232 bytes  free
```

Notice that the second line shows you the sub-directory. You can list the directory of the parent sub-directory by giving the command

```
 A>DIR ..
```

For more information about paths and sub-directories, see "Path Maintenance Commands" later in this chapter, and also Chapter 4.

Rules

The DIR listing does not list all files. Some files are hidden from the DIR command. These are files that have a special flag in their directory entry that tells the DIR command not to list them (these are also called "secret" files). You cannot create these files; they are created by the FORMAT command and the SYS command. You should know about them, since they will be listed in the output from the CHKDSK command.

Syntax

The syntax for the DIR command is

DIR [*d:* | *filespec*] [/P] [/W]

If you give the DIR command with no arguments, it will list the directory of the default disk. If you give a *d:*, the directory of that disk will be displayed; if you give a *filespec* (which can contain wild-card characters), only files that are in that *filespec* will be listed.

The /W argument displays the files in five columns across your screen, but does not show the file size or last update time. The /P argument causes the listing to pause at the end of each page.

FORMAT Command
External

The FORMAT command prepares a floppy or hard disk for use with MS-DOS. Some hard disk computer manufacturers require you to use a different command to format their disks. On the IBM PC, the FORMAT command can prepare diskettes so that they can be read by all versions of PC-DOS.

Common Uses

When you buy diskettes, they are usually unformatted; you must use the FORMAT command before attempting to write any files on a diskette. (Chapter 2 described some of the concepts behind formatting disks.) Since formatting a disk erases all of the information on a disk, you must use the command cautiously. Use the FORMAT command to prepare disks for use with MS-DOS.

The general syntax of the FORMAT command is

FORMAT [*d:*]

To format a disk in the B: drive, give the command

```
A>FORMAT B:
```

The FORMAT program responds

```
Insert new diskette for drive B:
and strike any key when ready
```

After you press a key, the program formats the disk and displays

```
Formatting...

Format complete.

Format another (Y/N) ?
```

If you want to format the same drive again, type Y.

Using FORMAT with arguments. The FORMAT command can be used with several arguments. The /S argument tells the FORMAT command to write the boot tracks and the system files on the diskette after it is formatted. This makes the diskette a system disk, which means that you can boot your system with it. The general syntax for the FORMAT command with the /S argument is

FORMAT [*d:*] /S

It is not necessary to use the /S argument on a disk unless you are going to use it as a system disk. This is because MS-DOS reads the system tracks off of a diskette when you boot up your computer. (This is different from other operating systems like CP/M, which read the tracks every time you exit a program.) Since the system files take up 39K of disk space, you can lose a fair amount of your disk space by putting the operating system on a disk where you don't need it.

For example, after formatting the disk with the /S argument, the FORMAT program will display

```
System transferred

   179712 bytes total disk space
    29936 bytes used by system
   139776 bytes available on disk
```

This shows you that some of the space on the disk is taken up by the system files.

The /S argument does not copy the file COMMAND.COM to the formatted disk. This file is not a system file, but it is necessary for running MS-DOS. Thus, if you want to make a disk that you are going to use as a bootable diskette, you have to copy COMMAND.COM to the disk as well.

For example:

```
A>FORMAT B: /S

A>COPY COMMAND.COM B:
```

The result is a bootable diskette.

You can, of course, copy all of the system files instead of COMMAND.COM alone. This will result in a system disk.

The /V argument (under version 2 of MS-DOS) permits you to put a *volume label* (also known as disk label) on the diskette. A volume label is not like the paper label on the outside of the diskette; it is a special 11-character piece of data stored on the diskette in the directory. Some application programs use these labels to identify the contents of a disk. However, volume labels are of limited use for most people.

The FORMAT command is the only MS-DOS command that lets you write a label on a disk, and you can only see this label with the DIR, VOL, and CHKDSK commands.

For example, if you use the /V argument, the program prompts you for the label after formatting the disk:

```
Volume label (11 characters, ENTER for none)?
```

Type in any characters that are valid in file names for the label of the disk.

Specifying tracks and sectors for the IBM PC. If you have double-sided floppy drives and want to make diskettes that someone with single-sided drives can read, you must use the / 1 argument in the FORMAT command. This is because FORMAT would normally format a diskette for double-sided drives (if you have them).

If you are using version 2 of MS-DOS and you want to make diskettes that someone with version 1 of MS-DOS can read, you must use the / 8 argument in the FORMAT command. This is because FORMAT would normally format a diskette for 9 sectors per track under version 2, while computers booted with version 1 can only read disks formatted for 8 sectors per track.

For instance, if you are using version 2 and want to format a diskette that can be used with single-sided drives under version 1 of MS-DOS, give the command

```
A>FORMAT /1/8
```

MS-DOS will ask you to insert the diskette to be formatted into the A: drive and will then format it as a single-sided, 8-sector diskette.

The / B argument is used to format a diskette with 8 sectors per track and space reserved for the hidden system files. This argument makes a diskette that is readable under either MS-DOS version 1 or 2. However, it does not put the files on the diskette. You must write the system files on with the SYS command, described in the next section of this chapter.

Therefore, after you use / B, you can give the formatted diskette to someone else without giving them the actual system tracks and files (which is not allowed under your license with Microsoft). The person receiving the diskette can then use the SYS command to make copies of the system files on the diskette.

Warnings and Common Errors

Remember that the FORMAT command erases all of the information on the destination disk. For this reason, when you format a disk that already has information on it, be sure that you do not want any of that information.

If you want the formatted diskette to eventually be a system diskette, it must be formatted with either the / S or / B argument. This is because of the way that the system files are found by the boot tracks.

If the first three entries on the diskette's directory are not the system files, the diskette will not work as a boot diskette. The SYS command (which writes the boot tracks and system files on a diskette) will only work if either the diskette has been formatted with the /S or /B argument or the diskette has not been written on since it was formatted.

Syntax

The syntax for the format command is

FORMAT [*d:*] [/S] [/1] [/8] [/V] [/B]

The order of the arguments is not important. *d:* is the disk drive to be formatted. If you do not specify a drive, the FORMAT command will assume that you want to format the default drive.

The /S argument causes the boot tracks and system files to be written on formatted diskette. The /1 argument indicates that you want to format the diskette for single-sided drives. The /8 argument indicates that you want to format the diskette for 8 sectors per track. The /V argument puts a volume label on the diskette. The /B argument is used to format a diskette with 8 sectors per track and space reserved for the hidden system files.

SYS Command
External

The SYS command copies the boot tracks and the system files from one diskette to another. However, the disk will not work as a boot diskette if the second diskette is not correctly formatted before running the SYS command.

Common Uses

The most common use for the SYS command is to make copy-protected disks bootable on your system. (These diskettes are usually application software that you buy.) You do this by putting a copy of your operating system on the application program diskette. The reason that application program diskettes come without the operating system is that it is illegal to sell or give a diskette with a copy of the operating system on it without the manufacturer's approval. However, you are allowed to make copies of MS-DOS as long as you run the copies on your computer only. The general syntax of the command is

SYS [*d:*]

If the diskette is not copy-protected, you could format a blank diskette with the FORMAT command and /S argument, copy the COMMAND.COM file from your system diskette to the new diskette, and then copy the files from the application diskette you received to this new diskette. In this case, you would not need to use the SYS command.

Before using the SYS command, the disks must be formatted, as discussed in the preceding section on the FORMAT command.

To add the boot tracks and system files to the diskette in drive B:, use the command

```
A>SYS B:
```

Rules

The disk you write on must either have been formatted with the /S or /B arguments from the FORMAT command or be unused since it was formatted.

Warnings and Common Errors

If you format a disk without the /S or /B arguments and then write on it, you cannot use the SYS command to turn the disk into a bootable disk, even if you erase the file. If you use the SYS command on such a diskette, you can lose data from the disk. Therefore, be absolutely sure that there are no files on a disk before giving the SYS command.

The SYS command does not copy the COMMAND.COM file, which is necessary for making a diskette bootable. You need to use the COPY command to copy COMMAND.COM.

For example:

```
A>SYS B:

A>COPY COMMAND.COM B:
```

This combination of commands copies the boot tracks, system files, and COMMAND.COM to the new disk.

Syntax

The syntax for the SYS command is

SYS *d:*

The *d:* argument is the disk that is to receive the boot tracts and system files.

**CHKDSK Command
External**

The CHKDSK command reports the size of the disk, the amount of space available on the disk, and amount of RAM available. It also reports and sometimes repairs many internal disk errors. However, you should use the RECOVER command instead of CHKDSK to resolve "Bad sector" error messages.

Common Uses

MS-DOS occasionally scrambles the internal directory map, which indicates what files are where on the disk. This sometimes happens while MS-DOS is writing information to a disk. There is little you can do to prevent this. However, if it happens, you can use the CHKDSK command to find out how much damage has been done and possibly fix it. The command is usually given without arguments.

You should use the CHKDSK command regularly to verify the internal correctness of important disks. If you have a hard disk, you should check the disk with the CHKDSK command each time you boot up the system. To do this, put a CHKDSK command in your AUTOEXEC.BAT file. Most of the time, you will give the CHKDSK command with no arguments.

```
For example:

A>CHKDSK
Volume APPOINTMENT created Nov 20, 1983 1:49p

    179712 bytes total disk space
     22016 bytes in 3 hidden files
```

```
    53760 bytes in 5 user files
   103936 bytes available on disk

   589824 bytes total memory
   170288 bytes free
```

The listing in the previous example contains four important pieces of information:

- Since the CHKDSK reported no errors, you can assume that the disk's directory has no internal errors. This does not mean that there are no bad sectors on the disk; it only shows that the directory is complete and all the entries are consistent. Bad sectors only show up when you try to read a file that is on the part of the disk with bad sectors.

- The first line tells you the volume label (APPOINTMENT) and when the label was created.

- The next set of lines gives the total disk space (which depends on how you formatted the disk, and whether it is single- or double-sided), the number and total size of the hidden files (described earlier under the DIR command), the number and size of user files (which are the regular files on your disk), and the amount of space left on the disk. In this case, it reports that the disk can possibly hold 179,712 bytes, that there are 3 hidden files and 5 normal files, and that there are 103,936 bytes free on the disk.

- The last set of lines reports the total RAM in your computer and the amount that is currently unused. The difference between these two numbers represents both the amount of RAM that MS-DOS uses and the amount of RAM that other *resident programs* use. (Resident programs are those that load themselves into memory and stay there, such as the PRINT command and RAM-disk programs.) In this case, there are 170,288 bytes of RAM free from a total of 589,824 in the computer.

If you are using sub-directories, the CHKDSK program will also report the amount of disk space taken by the directory entries.

```
For instance,
A>CHKDSK

   179712 bytes total disk space
    22016 bytes in 2 hidden files
     1024 bytes in 2 directories
```

```
    91648 bytes in 8 user files
    65024 bytes available on disk

    589824 bytes total memory
    171840 bytes free
```

Notice the extra line that tells you that 1024 bytes have been taken by two directories.

Using CHKDSK to test for fragmented files. You can also use the CHKDSK command to tell if a file is contiguous or not. A *contiguous file* is one which has all of its parts on adjacent sectors. The syntax for this form of the command is

CHKDSK *filespec*

In this case, the file name can have wild-card characters.

Figure 3-2 shows one track on a diskette laid out in a straight line with the contents of each sector of the track shown. The file SHOW.MEM takes up sectors 1, 2, and 3, and BAR.TXT takes up sectors 4 and 5; the last three sectors of this track are empty. Suppose you use your word processor and add text to SHOW.MEM so that the file is now 4 sectors long. Where is the new sector placed?

MS-DOS will not put the new data in sector 4, since this would erase part of BAR.TXT. Instead, MS-DOS allows the file to be *fragmented*, or split up on the disk. In this case, MS-DOS would see that sector 6 was empty and put the fourth sector of SHOW.MEM in it, giving a sector map like that shown in Figure 3-3. You do not need to worry about how MS-DOS knows that the different parts of the file are in different parts of the disk; MS-DOS handles that quite naturally.

If many of the files on your disk are fragmented, accessing them will be slower, since the disk heads have to move back and forth more often. If you have a diskette with many fragmented files, the best remedy is to format a new

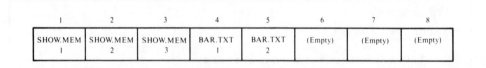

Figure 3-2. A track on a disk showing contiguous files

1	2	3	4	5	6	7	8
SHOW.MEM 1	SHOW.MEM 2	SHOW.MEM 3	BAR.TXT 1	BAR.TXT 2	SHOW.MEM 4	(Empty)	(Empty)

Figure 3-3.   Addition of a new sector produces fragmented file

diskette and use the COPY command to copy all of the files to the new diskette. Do not use the DISKCOPY command to eliminate fragmented files, since this simply copies each sector.

> For example, to see if the file CORPINV.DAT is fragmented, give the command
>
> ```
> A>CHKDSK CORPINV.DAT
> Volume APPOINTMENT created Nov 20, 1983 1:49p
>
>    179712 bytes total disk space
>     22016 bytes in 3 hidden files
>     53760 bytes in 5 user files
>    103936 bytes available on disk
>
>    589824 bytes total memory
>    170288 bytes free
>
> All specified file(s) are contiguous.
> ```
>
> If the file had not been contiguous, the message would have read
>
> ```
> CORPINV.DAT
>     Contains 2 non-contiguous blocks.
> ```

Using CHKDSK with arguments. The CHKDSK command can find a large number of different types of errors. Version 2 of MS-DOS permits you to use the /F (fix) argument to fix some of these errors. This procedure can cause you to lose some of the information on your disk; however, not fixing the disk can cause you to lose even more information. Therefore, if the CHKDSK command reports errors, you should probably run it again with the /F argument. Note, however, that version 1 of MS-DOS automatically fixes the disk and there is no /F argument. The general syntax for this form of the command is

CHKDSK /F

Sometimes, the CHKDSK command will find lost allocation units on your disk (these are also called lost clusters). You can recover these lost clusters by using the CHKDSK /F command. The CHKDSK command will put these clusters into new files where you can look at them. You should use your text editor to see if any of the information in the cluster is text. If you find text, you can move it into the correct files. If the clusters contain programs, you will not be able to read them with your text editor. The information you save will be put into files named FILE*nnnn*.CHK, where *nnnn* is a number starting with 0000.

The /V (verbose) argument is often used to further examine the disk after finding errors with CHKDSK. It causes MS-DOS to report the names of the files that it is examining in the directory as it progresses. If you have errors on the disk, this argument allows you to see where the CHKDSK command is finding them.

It is a good idea to include the CHKDSK command in your AUTOEXEC.-BAT file if you have one. In this way, your computer checks the integrity of your disk each time you boot the system.

Warnings and Common Errors

The /F argument of the CHKDSK command can result in a loss of some information that is readable by MS-DOS. Because of this, you should always first run the CHKDSK command without the /F argument. When CHKDSK reports errors on the disk, you should immediately attempt to copy all of the files off of the disk with the COPY command. You may or may not be able to, depending on the seriousness of the errors. If you come to files that you can't copy, simply skip over them. After you have copied all the files that you can, use the CHKDSK command with the /F argument.

Syntax

The following kinds of syntax may be used with the CHKDSK command:

CHKDSK [*d:*] [/F] [/V]

or

CHKDSK *filespec*

The *d:* argument is the disk drive you want to check. The /F argument indicates that you want the CHKDSK command to fix the disk if it finds errors. In version 2 of MS-DOS, CHKDSK normally only reports the errors to you.

The /V argument indicates that you want the CHKDSK command to work in its verbose mode and give you complete messages as it analyzes your disk.

If you give a *filespec*, the CHKDSK command checks whether the file or files are fragmented.

RECOVER Command
External
Version 2

The RECOVER command is used to restore files on a disk with bad sectors. It recovers files that have part of their data in the bad sectors, but it cannot recover the data in the bad sector. You cannot use the RECOVER command to restore a file that has been erased, nor can you use it to recover a program that has a bad sector. (A program will not run if a portion is missing.) The RECOVER command also recovers disks that have part of their directories in bad sectors.

Common Uses

The general syntax for the RECOVER command is

RECOVER *filespec*

If you get a "Bad sector" error message while running an application program, it probably means that the disk media (the magnetic coating on the disk) is damaged. Dust and fingerprints are common causes of this on floppy diskettes.

Chapter 5 discusses how to care for disks as well as how to recover from errors that the CHKDSK and RECOVER commands cannot handle. Chapter 5 also has information on commercial programs that perform the same functions as the RECOVER command. Some of these programs have creative ways of retrieving information that are less likely to lose information.

Generally, when you get a "Bad sector" error message, you will know which file it is referring to. For instance, if while you are writing a file with your word processor, you get a "Bad sector" message, you can assume that it is probably that file that has the bad sector. To recover as much file information as possible, give the RECOVER command with the file name.

For instance, to recover the file TIME.TBL, give the command

A>RECOVER TIME.TBL

Remember that the RECOVER command will not recover any information in the bad sector. Thus, don't be surprised if a recovered text file is missing a fair amount of text from the middle.

There is no way to recover a program with a bad sector because important program steps in the bad sector will have been lost. Similarly, it is very unlikely that you can do anything to salvage a data base file with a bad sector since most data base programs store the data in a compacted form that is similar to that of program files.

If the directory of your disk has a bad sector, you can use the RECOVER command to try to piece the directory together again; however, none of the files will have their correct names. Each file on the recovered disk will have the name FILE*nnnn*.REC, where *nnnn* is a number starting with 0000. To reconstruct your directory, you must determine the contents of each file individually, and give it its proper name again.

For example, if the disk directory of B: has a bad sector, the command for recovering it is

A>RECOVER B:

Since there is no way for the RECOVER command to know which parts of the disk directory are on good sectors, this form of the RECOVER command will reconstruct the whole directory (without the correct file names). This process becomes complicated if you have a hard disk with many files because deciphering which file is which can be incredibly time-consuming. Thus, be very sure that you have a bad sector in your directory before using this form of the RECOVER command.

Warnings and Common Errors

Remember that once you have used the RECOVER command on a file or directory, there is no way to reverse the order or "un-recover" it. Any information lost in the process of recovering a file or directory is lost forever.

Syntax

The syntax for the RECOVER command is either:

RECOVER *filespec*

or

RECOVER *d:*

The first form of the command is used to recover files with bad sectors. It is extremely unlikely that you will use the second form of the RECOVER command, which attempts to recover disks that have a bad sector in the directory.

DISKCOPY Command
External
IBM only

The DISKCOPY command copies an entire diskette to another diskette, erasing the previous contents of the destination diskette. Copying disks with the DISKCOPY command is usually faster than using the COPY command. Many manufacturers have similar commands.

Common Uses

The DISKCOPY command gives you a fast way to copy entire diskettes.
The general syntax is

DISKCOPY *source-disk: dest-disk:*

Instead of reading file by file like the COPY command, DISKCOPY reads all of the information from the sectors on the source diskette and then writes out those sectors on the destination diskette. (If the destination disk is unformatted or has a different format than the source disk, the DISKCOPY command will reformat it.) Thus, it makes an exact copy by copying the boot tracks, the directory, and the files.

For example, if you have two floppy disk drives, you would run the program with the following command:

```
A>DISKCOPY A: B:
```

In this example, the diskette you want to copy (the source diskette) is in A:, and the diskette receiving the copy (the destination diskette) is in B:. Since all information on the destination diskette (B:) will be erased, you should be absolutely sure that you have not switched these two. The program will now ask you to

```
Insert source diskette in drive A:

Insert target diskette in drive B:

Strike any key when ready
```

The DISKCOPY command is giving you one last chance to check that the proper diskettes are in the proper drives. Press any key, and the program will display

```
Copying 9 sectors per track, 2 side(s)
```

If you are copying from a diskette that was formatted with 8 sectors per track or 1 side, the numbers in this prompt will, of course, be different.

If the destination diskette is not formatted or is formatted differently than the source diskette, the DISKCOPY command will tell you

```
Formatting while copying
```

This means that you do not have to format the destination diskette before copying onto it. In fact, formatting while copying is faster than formatting first and then copying. You will hear the heads of the floppy disk drives moving, and after a few moments, the program will ask

```
Copy complete

Copy another (Y/N)?
```

If you want to make another copy, type Y; otherwise, type N.

If you have only one floppy disk drive, you can still use the DISKCOPY command. The program will first read the information off of the source diskette and then tell you to put in the destination diskette. Depending on the amount of memory in your computer, you may have to switch diskettes two or three times.

For example, to use the DISKCOPY command in one drive, give the command

```
A>DISKCOPY

Insert source diskette in drive A:

Strike any key when ready

Copying 9 sectors per track, 2 side(s)

Insert target diskette in drive A:

Strike any key when ready

Copying 9 sectors per track, 2 side(s)
```

Even though the DISKCOPY command verifies data after it is written, you may want to run the DISKCOMP command after you copy a diskette with the DISKCOPY command.

Since the DISKCOPY command copies all of the diskette, it is common to use this command to make backup copies of diskettes that contain software. DISKCOPY copies all of the files as well as any hidden files that the manufacturers have put on the disk. However, the DISKCOPY command will not work with copy-protected diskettes (see Chapter 5 for a discussion about backing up copy-protected diskettes).

Warnings and Common Errors

As with all the commands that can erase data on your diskette, you must be sure that you have the correct diskette in the correct drive before you run the DISKCOPY program. Another good way to prevent erasing information from the wrong disk is to use a write-protect tab on the source diskette before you run the DISKCOPY program.

Syntax

The syntax for the DISKCOPY command is

DISKCOPY [*d1:*] [*d2:*] [/1]

The argument *d1:* is the source diskette and *d2:* is the destination diskette.

You can specify either the same drive or different drives. If you give only one drive, the destination drive is assumed to be the default drive. If you do not give a drive, the DISKCOPY command will assume that you want to copy the diskettes using only one drive. The DISKCOPY command can work on one drive; it simply prompts you to switch the two diskettes in and out. Table 3-3 gives examples of using these arguments.

The / 1 argument indicates that you only want to copy one side of the diskette, regardless of whether it is a single- or double-sided diskette.

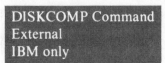

DISKCOMP Command
External
IBM only

The DISKCOMP command compares each sector of two diskettes to be sure they are exactly alike. It is only useful immediately after a DISKCOPY command has been given. This is because any change you make to a diskette (such as altering a file) will show up in the DISKCOMP command.

Common Uses

It is likely that the only time you will use the DISKCOMP command is after copying disks with DISKCOPY. The general syntax is

DISKCOMP *d1*: *d2*:

Table 3-3. Possible Arguments for the DISKCOPY Command

Command	Meaning
DISKCOPY A: B:	Copy from the diskette in A: to the diskette in B:.
DISKCOPY A: A:	Copy from the diskette in A: to another diskette, which will be switched into A:.
DISKCOPY B:	Copy from the diskette in B: to the diskette in the default drive.
DISKCOPY	Copy from the diskette in the default drive to another diskette, which will be switched into the default drive.

For example, if you copied from A: to B:, you can compare the diskettes to ensure that the copy is accurate. You would use the following command:

```
A>DISKCOMP A: B:
```

If the disks compare exactly (as they almost always will), the program prints

```
Diskettes compare ok
```

If the diskettes do not compare exactly, the DISKCOMP command will report the location (track and side) where the error occurs. The report lists the tracks that do not compare exactly:

```
Compare error(s) on
Track 04, Side 0

Compare error(s) on
Track 23, Side 1
```

Warnings and Common Errors

Remember that the DISKCOMP command is only useful after a DISKCOPY command, since other modifications that you might make to the diskette (such as changing a file or adding another file to the disk) will cause many mismatches on the diskettes to be reported. This is similar to the relation between the COPY and COMP commands.

Syntax

The syntax for the DISKCOPY command is

DISKCOMP [*d1:*] [*d2:*] [/1] [/8]

d1: and *d2:* are the source and destination diskettes respectively. This command has the same arguments as the DISKCOPY command. You can specify either the same drive or different drives; if you give only one drive, the destination drive will be assumed to be the default drive. If you do not give a drive, the DISKCOMP command will assume that you want to compare the diskettes using only the default drive. The arguments for the DISKCOMP command are the same as those for the DISKCOPY command.

The /1 argument indicates that you only want to compare one side of the diskette, regardless of whether it is a single- or double-sided diskette. The /8 argument should not be used unless your disks were formatted under version 1, which uses an 8-sector format. The /8 argument causes DISKCOMP to compare 8 sectors per track, even if the diskettes contain 9 sectors per track.

FDISK Command
External
Version 2
IBM only

The IBM PC/XT Fixed Disk can be separated into different partitions so that as many as four operating systems can run on it. These partitions act like separate hard disks: each operating system does not recognize the portion of the disk that belongs to the other operating systems. The FDISK command allows you to create the PC-DOS partition on the IBM Fixed Disk.

Common Uses

In addition to creating the PC-DOS partition on the IBM PC/XT Fixed Disk, the FDISK command also allows you to change the *active partition* (that is, the partition currently in use) to delete the PC-DOS partition, to display information about the current partition, and to use FDISK on another Fixed Disk. When you enter the FDISK command, a menu appears that allows you to select one of these options.

The FDISK command is only useful when you first set up your PC/XT (and then, only if your dealer did not install PC-DOS on the hard disk for you). It will work with the Fixed Disk that comes with the PC/XT, but may not work with other hard disks that are used with the IBM PC. In addition, FDISK can only be used to create the PC-DOS partition; other operating systems must be used to create or delete their own partitions. If you need to use this command, refer to your IBM PC-DOS manual.

BACKUP Command
External
Version 2
IBM only

The BACKUP command is used to make backup copies of files from the IBM PC/XT Fixed Disk to floppy disks. This program is difficult to use, and if it is used incorrectly, it can erase valuable information from your disks. The backup files produced using the BACKUP command cannot be used directly; they must first be copied again onto the Fixed Disk using the RESTORE command. Chapter 5 discusses better methods for backing up your data.

Common Uses

The general syntax for the BACKUP command is

BACKUP *filespec d:*

The *filespec* argument includes the Fixed Disk drive name, if it is not the default drive. For more information on the command, see the IBM PC-DOS manual.

RESTORE Command
External
Version 2
IBM only

The RESTORE command is used to restore files that were backed up onto a floppy diskette with the BACKUP command. The RESTORE command reconstructs the contents of the diskette onto the IBM PC/XT Fixed Disk. Like the BACKUP command, it is difficult to use. Chapter 5 discusses better methods for backing up your data.

Common Uses

The general syntax for the command is

> RESTORE *d: filespec*

The *d:* argument is the name of the floppy disk drive. The *filespec* argument includes the Fixed Disk drive name if it is not the default drive. For more information on the command, see the IBM PC-DOS manual.

SYSTEM SETTINGS

This section discusses the following commands:

DATE	*Sets the date*
TIME	*Sets the time*
VERIFY	*Tells MS-DOS to double-check when it writes on disks*
MODE	*Changes communication parameters*
VER	*Displays the MS-DOS version number*
VOL	*Displays the label of a disk*
PROMPT	*Changes the MS-DOS prompt*
BREAK	*Causes MS-DOS to check for user interrupts more often*
ASSIGN	*Changes the letters assigned to disks*
CTTY	*Changes the console to a serial port*
SET	*Changes environment strings*

Most of the commands in this section are used to set various *system settings* in MS-DOS. System settings are internal information kept by MS-DOS that tells it how you want it to act. Although these commands are not necessary to know, they are quite easy to learn and use.

Each time you boot MS-DOS, the system chooses many settings by default. If you don't like the default settings, you can use the commands in this section to change the setting. To change your setting automatically, you can include the appropriate commands in an AUTOEXEC.BAT file. For example, you could change the setting for MS-DOS's prompt (which is usually A>) to another string of characters.

The ASSIGN, CTTY, and SET commands are rarely used.

DATE Command
Internal

The DATE command sets the date that MS-DOS uses when it updates files. It acts like the date prompt you see when you boot up MS-DOS.

Common Uses

You can either give the date on the command line or have the DATE command ask you to enter it.

The general syntax is

DATE [*new-date*]

Note that this command sets the internal date that MS-DOS keeps in RAM, not the date of a file (the file's date is set when you write the file on the disk).

For example, to give a new date on the command line, enter

```
A>DATE 7/10/84
```

To have the DATE command prompt, you enter

```
A>DATE
Current date is Tue 7-10-84
Enter new date:█
```

You can also decline to give the date by pressing RETURN, which will leave the date the same as it was before you gave the command.

Some computers have internal clocks. Instead of setting the date and time manually, your manufacturer may have included a program you can run to read the internal clock and set the date and time for you.

Rules

The date must be typed in as three numbers separated by either dashes (-) or slashes (/). The complete rules for formatting the date were given in "Starting up MS-DOS" in Chapter 2.

Warnings and Common Errors

Some BASIC programs change the date. If you find that the date has been set incorrectly after running a program, you may want to reset it with the DATE command.

Syntax

The syntax for the DATE command is

DATE [*mm-dd-yy*]

mm-dd-yy is the month, day, and year. You can give this parameter with either dashes (-) or slashes (/) between the numbers. If you do not give a date on the command line, the DATE command will ask you for one.

TIME Command
Internal

The TIME command sets the time that MS-DOS uses when it updates files. It acts as the time prompt when you boot up MS-DOS.

Common Uses

The general syntax of the TIME command is

TIME [*new-time*]

You can either give the time on the command line or have the TIME command prompt you.

For example, to give a new time on the command line, enter

```
A>TIME 9:41
```

To have the TIME command prompt, you enter

```
A>TIME
Current time is 9:41:03
Enter new time:
```

You can also decline to give the time by pressing RETURN, which will leave the time the same as it was before you gave the command.

Some computers have internal clocks. Instead of setting the date and time manually, your manufacturer may have included a program you can run to read the internal clock and set the date and time.

Rules

The only format acceptable for the time is in hours, minutes, and seconds separated by colons (:). The complete rules for formatting the time were given in "Starting up MS-DOS" in Chapter 2.

Warnings and Common Errors

Some BASIC programs change the clock in order to time events. If they do, they usually set it to midnight (00:00:00). Thus, if you find that the time has been set incorrectly after running a program, you may want to reset it with the TIME command.

Syntax

The syntax for the TIME command is

TIME [*hh:mm:ss.xx*]

hh:mm:ss.xx is the hours, minutes, seconds, and hundredths of seconds. You must give the time with colons (and a decimal point, if you are very accurate). The seconds and hundredths of seconds are optional.

VERIFY Command
Internal
Version 2

The VERIFY command makes MS-DOS verify the information it writes on a disk every time it does so. MS-DOS checks the information by rereading it off the disk and comparing it to the information that was supposed to be written out.

Common Uses

Although it is unlikely that MS-DOS will incorrectly write out information on a disk, the consequences can be disastrous if it does happen. The benefits of forcing MS-DOS to verify after writing far outweigh the fraction of a second it takes to do so. Unless the increased disk-writing speed is critical to you, you should probably have verify set to ON.

To cause MS-DOS to verify when it writes to a disk, give the command

```
A>VERIFY ON
```

To find out whether the verify setting is ON or OFF, give the VERIFY command with no arguments.

For example, enter

```
A>VERIFY
VERIFY is on
```

MS-DOS will display a message that lets you know VERIFY's current status.

Syntax

The syntax for the VERIFY command is

VERIFY [{ON | OFF}]

When VERIFY is set to ON, MS-DOS will verify all data it writes. The OFF argument tells MS-DOS not to verify data. As an alternative, you can tell the COPY command to verify single copy operations by using the /V argument, regardless of the status of the VERIFY command.

The MS-DOS default is not to verify after writing. If you give the VERIFY command without either argument, it will print out its current status.

MODE Command
External
IBM only

The MODE command changes the way in which MS-DOS communicates with external devices. It allows you to set the communications for the printer, the color and monochrome graphics adapters, and the communications ports.

Common Uses

The MODE command has many different purposes. In general, you use it to change the way that MS-DOS communicates with your computer's hardware or *peripherals* (devices that you add to your computer). This is often necessary if you use hardware that uses different communications *protocols* than the ones that MS-DOS assumes by default. Protocols are the electronic method MS-DOS uses to talk to devices. Protocols are the rules that devices and computers use to communicate, just like diplomatic protocols in real life.

Changing print spacings. One use of the MODE command is to change MS-DOS's default assumptions about your printer. The general syntax for this form of the MODE command is

MODE LPT*n*: *linewidth*, *linesize*

In this form, the *n* specifies which printer port number (1, 2, or 3) you are resetting; the *linewidth* is the number of characters per line that the printer can handle; and *linesize* is the number of lines per inch. The *linewidth* argument must be either 80 or 132, and *linesize* must be either 6 or 8. (The defaults are 80 and 6.)

For example, to change the default settings for LPT1: to 132 characters per line and 8 lines per inch, give the command

```
A>MODE LPT1: 132,8
```

Until you turn off your computer or use MODE to change the settings again, your printer will print condensed characters.

If your printer is not turned on or working, the parallel port may not always respond. Instead, it will produce a *time-out error.* You should use the P argument for the MODE command, which specifies that if the port does not respond, MS-DOS should continuously try to send data to the port. If, however, the port never responds, you must reboot your system.

For example, to change the default settings for LPT1: to 132 characters per line, 6 lines per inch, and a continuous retry, give the command

```
A>MODE LPT1: 132,6,P
```

(Notice that you do not use a slash for the P argument.)

Setting the display adapters. The MODE command can also be used for setting the display adapters (the optional boards used to control the monitor of your system) or for switching between two adapters. For this use, the general syntax for the MODE command is

MODE *screenwidth*

Table 3-4 explains the possible values for *screenwidth.*

Table 3-4. MODE Command Arguments for Display Adapters

Argument	Meaning
40	Set the color adapter to 40 characters across.
80	Set the color adapter to 80 characters across.
CO40	Switch to the color adapter and set it to 40 characters across.
CO80	Switch to the color adapter and set it to 80 characters across.
BW40	Switch to the color adapter, set it to 40 characters across, and disable the color on the screen (only use black and white).
BW80	Switch to the color adapter, set it to 80 characters across, and disable the color on the screen (only use black and white).
MONO	Switch to the monochrome adapter (which always uses 80 columns across).

For example, if you have both adapters installed and are currently using the monochrome adapter, you can switch from the monochrome to the color adapter by using the following command:

```
A>MODE C080
```

If you are already using the color adapter in 80-column mode and want to switch to 40-column mode, give the command

```
A>MODE 40
```

You cannot change the monochrome adapter to 40 columns.

If you are using a color adapter card, you can use the R or L arguments to shift the whole screen display one character to the right or left. You would use this to center the display in the screen area if it isn't correctly centered (this rarely occurs). To check the centering, use the T (test) argument.

For example, if you notice that you can't read the rightmost letter on the screen properly, give the command

```
A>MODE 80, L, T
```

MS-DOS will move the screen display one character to the left and test if it is centered.

Setting communication protocols. Another use of the MODE command is to set the protocols for the communication, or serial, ports. The devices usually connected to communications ports are serial printers, modems, and terminals.

Before you attach a device to the serial port, check the manual to determine which protocol the device expects. If the protocol is different, you can usually set the protocol in the device with switches. (Consult your hardware manual for more information on how to do this.) The protocols for the communications ports are the baud rate, parity, data bits, and stop bits. These terms will be described shortly.

The general syntax for the communications port is

MODE COM*n*: *baud, parity, databits, stopbits*

The *n* indicates the number of the communications port. All arguments after the *baud* are optional, but you usually specify them anyhow. The list that follows defines each of these arguments. Note that they can only have the values described in Table 3-5.

- *Baud rate.*   This is the number of bits per second at which you communicate. Table 3-6 lists some common baud rates for many devices.

- *Parity.*   The parity is a way of checking that each byte of information was passed correctly. Parity can be even, odd, or none (if your device manual talks about "ignore" for parity, it is the same as none).

- *Data bits.*   This is the number of bits, always either 7 or 8, that contain data in each byte.

- *Stop bits.*   These are the number of bits, always either 1 or 2, that are transmitted after the data bits in each byte.

Table 3-5.   MODE Command Arguments for the Communications Port

Argument	Possible values
baud	110, 150, 300, 600, 1200, 2400, 4800, 9600
parity	N (ignore parity) O (odd parity) E (even parity)
data bits	7, 8
stop bits	1, 2

Table 3-6.   Common Baud Rates for Devices

Device	Common rates (in baud, or bits per second)
Modem	300 or 1200 (rarely, 110)
Printer or Plotter	4800, 9600, 19200 (most can be set to any rate)
Terminal	9600, 19200 (most can be set to any rate)

To find out which settings are used for your device, read the instruction manual for that device. If you still can't figure out the settings for your device, try using the most common setting: no parity, 8 data bits, and 1 stop bit. MS-DOS's default is 7 data bits, 1 stop bit, and even parity.

> For example, suppose you wanted to set communications port (COM2:) to 9600 baud, no parity, 8 data bits, and 1 stop bit (a typical setting for many serial printers). You would give the command
>
> ```
> A>MODE COM2: 9600,N,8,1
> ```

When you change some of the protocols, use the comma to maintain the parts you want to remain the same. Thus, if you have a MODE command with many arguments and you want to leave some of the current settings alone, simply include the commas in the place of these arguments. You must include one comma for each argument you skip.

> For instance, the command
>
> ```
> A>MODE COM2: 9600,,,2
> ```
>
> leaves the parity and data bits set to what they were originally, but changes the stop bits to 2.

As in setting the parallel ports, you can tell MS-DOS to ignore time-out errors by adding a P argument to the end of this form of the MODE command.

Redirecting printer output. Another use of the MODE command is redirecting printer output to a communications port. This means that any time a command sends a file to the printer (PRN:), the data will be redirected to a communications port (such as COM1:) instead. This is especially useful if you have a serial printer. The syntax for this form of the MODE command is

MODE LPTn:=COMn

> For example, if you want all of the information that MS-DOS would normally send to the parallel printer port (PRN:, which is also LPT1:) to be sent to the serial COM1: port, give the command
>
> ```
> A>MODE LPT1:=COM1:
> ```

Syntax

The MODE command uses the following general kinds of syntax:

For setting printer ports:

MODE LPT*n*: [*linewidth*] [,[*linesize*] [,P]]

For the color or monochrome display adapters:

MODE *screenwidth* [, {R | L} [,T]]

For the serial ports:

MODE COM*n*: *baud* [,*parity* [,*databits* [,*stopbits* [,P]]]]

For redirecting the printer output:

MODE LPT*n*:=COM*n*

The *n* is a number in all forms of the commands.

In the first syntax (for the printer ports), *linewidth* is the number of characters, 80 or 132, on the line. *linesize* is the number of lines, 6 or 8, per inch. The P argument specifies continuous retry. The defaults for the line printer are 80 characters per line, 6 lines per inch, and no retry.

In the second syntax (for communicating with the color or monochrome display adapters), *screenwidth* may be 40, 80, BW40, BW80, CO40, CO80, or MONO. If you are using a color adapter card, the R and L arguments shift the display to the right or left respectively. You can check for the correct alignment by using the T argument, which puts a test pattern on the screen.

In the third syntax (for setting the serial ports), the arguments are the baud rate, parity checking, and the number of data bits and stop bits for the port. The P argument is similar to the P argument used in the printer port syntax in that it instructs MS-DOS to retry the port if it does not respond. The defaults are E (parity), 7 (data bits), and 1 (stopbit); if you set the baud rate to 110, the default for *stopbits* will be 2.

In the fourth syntax (for redirecting the printer output), the two *n*'s are the numbers of the printer and serial port respectively.

VER Command
Internal
Version 2

The VER command displays the version number of MS-DOS.

Common Uses

This command is used if you forget which version of MS-DOS you are using. To use it, you simply enter VER and press the RETURN key.

For instance, on an IBM PC running MS-DOS version 2, this command would display

```
A>VER

IBM Personal Computer DOS Version  2.00
```

VOL Command
Internal
Version 2

The VOL command displays the volume label for a disk. Volume labels are set with the FORMAT command, described earlier in this chapter.

Common Uses

The VOL command is extremely easy to use. The general syntax is

VOL [*d:*]

where *d:* is the drive name of the disk in question.

For example, to see the label on B:, give the command

```
A>VOL B:
 Volume in drive B is TRUCK1A
```

If the volume has no label, the VOL command will print

```
 Volume in drive B has no label
```

Syntax

The syntax for the VOL command is

VOL [*d:*]

The *d:* argument is the drive that contains the disk whose label you want to see. If you do not specify a drive, the label of the default drive will be shown.

PROMPT Command
Internal
Version 2

The PROMPT command will change the MS-DOS prompt to any string of characters. The usual prompt is the default drive letter followed by a greater than sign (for example, A>). If other people use your computer, it is unlikely that you will want to change your system prompt.

Common Uses

You can use the PROMPT command to change the MS-DOS prompt. In changing the prompt, you can get more information on your screen whenever you get the MS-DOS prompt. Table 3-7 lists the special characters you can

Table 3-7. Special Characters in a Prompt String

Character*	Meaning
t	Current time
d	Current date
n	Default drive
p	Current path (including drive)
v	MS-DOS version number
g	Greater than character ($>$)
l	Less than character ($<$)
b	Vertical bar character ($\mid$)
q	Equals sign character ($=$)
—	Carriage return and line feed characters
h	Backspace, which erases the last character
e	ESCAPE character (ASCII code 27)
$	$ character

*Special characters must be preceded by a $ when entered in the PROMPT command line.

use to add information to the prompt. To use a special character, you must precede it in the argument string with a dollar sign ($). You can also include any other text in the prompt. The general syntax is

PROMPT *prompt-string*

Suppose you wanted to find out the date and time whenever you reach the MS-DOS prompt. In order to change the prompt to look like this

```
17:02:33.91 ¦ Tue 7-10-84 ¦ A>▓
```

(that is, with the time and date added), you would give the command

```
A>PROMPT $t $b $d $b $n$g
17:02:33.91 ¦ Tue 7-10-84 ¦ A>▓
```

Notice that there are spaces between all of the characters and symbols except between the $n and $g. A space in the prompt string causes a space in the prompt, as you can see in the line below it, which shows the new, more detailed prompt. Note that any character not preceded by a dollar sign is interpreted as a normal character with no special function (such as "Hi, Sally!").

For example, if you want to add a friendly prompt that combines a message with special characters, enter

```
A>PROMPT Hi, Sally!$ You are in $p$ Your command $q
Hi, Sally!
You are in a:\reports\sally
Your command =▓
```

Note that the characters after the first and third dollar signs are underscores.

Rules

Every special character in the prompt string must be preceded by a dollar sign. If the PROMPT command does not recognize the character, it will be ignored, even if it is preceded by a dollar sign.

Warnings and Common Errors

If many people use your computer, be sure that the novices know what to do when they see a prompt other than A>. An altered MS-DOS prompt in an AUTOEXEC.BAT file can also be very confusing if someone else starts up the computer. However, simple prompt changes (such as adding the date and time on other lines) probably won't cause much confusion. Be sure to test any prompt change before putting it in an AUTOEXEC.BAT file.

The PROMPT command writes information into the *environment,* which is a special part of RAM that MS-DOS uses to hold information (see the SET command for more information on this concept). The environment has limited space, however. If you give the PROMPT command and get the error message "Out of environment space," you cannot change the prompt until you reboot your computer.

Syntax

The syntax for the PROMPT command is

PROMPT [*prompt-string*]

The *prompt-string* is a string of characters that contains the information you want in the MS-DOS prompt. If you do not give a *prompt-string*, the MS-DOS prompt will return to its default.

BREAK Command
Internal
Version 2

The BREAK command sets MS-DOS to check whether CONTROL-C or the BREAK key has been pressed. (This key differs from computer to computer; on the IBM PC, it is the CONTROL-BREAK combination.) This command is useful if you are running programs that only do computations and memory management without printing characters on the screen or taking input from the keyboard.

Common Uses

BREAK may be set to ON or OFF (The default is OFF). The ON argument tells MS-DOS that whenever a program performs any internal command it should check if the CONTROL-BREAK key combination has been pressed. The OFF argument tells MS-DOS to check only when a program performs a screen or keyboard system call. Thus, setting BREAK to ON makes the system check for the abort key sequence more often.

The only use of this command is to make MS-DOS check whether you have pressed the CONTROL-C or BREAK key more often than normal.

For instance, enter

```
A>BREAK ON
```

to set BREAK to ON.

To get the current status of the system setting, give the command with no argument.

For example, enter the following command to see whether BREAK is ON or OFF:

```
A>BREAK
BREAK is on
```

Syntax

The syntax for the BREAK command is

BREAK [{ON | OFF}]

The only choices for the argument are ON and OFF. If the BREAK command is given without either argument, it will print its current status.

ASSIGN Command
External
Version 2

The ASSIGN command makes MS-DOS temporarily reassign the disk letters so that when a program asks for information from one disk, it actually gets it from another. This command is rarely used, and unless used carefully, it can cause disastrous results.

Common Uses

It is unlikely that you will need to use this command since most programs written for MS-DOS do not contain the programming error that the ASSIGN command is designed to overcome. The ASSIGN command is only useful before running a program that includes drive names in the files it accesses or writes. Very few programs specify the drive name in file names; usually, they assume that all files are on the default drive. The general syntax is

ASSIGN *old-letter = new-letter*

where old-letter represents the drive name written in the program and *new-letter* is the drive name that should be used instead.

For example, consider what would happen if your computer had only drives A: and B:, and you had an application program that tried to read the file C:TENURE.DAT. Since you have no C: drive, the program would never find the file. If, however, you had a copy of the file on B:, you could give the following command before running the program:

```
A>ASSIGN C=B
```

This tells MS-DOS that whenever a program tries to read or write a file on C:, MS-DOS should look on B: instead.

You can, if necessary, make more than one reassignment in one ASSIGN command.

For example, to assign requests for both A: and B: to C:, give the command

```
A>ASSIGN A=C B=C
```

MS-DOS will now look on C: for all requests for data from A: and B:.

Once you are finished with the program, be sure to clear the assignment by giving the ASSIGN command with no arguments.

Give the command as

```
A>ASSIGN
```

The disk drives will be reassigned their regular names.

Rules

You cannot use colons in the ASSIGN command. Some programs, such as IBM's DISKCOPY and DISKCOMP commands, will ignore the reassignments made with the ASSIGN command.

Warnings and Common Errors

The ASSIGN command can be dangerous if not used carefully. For instance, you might make an assignment that you did not intend, and subsequent programs that you run would not look for files on the correct drives. For instance, if you first give an ASSIGN command and then use the ERASE command, you could erase files from the wrong disk.

Another problem with the ASSIGN command occurs when you try to reassign the letter of the disk that contains the ASSIGN program. When this happens, you cannot clear the assignment without rebooting your computer since you can no longer access the disk that has the ASSIGN program.

Syntax

The syntax for the ASSIGN command is

ASSIGN [*d1*=*d2* ...]

d1 and *d2* are the drive letters that you want to reassign. If a program requests to read or write to the *d1* disk after receiving the ASSIGN command, MS-DOS actually reads or writes to the *d2* disk. You cannot use colons in the ASSIGN command.

If you give no argument to the ASSIGN command, all drive assignments will return to normal.

CTTY Command
Internal
Version 2

The CTTY command allows you to change from the standard console (keyboard and screen) to one of your serial communications ports. This command is rarely used.

Common Uses

The only time you might use this command is if you wanted to connect a terminal to one of your communications ports. The general syntax for the command is

CTTY *device*

The *device* is where you want the console to be. Note that you do not use the colon in the device name (in most commands, you do).

For example, if you attached a terminal to the first auxiliary port (which is called AUX: or COM1:), you can turn that into the MS-DOS console by giving the command

A>CTTY AUX

or

A>CTTY COM1

To switch back to your normal console, give the command

    A>CTTY CON

Rules

Do not include the colon in the device name. The only acceptable devices are AUX, CON, AND COM*n* (where *n* is a number).

Warnings and Common Errors

Once you have switched the console to one of the communications ports, you cannot switch back without giving some commands to a device (such as a terminal) that is connected to that port. To give commands, you must use the newly assigned console. Thus, be absolutely sure that the terminal you have hooked on that port is set at the correct baud rate and data protocols (see your device manual for these specifications). If you have an error here, you must reboot your computer.

Syntax

The syntax for the CTTY command is

  CTTY *device*

device is the device that you want MS-DOS to respond to as the console. Do not include the colon in the device name.

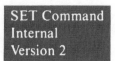

SET Command
Internal
Version 2

   The SET command defines the *environment variables,* which are kept in memory with MS-DOS. Some of these variables are defined by other commands (such as PROMPT and PATH).
   The SET command is rarely used except for cases in which a specific software program instructs you to use it before running the software. In this

case, the documentation for the program will probably specify the exact SET command you need.

Common Uses

There is no common use for the SET command. However, if by some slim chance you have an application program that tells you to use the SET command, it is very simple to use.

> For instance, to see all of the current variables in memory, use the command
>
> ```
> A>SET
> COMSPEC=A:\COMMAND.COM
> PATH=
> ```
>
> This shows that the variables COMSPEC and PATH are defined. MS-DOS defined them when you booted up your system; however, MS-DOS does not do anything with these definitions. If you want to add the variable DATDISK and give it the value A:, you would give the command
>
> ```
> A>SET DATDISK=A:
>
> A>SET
> COMSPEC=A:\COMMAND.COM
> PATH=
> DATDISK=A:
> ```

You can also use the environment variables inside of batch files. Their use is similar to command line arguments. To retrieve a variable from the environment, put the variable name between percent signs, as was discussed in "Using Arguments Inside of Batch Files" in Chapter 2.

> For instance, to retrieve the DATDISK variable from within a batch file, you would refer to it as %DATDISK%. To type out the file ACCREC.FIL from the disk named in DATDISK, give the following line in your batch file:

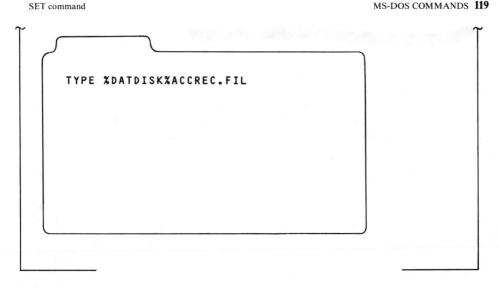

```
TYPE %DATDISK%ACCREC.FIL
```

Rules

If you have loaded any programs or commands that remain in memory (such as PRINT), the amount of RAM that MS-DOS uses for the environment will be limited to 127 bytes. This means that the total length of all the strings you put into the environment with the SET command is limited. However, since very few programs use the environment, you probably don't need to worry about running out of space when you add variables.

Syntax

The syntax for the SET command is

    SET [*varname*=[*string*]]

The *varname* argument is the name of the variable you want to define, and *string* is the value you want to set the variable to. The SET command converts the *varname* to all uppercase letters, but leaves the *string* alone.

If you give a *varname* without a *string,* that variable is taken out of the MS-DOS environment. This is like erasing the variable. If you give no arguments to the SET command, it will list all of the environment variables that are defined.

PATH MAINTENANCE COMMANDS

This section discusses the following commands:

MKDIR (also MD)	*Adds sub-directories to a disk*
CHDIR (also CD)	*Changes the default sub-directory*
RMDIR (also RD)	*Removes sub-directories from a disk*
TREE	*Prints out list of sub-directories*
PATH	*Changes the command search list*

The commands in this section let you use the tree-structured directories available in MS-DOS version 2. These commands (often called path commands or tree commands) all involve splitting the directory of a disk into many sub-directories. A path is the method that MS-DOS uses to find its way around your sub-directories. The sub-directories are arranged like the roots of a tree with the top sub-directory being called the "root."

If you have a hard disk, these commands are very useful because they allow you to manage a large number of files on your disk. Unfortunately, these commands only apply to MS-DOS version 2 or later; they do not exist in any form under MS-DOS version 1.

If you are not familiar with tree-structured directories, they are described in detail in Chapter 4. You should probably read Chapter 4 before you read about the commands in this section, since you need to understand what paths are in order to use them.

> MKDIR Command
> MD Command
> Internal
> Version 2

The MKDIR command is used to create a new sub-directory. The MD command is identical to the MKDIR command.

Common Uses

The MKDIR command can be used to create a new sub-directory when you want to further divide your sub-directory tree. The general syntax is

MKDIR *path*

For example, if you want to add the sub-directory TELE to your current sub-directory, you would give the command

```
A>MKDIR TELE
```

or

```
A>MD TELE
```

MKDIR does not restrict you to only adding a sub-directory to the current sub-directory. You can also use it to create a sub-directory within a different sub-directory.

For example, suppose you wanted to add the sub-directory BOOKS to the \MATERIAL\OFFICE sub-directory. Regardless of which sub-directory you are currently in, you can give the command

```
A>MKDIR \MATERIAL\OFFICE\BOOKS
```

The backslash (\ ) directly following the MKDIR command tells MS-DOS to begin its path at the main directory; and the subsequent backslashes indicate a path from one sub-directory to another within it.

You can also add sub-directories to sub-directories on other disks.

For example, to add the sub-directory JONES to whatever is the default sub-directory on the B: drive, give the command

```
A>MKDIR B:JONES
```

Warnings and Common Errors

The entire name of the sub-directory you create must not be greater than 63 characters in length including the backslashes. This is because MS-DOS can only keep 63 characters internally as names. Unless you have more than five levels of sub-directories, the name length should not be a problem.

Syntax

The syntax for the MKDIR command is

MKDIR [*d:*]*path*

If you specify a *d:*, a new sub-directory will be created on that disk; otherwise, it will be created on the default drive. The *path* argument is the path you want to create.

> CHDIR Command
> CD Command
> Internal
> Version 2

The CHDIR command is used to change your current sub-directory or to display its name. The CD command is identical to the CHDIR command.

Common Uses

The CHDIR command is often used to switch to a different sub-directory. The general syntax is

CHDIR *dir-name*

For instance, if you are in the \BASIC\TIMEACCT sub-directory and you want to switch to the \WP\LETTERS\JIM sub-directory, give the command

```
A>CHDIR \WP\LETTERS\JIM
```

or

```
A>CD \WP\LETTERS\JIM
```

You can change to the root directory with the command

```
A>CHDIR \
```

You can check your current (or default) sub-directory simply by giving the CHDIR command with no arguments.

Thus, after the CHDIR command given in the previous example, the result would be

```
A>CHDIR
A:\wp\letters\jim
```

Notice that the CHDIR command prints out the path name in lowercase letters.

You can also change your default sub-directory on another disk. To do this, simply add the new name and the drive name. The CHDIR command will not change the default drive.

For instance, if you want to change your current sub-directory on drive B: to PAYABLE.FIL, give the command

```
A>CHDIR B:\PAYABLE.FIL
```

To see the name of the current sub-directory on the other disk, give the command

```
A>CHDIR B:
B:\payable.fil
```

Notice that the default drive is still A:.

Many MS-DOS application programs cannot use tree-structured directories. This means that they can't access files from other sub-directories. If you are using a program of this sort, you must be sure that all the files you want to access are on your current sub-directory.

Rules

If you are changing the current sub-directory of a different disk, you cannot include a space between the disk name and the sub-directory.

For instance,

```
A>CHDIR B: \PAYABLE.FIL
Invalid directory
```

MS-DOS gives you an error message because of the space between the disk name and the sub-directory.

Syntax

The CHDIR command takes the following syntax:

> CHDIR [[*d:*]*path*]

or

> CHDIR [*d:*]

The first form of the command is used to change the current sub-directory on a drive, and the second form is used to display the current sub-directory. In both forms, *d:* is the drive you want; if you don't specify it, the CHDIR command will assume the default drive. *path* is the path name of the sub-directory you want to switch to.

RMDIR Command
RD Command
Internal
Version 2

The RMDIR command removes a sub-directory from a disk if it contains no files. The RD command is identical to the RMDIR command.

Common Uses

The RMDIR command is used to remove a sub-directory that you do not want. Since it will only remove sub-directories if they contain no files, you must first remove the files with the ERASE command. The RMDIR command will not remove a sub-directory if it contains other sub-directories, even if those sub-directories are empty. The general syntax is

> RMDIR *dir-name*

where *dir-name* is the name of the sub-directory you want to remove.

For example, if you wanted to remove the sub-directory SHARON from the current sub-directory, you would give the command

```
A>RMDIR SHARON
```

or

```
A>RD SHARON
```

You can also remove sub-directories from another disk. You can use the DIR command to check that the directory was removed.

For example:

```
A>RMDIR B:BENCHMRK
```

removes the sub-directory BENCHMRK from the disk on the B: drive.

If you give a path with more than one name, only the last sub-directory named will be removed.

Thus, to remove the sub-directory OVERDUE from the sub-directory \ACCOUNTS\PAYABLE, give the command

```
A>RMDIR \ACCOUNTS\PAYABLE\OVERDUE
```

Rules

The RMDIR command will not let you remove a sub-directory that has any files in it. If you try to remove such a sub-directory, you get the message "Invalid path, not directory, or directory not empty."

Syntax

The syntax for the RMDIR command is

RMDIR [*d:*]*path*

The *d:* argument is the disk that contains the empty sub-directory that you want removed. If you specify a *d:,* the empty sub-directory will be removed from that disk; otherwise, it will be removed from the default drive. The *path* argument is the name of the path you want to remove. Only the last sub-directory in the path will be removed.

TREE Command
External
Version 2
IBM only

The TREE command displays all of the sub-directory paths on a disk. It does not, however, display the tree form of the sub-directories. Instead, it uses paths with backslashes to separate sub-directories in a path.

Common Uses

The general syntax for the TREE command is

TREE [*d:*]

Remember that each disk has a different tree on it, depending on which sub-directories you have created, so you can run the TREE command for each disk.

Figure 3-4 shows a simple tree. The output for the TREE command for this tree will have the following appearance although the output has been compacted for clarity.

```
A>TREE

DIRECTORY PATH LISTING FOR VOLUME ??????????

Path: \HARRIS
Sub-directories:   CHRIS
                   SANDY

Path: \HARRIS\CHRIS
Sub-directories:  None

Path: \HARRIS\SANDY
Sub-directories:  None
```

```
Path: \POWERS
Sub-directories:   GENE

Path: \POWERS\GENE
Sub-directories:   None
```

If you use the TREE command on a disk with no sub-directories, the TREE command responds "No sub-directories exist." This is a quick way of telling whether or not a disk has sub-directories.

The /F argument tells the TREE command to list all of the files in each sub-directory.

For instance, if the \POWERS\GENE sub-directory had the files LIGHTS.DOC and MAKEPROG.BAS, the TREE /F command would show

```
Path: \POWERS\GENE
Sub-directories:   None
Files:             LIGHTS  .DOC
                   MAKEPROG.BAS
```

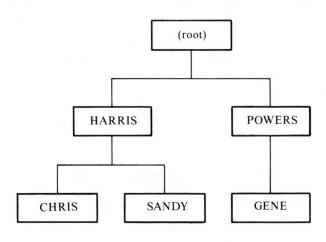

Figure 3-4.   A simple tree-shaped directory

Syntax

The syntax for the TREE command is

TREE [*d:*] [/ F]

d: is the disk that contains the paths you want to see. If a drive is not specified, the paths on the default drive will be displayed. The / F argument causes the TREE command to list the names of all of the files in the sub-directory.

PATH Command
Internal
Version 2

Normally, MS-DOS looks for commands or application programs in the same directory where that program's files reside. The PATH command tells MS-DOS where to look for commands and batch files if it cannot find them on your current sub-directory.

Common Uses

If you keep your commands, batch files, or application programs on many different sub-directories, the PATH command lets you tell MS-DOS where they all are. This means that you can have one sub-directory with your word processing commands and another with your MS-DOS command files, and still be able to run any of the commands from any sub-directory.

The general syntax of the PATH command is

PATH *path; paths* ...

The *path* argument is the path name that you want searched. If more than one path is included, the path names are separated by semicolons.

Suppose you want your word processing program to be able to access commands from the \HARRIS\SANDY and the \POWERS sub-directories shown in Figure 3-4 and that the disk described in Figure 3-4 is the C: disk. You would give the command

```
A>PATH C:\HARRIS\SANDY;C:\POWERS
```

Notice that a semicolon is used to separate the two paths named in the command.

The order in which you give the commands is the order in which MS-DOS will search the sub-directories (with the exception that MS-DOS will always first search on the current sub-directory).

To see the search path MS-DOS is using, give the PATH command without an argument.

For instance,

```
A>PATH
PATH C:\HARRIS\SANDY;C:\POWERS
```

causes MS-DOS to display the current search path.

You can mix drives in a path command if you wish. However, you must be sure that all of the drives are active (meaning that they are ready to be read; a floppy drive with its door open is not ready to be accessed).

For example:

```
A>PATH A:\;B:\;C:\;C:\POWERS
```

The PATH command only tells MS-DOS where to find commands and batch files, not other files. Thus, it does not affect how MS-DOS finds data files, overlay files, and other files that you might name in commands. There is no way to specify the search order for these files.

Warnings and Common Errors

If MS-DOS is searching for a sub-directory in the path list and that sub-directory does not exist, it will simply continue searching. Thus, you will not get an error message if you give incorrect sub-directory names to the PATH command.

You should always include the disk name with each path name, since without it MS-DOS will look for the path name on the default disk.

For example, your PATH command might be

```
B>PATH \POWERS;\
```

If your default drive is B: and you give a command that cannot be found in your current sub-directory, MS-DOS will look for the command on B: \POWERS and B: \. If you really wanted it to look on A: \POWERS and A: \, you should have given the command

```
B>PATH A:\POWERS;A:\
```

Syntax

The syntaxes for the PATH command are

PATH [*d:*]*path*[;[*d:*]*path* ...]

or

PATH

Each part of the list of paths must include a *path* name and can optionally include a drive name (*d:*). The members in the list are separated by semicolons. You cannot include any spaces in the list of paths. If you do not give an argument, PATH prints your current path.

To reset the search order to the default (no paths), give an argument of a single semicolon.

BATCH FILE COMMANDS

This section discusses the following commands:

ECHO	*Prints a message on the screen*
PAUSE	*Waits for a key to be pressed*
IF	*Executes commands based on a decision*
FOR	*Repeats a command for many choices*
GOTO	*Jumps to a different part of a batch file*
SHIFT	*Moves the command line arguments*
REM	*Puts a note in batch files*
COMMAND	*Runs another program*

These commands are called *batch file commands* because they are only used inside of batch files.

You learned how to write batch files in Chapter 2. To summarize the discussion briefly, batch files are files that contain a list of commands you would normally give to MS-DOS. The commands in a batch file can include MS-DOS commands, the names of application programs, or the name of another batch file. You also learned about the AUTOEXEC.BAT file, which is a batch file that is automatically run when you boot up your system.

Now that you have read about most of the common MS-DOS commands, you probably have discovered some other commands that you could include in your AUTOEXEC.BAT file.

One example of a useful AUTOEXEC.BAT file that uses some of these other commands is

AUTOEXEC.BAT

```
VERIFY ON
PATH A:\DOS;A:\WP;A:\OTHERS
MODE COM1:9600,N,8,1,P
PROMPT $t$_$n$g
MODE MONO
CHKDSK
```

The commands in the typical AUTOEXEC.BAT file shown here will automatically set up several of the system settings for you. This file sets the VERIFY system flag ON, sets the command search path, sets up the communications port, changes the MS-DOS prompt to include the time on a separate line, chooses the monochrome screen as the primary console, and checks the default disk for internal consistency.

Of the eight batch commands presented in this section, the most commonly used ones are the ECHO, PAUSE, COMMAND, IF, and FOR commands.

ECHO Command
Internal
Version 2

The ECHO command allows you to turn on or off the displays of individual lines that appear as a batch file is executed. It also lets you display a message on the screen.

Common Uses

The ECHO command controls whether or not you see each line of a batch file as it is executed. Normally, MS-DOS displays each line (with the arguments substituted) so you can see what is happening.

If you do not want to see each line, include in your batch file the ECHO OFF command. You would use this if there were many lines in your batch file and you didn't want to see them printed each time you ran the file. This is mostly an aesthetic choice. To turn the echo back on, include the ECHO ON command.

You can display a message on the screen by using the ECHO command followed by your message.

For example, you might write a batch file containing the command

```
ECHO Insert the new disk in A:
```

When the batch processor executes the line, it will display "Insert the new disk in A:" on the screen.

Since ECHO is always set on when you are giving MS-DOS commands, the first line of any batch file will always be displayed. If you do not want any of the commands in a batch file displayed, give an ECHO OFF command on the first line of your batch file.

Syntax

The syntax for the ECHO command is

ECHO [{ON | OFF | *message*}]

The ON argument turns the command echoing on, and the OFF argument turns command echoing off. If you give a *message*, it is displayed on the screen. If you give no parameters, the ECHO command will report the status of ECHO.

PAUSE Command
Internal

The PAUSE command displays the message "Strike a key when ready . . ." and then waits for a key to be pressed before continuing.

Common Uses

The PAUSE command is useful if the operations you are about to perform require some mechanical setup.

For example, if you set up your batch file to print the file PAYROLL.RPT on the printer, you first might want to ask the user to check if the printer is on. You could add the sentence, "Be sure that the printer is turned on and ready" after the PAUSE command, as in the batch file shown.

```
PRNPAY.BAT

ECHO Be sure that the printer is turned on and ready.
PAUSE
COPY PAYROLL.RPT PRN:
```

This batch file allows you to check that the printer is ready before sending a
file to it. While using the PAUSE command, you can do whatever you want
except use the keyboard. To continue the batch file, you press any key.

Another common use for the PAUSE command is to allow the user to put a
new diskette in a drive.

For example, a file that asks the user to insert a diskette would look like
this:

```
TOARLEEN.BAT

ECHO Put the diskette labelled
ECHO "Arleen's Data" in the left-hand drive
PAUSE
COPY %1 A:
```

This batch file asks the user to put a diskette in a drive before copying the file
named in the first argument of the command. (Note that the ECHO command must be repeated for a two-line message.)

Syntax

The PAUSE command is entered as follows:

PAUSE

It is included in a batch file.

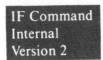
IF Command
Internal
Version 2

The IF command instructs MS-DOS whether or not to execute commands based on a variable condition.

Common Uses

The general syntax of the IF command is

IF *condition command*

The IF command checks if the *condition* is true. If it is, the *command* is executed; if not, the *command* is skipped. This is just like using the word "if" in English: "if it is raining, don't go outside." Table 3-8 lists and describes the three forms that the *condition* argument may take.

Table 3-8.   Conditions Used in the IF Command

Condition	Function
EXIST *filespec*	To check whether or not the file exists. If you use wild-card characters in the *filespec,* this condition will be true if any file matches the specification.
string1 == string2	To determine if the two strings match exactly. This is usually used to check whether or not a particular argument was given.
ERRORLEVEL *number*	To check whether or not the error level set by the last command matches the number. Since very few commands set the error level, this form is rarely used.

The IF command can be used to check whether or not a file exists before executing a command. To do this, use the EXIST form of the condition.

For example, suppose you are about to type out the file NEWMSG.TXT. By using the EXIST condition, you can check whether it exists first to avoid getting a "File not found" message. Include the following command in your batch file:

```
IF EXIST NEWMSG.TXT TYPE NEWMSG.TXT
```

A common use for the EXIST condition is to check that the file exists before creating a file with the same name.

If you are about to rename MANUAL.NEW to MANUAL.OLD, you should check to see whether MANUAL.OLD already exists (if it does, you should type out a message on the screen). To automate this process, you might include the following command:

```
IF EXIST MANUAL.OLD ECHO Can't rename MANUAL.NEW
```

In this case, if the file exists, the ECHO command will display "Can't rename MANUAL.NEW."

The string condition of the IF command (the second condition in Table 3-8) is used to check whether or not a particular argument was given. It does this by comparing the two strings.

For example, you may want to copy the file TOTCOST.TXT to the B: disk if the third argument given on the command line is the word MOVE. To do this, you would use the command

```
IF %3==MOVE COPY TOTCOST.TXT B:
```

Unfortunately, the strings must compare exactly (including upper- and lowercase letters) and you must tell MS-DOS which argument contains the string. This limitation is not what you are used to with other MS-DOS commands; usually, MS-DOS doesn't care about upper- or lowercase letters and sometimes doesn't care about the order of arguments.

You can also use the NOT argument after the IF command to negate the condition.

Thus, the line

```
IF NOT EXIST MACHINE.TXT COPY B:NEWMACH.TXT
```

would perform the COPY command if the file MACHINE.TXT did not exist.

A third use of the IF command is to check the error level. In this case, the IF command checks how successfully certain commands have performed (this is the third case in Table 3-8). Very few commands set the error level, so this condition may not be useful to you.

The *error level* is a number a command gives that indicates if it finished successfully or not. The number is stored in RAM by MS-DOS, and you can read it with this form of the IF command. Programs set the error level to let other programs know if they completed successfully or not. For instance, a particular program might set the error level to 4 to indicate that it was not able to find a certain file. Unfortunately, there is no standard for understanding what the error level numbers mean. However, each command that uses the error level has a specific meaning for each number. You can determine the error level of the last command performed, resolve the problem, and decide which MS-DOS command to perform next based on the meaning of the error level.

Since very few MS-DOS commands set the error level, this form of the IF command is not useful yet. Future revisions of MS-DOS and future application packages may have more commands that set the error level.

Rules

If you use the string condition to compare two strings, the two strings must match exactly.

For example, if a line in your batch file is

IFSTRING.BAT

```
IF %3==MOVE COPY TOTCOST.TXT B:
```

you must type in "MOVE" to execute the COPY command. MS-DOS will not consider the strings as matching if you enter "move" or "Move."

If you have not entered as many arguments as the batch file specifies, MS-DOS will give you an error.

For instance, if you only give two arguments on the command line when you execute the line in the previous example, MS-DOS will display "Syntax error" and continue.

Warnings and common errors

You cannot use path names with the EXIST condition.

Syntax

The syntax of the IF command is

IF [NOT] *condition command*

The three available *conditions* were described in Table 3-8. The *command* is any command (such as an MS-DOS command, application program, or batch file command). NOT negates the *condition.*

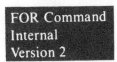

FOR Command
Internal
Version 2

The FOR command allows you to repeat a command for many different arguments. It also lets you repeat a command for all files that match a file name that contains wild-card characters.

Common Uses

The FOR command is used to perform a command repeatedly on a list of arguments. The first general syntax of the FOR command is

FOR *%%letter* IN (*list*) DO *command*

The *letter* is any letter of the alphabet; it is like a label for a piece of RAM. Each element in the *list* is copied into that place in RAM one at a time, and the *command* is executed using that element of the list. The next element is then copied and the procedure is repeated. This concept is best explained with an example.

For example, to get the directory of A:, B:, C:, and D:, you could include the following commands in a batch file:

```
HARDWAY.BAT

    DIR A:
    DIR B:
    DIR C:
    DIR D:
```

An easier way of performing this batch file would be to use the FOR command. In this case, the command would be

```
EASYWAY.BAT

    FOR %%A IN (A: B: C: D:) DO DIR %%A
```

This command tells MS-DOS to perform a DIR command on the A:, B:, C:, and D: disks.

You might also use this form of the FOR command to copy all of the files from the command line of a batch file to another disk in the B: drive. The command would be

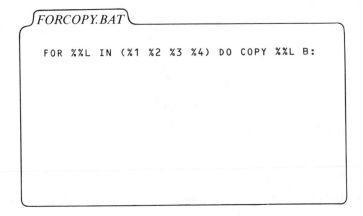

FORCOPY.BAT

```
FOR %%L IN (%1 %2 %3 %4) DO COPY %%L B:
```

This command will copy up to four files that you name on the command line to B:.

The second syntax form of the FOR command is

FOR *%%letter* IN (*filespec*) DO *command*

In this form, the *filespec* is a file specification that contains wild-card characters. In this case, MS-DOS performs the *command* on each file that matches the specification. This form only uses one argument in the parentheses.

For example, to perform a TYPE command on each file on a disk that has an extension of BAS, give the command

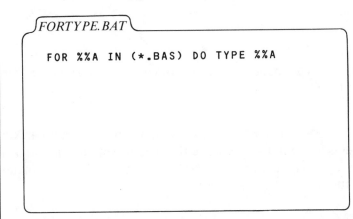

FORTYPE.BAT

```
FOR %%A IN (*.BAS) DO TYPE %%A
```

Rules

If you use the first form of the command, each item in the list must be separated by exactly one space.

If you use the second form of the command, only one *filespec* can be given.

Syntax

The FOR command uses the following syntaxes:

FOR *%%varname* IN (*list*) DO *command*

or

FOR *%%varname* IN (*filespec*) DO *command*

The *varname* argument is a name you assign that contains one letter. The double percent signs before *varname* are required.

In the first form, *set* is a list of arguments, each argument separated by a space. In the second form, *filespec* is a file specification that contains wildcard characters; the FOR command treats it like a list of files that match the *filespec*. The *command* is executed on each element in the *list*.

GOTO Command
Internal
Version 2

The GOTO command permits you to jump to another place in a batch file.

Common Uses

You can use the GOTO command to skip to another part of a batch file. The general syntax of the GOTO command is

GOTO *label*

The *label* is the place in your batch file that you want to go to. You always skip to a label. A label is a line in the batch file that begins with a colon and is followed by as many as eight characters. Notice that the GOTO command does not include the colon before the label.

A label is like a signpost that tells the batch processor where to start again after a GOTO command has been given. When you run a batch file, the labels are not displayed on the screen.

For example, you may want to write a batch file that tells you whether or not a file exists. The following IFGOTO.BAT file shows how this is done, using the GOTO command with an IF command in a batch file.

```
IFGOTO.BAT

IF EXIST %1 GOTO WASTHERE
ECHO The file %1 was not there
GOTO DONE
:WASTHERE
ECHO The file %1 was there
:DONE
```

This batch command displays a message about whether the file named in the first argument of the command exists. The first line checks whether a file exists. If it exists, the batch processor jumps to the line

```
:WASTHERE
```

If it does not exist, the batch processor continues with the next line (the first ECHO command).

You can also skip to a label that is before the GOTO command. This causes the program to run in an endless loop. This can be useful if you want to perform the same task over and over. To exit from the endless loop, you simply press CONTROL-C while the batch file is executing.

For instance, a batch file that allows you to run the CHKDSK command on as many diskettes as you want might look like this:

GOTOLOOP.BAT

```
ECHO OFF
:LOOP
ECHO Insert a disk in C:
PAUSE
ECHO Testing...
CHKDSK C:
GOTO LOOP
```

The GOTOLOOP.BAT file continues to run the CHKDSK command until the user presses CONTROL-C.

Rules

If you give label names that are longer than eight characters, all characters after the eighth character will be ignored.

Syntax

The syntax for the GOTO command is

GOTO *label*

The *label* is the line in the batch file you want to go to.

REM Command
Internal

The REM command is used to add comments to a batch file. It does not produce any result.

Common Uses

The REM command is used to put notes in a batch file. This command can be used to describe the contents of a batch file. When you write a batch file, you may want to leave yourself notes about what it does.

For example, the following REMARK.BAT file includes comments in REM commands:

```
REMARK.BAT

ECHO OFF
REM        This file was written by Les
REM        Sanders to test diskettes
:LOOP
ECHO Insert a disk in C:
PAUSE
ECHO Testing...
CHKDSK C:
GOTO LOOP
REM        This GOTO causes an endless loop
```

Remember that the REM comments do not do anything. If ECHO is ON, they will be displayed on the screen. If ECHO is set to OFF, as it is in this batch file, the REM message will be visible only by displaying the REMARK.BAT file.

It is always a good idea to put at least one REM command in a batch file to remind yourself why you wrote the file.

Syntax

The syntax for the REM command is

REM *comment*

The *comment* argument is any text. The REM command can be placed anywhere in a batch file.

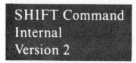

The SHIFT command shifts all of your arguments down by one number, allowing you to access arguments that are greater than %9. Unless you use the SHIFT command, MS-DOS limits you to using nine arguments on the command line of a batch file. The SHIFT command is rarely used.

Common Uses

The only time you would use the SHIFT command is to access more than nine command-line arguments; it is unlikely that you will ever want to give more than nine arguments to a batch file.

The SHIFT command changes the argument %0 in the batch file to read %1 from the command line, %1 to %2, and so on, up to %9 to %10, thus letting you access one more argument. After a SHIFT command, you cannot look at the original contents of the argument %0. You must give the SHIFT command for each argument past the ninth that you want to use. Thus, if you want to use 12 arguments, you must include three SHIFT commands in your batch file.

The following is a simple example of a batch file that might use the SHIFT command:

```
SHIFTEX.BAT

ECHO OFF
ECHO %1 %2
ECHO %2 %3
SHIFT
ECHO %1 %2
```

When this batch file is executed, the display looks like this:

```
A>SHIFTEX AAA BBB CCC DDD

A>ECHO OFF
AAA BBB
BBB CCC
BBB CCC
```

Syntax

The syntax for the SHIFT command is

SHIFT

SHIFT automatically shifts all % arguments in a batch file down one number.

COMMAND Command
External
Version 2

Here's an interesting tongue twister: the COMMAND command is MS-DOS's command processor. You can use the /C argument of the COMMAND command to execute a batch file from within a batch file.

Common Uses

The discussion of batch files in Chapter 2 described how you could link one batch file to another by giving the name of the second batch file. It was stated that you could link at the end of a batch file because MS-DOS almost never returns to the first batch file. The COMMAND command is the one exception to this generalization: it allows you to proceed from one batch file to another and then return to the original one when the second is finished. The general syntax for doing this is

COMMAND /C *command*

There are other ways to use the COMMAND command, but the /C argument is the most important way and is the only one described here.

Compare the two examples that follow. They illustrate the difference between a batch file that does not include a COMMAND command and one that does.

This example is only meant to show you why the COMMAND command is important; it is not useful otherwise. Here are the two batch files:

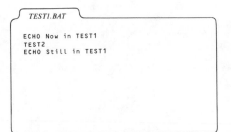

```
TEST1.BAT

ECHO Now in TEST1
TEST2
ECHO Still in TEST1
```

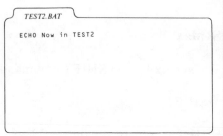

```
TEST2.BAT

ECHO Now in TEST2
```

When you execute TEST1, the following will appear on your screen:

```
A>TEST1

A>ECHO Now in TEST1
Now in TEST1

A>TEST2

A>ECHO Now in TEST2
Now in TEST2

A>
```

Since you see the cursor here, you can tell that MS-DOS is finished. This means that after the one line in TEST2 is executed, MS-DOS does not return to TEST1, and the last line of TEST1 is never executed. This is because MS-DOS links to the second batch file and does not remember where to return to.

You might find it convenient to run one batch file from another and, when the second file is finished, continue processing the original batch file. The COMMAND command gives you that capability.

You can change the TEST1 file to cause MS-DOS to return to it after executing the TEST2 batch file:

```
TEST1.BAT

ECHO Now in TEST1
COMMAND /C TEST2
ECHO Still in TEST1
```

```
TEST2.BAT

ECHO Now in TEST2
```

Notice how the line that previously read

```
TEST2
```

now reads

```
COMMAND /C TEST2
```

The /C option tells the COMMAND command that the other arguments are a command that should be executed. This line in the batch file will now cause MS-DOS to execute the second batch file and return to the first:

```
A>TEST1

A>ECHO Now in TEST1
Now in TEST1

A>COMMAND /C TEST2

A>ECHO Now in TEST2
Now in TEST2

A>ECHO Still in TEST1
Still in TEST1

A>
```

As you can see, this gives MS-DOS batch files much greater flexibility. If you are writing a large batch file, you can break it down into smaller files and use the COMMAND command for each part.

Warnings and Common Errors

Be careful not to overload your system's memory. The COMMAND.COM file takes up about 5K of RAM. If you use the COMMAND command with a program that needs the memory that is normally free in your system, the program may run out of memory. This rarely happens, however.

If you give the COMMAND command without the / C argument, you will lose a bit of free RAM (there is really no reason for you to do this). To free up this memory, give the EXIT command. The EXIT command is only useful for this purpose, so it is not described elsewhere in this book.

Syntax

The syntax for the COMMAND command is

COMMAND /C *command*

The /C argument tells MS-DOS to temporarily load in memory a new copy of the command processor, execute the *command*, and then remove the copy of the command processor.

OTHER COMMANDS

This section discusses the following commands:

FIND	*Searches for text in a file*
SORT	*Sorts a text file*
CLS	*Clears the screen*
GRAPHICS	*Allows you to print graphics screens*

The commands in this section do not fit into any of the other categories. The FIND and SORT commands are sometimes used to manipulate files, and they are handy for quick searching or sorting. The CLS command is useful for clearing text from your screen.

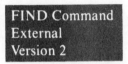

FIND Command
External
Version 2

The FIND command finds all lines in a file (or group of files) that contain a string and displays them on the screen. The FIND command uses input and output redirection. Input and output redirection are described in Chapter 4, but you do not need to know how to use them before you use the FIND command.

Common Uses

If you wanted to display each line of a file that contains a string you are interested in, you would use the following syntax:

FIND *"string" file*

The *string* argument must be enclosed in quotation marks.

For example, to search the file DAILYRPT.TXT for all lines containing the phrase "well written", give the command:

```
A>FIND "well written" DAILYRPT.TXT

---------- DAILYRPT.TXT
project was well written in a timely fashion. I do not feel
to the company. Another important job that can be well written
```

The first line is the FIND command's way of telling you the file that it is working on. The next two lines are the lines in the file that it found with the string "well written."

The FIND command displays each line with the string that you specify; this may be a bit disconcerting, since you can't see the whole sentence that contained the phrase. Unfortunately, the FIND command does not know anything about sentences, only lines and files.

You can also use the FIND command with a list of files.

For example, to find all the lines in both the DAILYRPT.TXT file and the JEAN.RPT file containing the string "well written", enter:

```
A>FIND "well written" DAILYRPT.TXT JEAN.RPT

---------- DAILYRPT.TXT
project was well written in a timely fashion. I do not feel
to the company. Another important job that can be well written

---------- JEAN.RPT
I cannot find a well written sample of his writing that
```

The /C argument tells the FIND command only to count the lines, not display them. The /C argument, like all of the FIND command's arguments, must precede the string. Thus, for the /C argument, the general syntax is

FIND /C *"string"* *file*

For example:

```
A>FIND /C "well written" DAILYRPT.TXT

---------- DAILYRPT.TXT: 2
```

MS-DOS displays the number of times the string appears in DAILYRPT.TXT.

If you want to see all of the lines that do not contain a certain string, use the /V argument.

For instance,

```
A>FIND /V "well written" DAILYRPT.TXT
```

As you might guess, this will cause a huge listing of lines. However, you can combine arguments so that you can count the number of lines that do not contain a certain string.

```
A>FIND /V/C "well written" DAILYRPT.TXT

---------- DAILYRPT.TXT: 189
```

The /N argument tells the FIND command to print the line number with the line.

For example:

```
A>FIND /N "well written" DAILYRPT.TXT

---------- DAILYRPT.TXT
[17]project was well written in a timely fashion. I do not feel
[131]to the company. Another important job that can be well written
```

The line number appears at the beginning of each line that contains the string.

Rules

You cannot use wild-card characters in the file names for the input files. You must put any arguments you use before the string and file names.

If the string you want to search for has a double quote (") in it, you must put a second double quote before it.

For example, to search the file DICKENS.TXT for the phrase

```
home," he said.
```

give the command:

```
A>FIND "home,"" he said." DICKENS.TXT
```

Syntax

The FIND command uses the following syntax:

FIND [/V] [/C] [/N] *"string"* [*filespec* ...]

The FIND command looks for the *string* in the list of *filespec*s (the list has spaces between each *filespec*). The *string* must be enclosed in quotation marks.

The /V argument causes the FIND command to display each line not containing the *string*. The /C argument indicates that you only want to display the total number of lines found, not the lines themselves. The /N argument causes the line number of the input file to be included at the beginning of the line with square brackets ([ ]) around it.

SORT Command
External
Version 2

The SORT command displays a file in a sorted order. The SORT command also uses input and output redirection, but you do not need to know how to use these before you use the SORT command.

Common Uses

The SORT command sorts a file based on the ASCII values of the characters in the file. This means that most punctuation comes first followed by numbers, capital letters, and lowercase letters (most programming books contain an ordered list of the ASCII codes).

The simple form of the SORT command is

SORT <*file*

Notice that the less-than sign (<) is required.

For example, to see the file INVITE.LST sorted, give the command

```
A>SORT <INVITE.LST
Gardner, Karen        x421
Hodges, Ralph         x120
Nance, Coleman        x0
Sanders, John         x425
Sanders, Susan        x419
d'Tang, Irene         x430
```

Notice that d'Tang is listed last because it begins with a lowercase letter.

If you want to see the file in reverse order, include the /R argument. All of the arguments in the SORT command must precede the redirected files. Thus, for the /R argument, the general syntax is

SORT /R <*file*

For example:

```
A>SORT /R <INVITE.LST
d'Tang, Irene         x430
Sanders, Susan        x419
Sanders, John         x425
Nance, Coleman        x0
Hodges, Ralph         x120
Gardner, Karen        x421
```

You can also tell the SORT command to begin sorting other than with the first column; for this, you use the /+ argument with the column number.

For example, to sort the list by phone numbers (which start in column 21 in the previous file), give the command:

```
A>SORT /+21 <INVITE.LST
Nance, Coleman        x0
Hodges, Ralph         x120
Sanders, Susan        x419
Gardner, Karen        x421
Sanders, John         x425
d'Tang, Irene         x430
```

Syntax

The syntax for the SORT command is

SORT [/R] [/+n] <*filespec*

The less than sign (<) is required for the SORT command to work. The *filespec* argument represents the file to be sorted and displayed.

The /R argument causes the file to be displayed in reverse sorted order. The /+n argument tells the SORT command to sort beginning with column *n*.

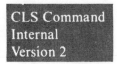

CLS Command
Internal
Version 2

The CLS command clears the screen and displays the MS-DOS prompt.

Common Uses

You use the CLS command to clear the screen of your computer. The main reason you would want to do this is to get rid of distracting text and graphics from the screen. If you leave characters in the same place on the screen for a long time, you can accidentally etch the image of the letters in the screen. (Another way to avoid this is to turn down the brightness control on your monitor.)

Syntax

The syntax for the CLS command is

CLS

GRAPHICS Command
External
Version 2
IBM only

The GRAPHICS command allows you to copy the graphics on the screen to a printer on the IBM PC. It only works with screens that have only regular text characters or are in one of the graphics modes.

Common Uses

The GRAPHICS command causes a graphics screen-dump program to be loaded into RAM that extends the use of the PRTSC (PrintScreen) key of the IBM PC. After running the GRAPHICS command, you can use the PRTSC to print screens from the graphics modes as well. The IBM PC-DOS manual gives more detail about the graphics modes and screen-dump procedures.

Syntax

The syntax for the GRAPHICS command is

    GRAPHICS

PROGRAMMING TOOLS

This section discusses the following commands:

    LINK   *Combines object files*
    DEBUG   *Examines and changes binary files*
    EXE2BIN *Converts EXE files to COM files*

The three programming tools, also called *utilities* (LINK, DEBUG, and EXE2BIN) are only useful to advanced programmers. Even if you learn BASIC, they are not useful to you; they are really only for people who program in assembly language (although LINK is sometimes used by other high-level languages). It is unlikely that you will need to learn how to use these commands (although the DEBUG command can be useful).

The following descriptions of these commands are only meant to serve as an overview. Complete technical descriptions of the commands can be found in the documentation provided by your computer manufacturer.

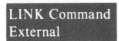

LINK Command
External

The LINK command combines object modules into programs that can be executed. It can access libraries to aid in defining the external references in each program.

Syntax

The LINK command uses the following kinds of syntax:

LINK

or

LINK @*filespec*

or

LINK *objectlist, outfile, mapfile, liblist,*
[/DSALLOCATION] [/HIGH] [/LINE] [/MAP] [/PAUSE] [/STACK:*n*]

The first form of the LINK command causes LINK to ask you for all of the arguments on the screen. This is useful if you don't want to make a long LINK command line. The second form assumes that you have created a file containing the answers to the questions the LINK command interactively asks. The at sign (@) is required.

The arguments for the third form of the LINK command are defined in Table 3-9. Each of the arguments can be abbreviated to one letter.

Table 3-9.   Arguments in the LINK Command

Argument	Meaning
objectlist	A list of the object files to be linked; they are separated with plus signs (+).
outfile	The name of the EXE file to be produced.
mapfile	The name of the map file for the linker to produce.
liblist	The list of the libraries for the linker to search; they are separated with plus signs (+).
/DSALLOCATION	Indicates you want the LINK command to load DGROUP data at the high end of the group.
/HIGH	Causes the LINK command to place the run image as high as possible in RAM.
/LINE	Indicates that you want the line numbers to be included in the map file.
/MAP	Causes the LINK command to list all global symbols in the map file.
/PAUSE	Tells the LINK command to display a message before it generates the EXE file so that you can change disks.
/STACK*n*	Sets the size of the stack to *n*, regardless of its previous value.

DEBUG Command
External

The DEBUG command is used to test programs and to inspect and alter programs (as well as other binary files). The DEBUG command is like a line editor except that it allows you to change the steps and data in a program instead of the letters and words in a text file.

Syntax

The syntax for the DEBUG command is

DEBUG [*filespec*] [*args*]

filespec is the file that you want to modify or execute. *args* are the arguments that will be used by a command if you are using DEBUG on a COM or EXE file.

EXE2BIN Command
External

The EXE2BIN command converts an EXE file to a COM file, as long as the EXE program does not have a stack segment and is smaller than 64K. Some manufacturers have renamed this command LOCATE.

Syntax

The syntax for the EXE2BIN command is

EXE2BIN *filespec1* [*filespec2*]

The *filespec1* argument is the file to be converted. The *filespec2* argument is the name of the output file. If you do not specify an output file, the EXE2BIN command uses the same name, with the extension of BIN.

4

ADVANCED
MS-DOS USAGE

Using Sub-Directories and Paths to
   Organize Files
Redirecting I/O
Pipes
Editing MS-DOS Command Lines

This chapter explores three concepts that Microsoft introduced with version 2 of MS-DOS: paths, I/O redirection, and pipes. Of these three features, which are available only in MS-DOS version 2, most users will probably find paths the most useful, although I/O redirection may be easier to understand. This chapter also explains how to use special keys on your keyboard to edit the command line as you type it in. These keys are useful regardless of which version of MS-DOS you own.

If you don't own MS-DOS version 2, you should at least read through this chapter quickly so that you will know what capabilities are available in version 2. If you later hear about some of the ideas presented here, you will be familiar with the general concepts. Many computer manufacturers will sell you newer versions of MS-DOS as they become available, so knowing what is available will let you know what is coming in the future.

USING SUB-DIRECTORIES AND
PATHS TO ORGANIZE FILES

A directory is a list of the files on a disk. When you give the DIR command, MS-DOS displays that list of files on the screen. You can probably think of ways that you might subdivide the directory into groups of files; in fact, some of those groups might even have subgroups.

Grouping your files in this way would be the same as constructing a *tree-shaped directory*. A tree-shaped directory is like a corporate chart of upper- and lower-level management. Each part of the sub-directory tree can have other sub-directories and files beneath it. For example, you can group all of the text files on a disk in one sub-directory with its own sub-directories, and all of the command files and programs in a different directory.

Figure 4-1 shows a picture of a sub-directory tree. (You will see how to construct this tree on your disk shortly.) This figure shows how sub-directories might be organized on a disk, and it will be referred to frequently. Each box contains the name of a sub-directory; the files in each sub-directory are shown extending from the right side of the sub-directory. As you can see, some sub-directories have additional sub-directories beneath them, while others do not; some have files, while others have only sub-directories.

The sub-directories in Figure 4-1 form a pattern that looks like the roots of a tree with the *root directory* (main directory) at the top. The sub-directory just above another sub-directory is called its *parent*, and those below it are called its *children*. In the figure, STEIN and SMITH are children of CLIENTS.

If you have a large number of files on a hard disk, being able to separate the files into sub-directories will help you organize your files. If you do not subdivide your directory, when you use the DIR command, you will see all of your files in no apparent order, often filling up many screens. If you have a complicated system of directories and sub-directories, you will need a *path*, which provides directions for finding a particular directory. As you will see, paths allow you to find your way around a tree-shaped directory.

Each directory can have virtually as many files or sub-directories as you can fit on a disk, although in some version 2 releases, the root directory is limited to 64 files and sub-directories. This should never get in your way, though. Too many sub-directories may get confusing. In Figure 4-1, the root has three sub-directories, the PROGRAMS sub-directory has two sub-directories, and the TEXT sub-directory has three sub-directories.

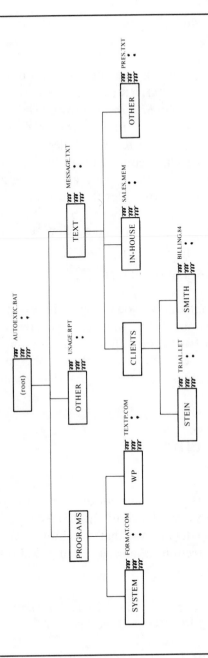

Figure 4-1. A tree-shaped directory showing sub-directories with files

Basic Commands Used
With Sub-Directories

There are three basic commands you will use with sub-directories: MKDIR to make a new sub-directory, RMDIR to remove an existing sub-directory, and CHDIR to change to another sub-directory. (Unfortunately, there is no command to show you the structure of your tree on a disk. The TREE command lists all of the sub-directories and files, but does not put them into a display like Figure 4-1.) These commands were all introduced in Chapter 3.

Remember that you are constructing a sub-directory tree to set up a convenient structure to hold your files. The general way you create a tree is to

- Use the MKDIR command to make a new sub-directory
- Move to that sub-directory with the CHDIR command
- Make the next level of sub-directories.

In the discussion that follows, you will learn how to make the tree shown in Figure 4-1. Since it is unlikely that this is the exact tree that you want for your disk, you should construct it on a floppy diskette that you can then use for experimenting with the commands described here. You should use a diskette that does not have any files on it. Put the new diskette in the B: drive, and set the default drive to B:.

Using MKDIR and CHDIR
To Construct a Tree

MS-DOS always starts you in the root directory. You can see that there are three sub-directories under the root: PROGRAMS, OTHER, and TEXT. You will create these first. (The way that you choose names for sub-directories is explained in the section "Rules for Using Sub-Directories and Path Names.")

To start, be sure that your default drive is B: (the prompt will be B>), and then create the PROGRAMS sub-directory:

```
B>MKDIR PROGRAMS
```

The MKDIR command does not move you to this new sub-directory; you are still in the root. Now create the OTHER and TEXT sub-directories:

```
B>MKDIR OTHER

B>MKDIR TEXT
```

You can use the DIR command to verify that you made these sub-directories. The output of the DIR command is described in greater detail in the section "Understanding the DIR and TREE Command Listings."

Once you have made these sub-directories, you can move to them with the CHDIR command and put files in them, or you can make sub-directories under them. (Of course, you can also put files in the root directory.) To do this, use the CHDIR command, which was also introduced in Chapter 3.

Use the CHDIR command to move to the PROGRAMS sub-directory, and then add the SYSTEM and WP sub-directories under it:

```
B>CHDIR PROGRAMS

B>MKDIR SYSTEM

B>MKDIR WP
```

To put files in a sub-directory, you simply change to that sub-directory and use the COPY command, just as you normally do.

For example, assume that the disk that contains your word processor is in the A: drive and you want to copy all of the files from it to the WP sub-directory. You would give the commands

```
B>CHDIR WP

B>COPY A:*.*
```

To move back to the root directory to construct the rest of the tree, you need to give the command

```
B>CHDIR \
```

The backslash (\ ) is a special name that MS-DOS uses for the root; its use is explained in the next section. Once you are back at the top, you can finish creating the tree.

To finish constructing the tree, be sure you are in the root directory. (If you are not, give the CHDIR \ command just described.) Then give the following commands:

```
B>CHDIR TEXT

B>MKDIR CLIENTS

B>MKDIR IN-HOUSE

B>MKDIR OTHER

B>CHDIR CLIENTS

B>MKDIR STEIN

B>MKDIR SMITH

B>CHDIR \
```

You have now created the whole tree. You can use the CHDIR command to move down levels and then use the COPY command to put files in each of the sub-directories. As you move around the tree, the only way you can move up is to use the CHDIR \ command to get to the root, and then move down to where you want to go. Later you will learn to use paths so you won't need to keep returning to the root.

Remember that each disk can have a different set of sub-directories on it, so that the tree on your A: disk can look very different from the tree on your B: disk. Generally, you will only have to remember the shape of one or two different trees. If you do not use the sub-directory feature of MS-DOS, all of your files will be considered part of the root directory of that disk.

When you use the CHDIR command to move around in the tree, you are actually changing your *default sub-directory.* The default sub-directory is the sub-directory on which MS-DOS will look for files (unless you tell it differently). For example, when you give the DIR command from within a sub-directory, you only see a list of the files on that sub-directory. When you give an external command, MS-DOS will only look for it on your default sub-directory (unless you have given the PATH command). If you want to see your default sub-directory, use the CHDIR command with no arguments.

Rules for Using
Sub-Directories and Path Names

There are a few rules to follow when defining sub-directories. Each sub-directory must have a name. Just as with files, it is important to give sub-directories descriptive names to make them easier to manage. In Figure 4-1 some of the sub-directory names are PROGRAMS, WP, and SMITH. The rules for naming sub-directories are exactly the same as those for naming files (covered in Chapter 2). You usually do not use an extension when you name a sub-directory, although it is allowed. The files within sub-directories, of course, can have extensions.

Although the rules for naming sub-directories are the same as those for naming files, the files in sub-directories cannot be accessed in the same way as the files in the root directory. This is because each sub-directory has a unique *path name* that MS-DOS uses to find the sub-directory. The path describes how the sub-directory is linked to the root. The root directory has no path name; it is indicated by a single backslash character (\ ). Each successive name along the path is also separated by a backslash. For instance, in Figure 4-1 the path name for the PROGRAMS sub-directory is \PROGRAMS, since it is connected directly to the root; the path name for the STEIN sub-directory is \TEXT\CLIENTS\STEIN.

This method of giving path names allows you to have the same sub-directory name at different places in the tree. Notice that there are two sub-directories called OTHER in Figure 4-1: one is the child of the root, and the other is the child of TEXT. MS-DOS can tell the difference because the path names are different (\OTHER and \TEXT\OTHER). However, you cannot have two sub-directories with the same name connected to the same sub-directory.

To access a file in a particular sub-directory, you simply add another backslash to the end of the path name and the name of the file you want.

For instance, if the file SALES.MEM were in the \TEXT\IN-HOUSE sub-directory, you would display it on the screen with the following command:

```
B>TYPE \TEXT\IN-HOUSE\SALES.MEM
```

This will type out the file from the default disk.

If you need to give a drive name in a file specifier that has a path name, you would add it to the beginning of the path name.

Thus, if the previous file was on the A: disk, the new TYPE command would be

```
B>TYPE A:\TEXT\IN-HOUSE\SALES.MEM
```

Be sure that you do not put a space between the disk drive designation and the beginning of the path.

You can use path names in the CHDIR command to move directly from one sub-directory to another. This makes moving around much easier than always having to return to the root.

For example, to move to the SMITH sub-directory in Figure 4-1, you would give the command

```
B>CHDIR \TEXT\CLIENTS\SMITH
```

Notice that when you give the CHDIR command it does not matter what sub-directory you start from. Placing a backslash (\ ) at the beginning of the path name tells MS-DOS to start at the root directory. Of course, returning to the root directory from any sub-directory is always easy since it has such a short path name:

```
B>CHDIR \
```

When you use the CHDIR command, it is not always necessary to begin the path name at the root directory. In fact, you can move to a sub-directory of the current directory you are in. Remember that in previous examples when you gave a full path name it included a backslash for the root directory (\TEXT\CLIENTS\SMITH). You would omit this backslash in your path name to move to a sub-directory that is a child of your default sub-directory. You simply tell CHDIR the name of that child, without giving its entire path name.

For example, to move from \TEXT to \TEXT\CLIENTS, you would give the command

```
B>CHDIR CLIENTS
```

Notice that the full path name was not necessary in this example. This is how you moved around in the first part of this chapter.

You can use the sub-directory's child's name to move from the parent to the child in a sub-directory. Simply follow the child's name with a backslash and continue the path name.

For example, if you wanted to move the default subdirectory from \TEXT to \TEXT\CLIENTS\SMITH, you would give the command

```
B>CHDIR CLIENTS\SMITH
```

A path name that shows the path all the way from the root is called an *absolute path name,* since you are giving the most complete name possible. Giving a path name that is based on your current position is called a *relative path name.* Starting a path name with a backslash always means that you are starting from the root directory; starting a path name without a backslash always means that you are starting from the current sub-directory.

Changing to a child sub-directory with a relative path name can cause some confusion, since the command is similar to changing to a child of the root.

For example, if you are in the TEXT sub-directory and you want to move to the PROGRAMS sub-directory, you use the backslash:

```
B>CHDIR PROGRAMS
Invalid directory

B>CHDIR \PROGRAMS

B>
```

To move to the parent of your default sub-directory, you use a special path name, which is two dots (..). This is often called the *double-dot.* This double-dot simply represents the parent of your default sub-directory, regardless of where you are in the tree.

For example, if your default sub-directory is WP and you want to move to its parent, the PROGRAMS sub-directory, you would give the command

```
B>CHDIR ..
```

Moving to the parent sub-directory with the double-dot is similar to moving to the child sub-directory because you can use the double-dot as the beginning of a longer path name. In fact, using the double-dot is a common way to move to a directory on the same level of the tree as the current sub-directory.

For example, to move from WP to SYSTEM, give the command

```
B>CHDIR ..\SYSTEM
```

You can also use a string of double-dots to move up the tree. To move from STEIN to TEXT, you can give the command

```
B>CHDIR ..\..
```

Using path names in the MKDIR command allows you to add sub-directories anywhere on the tree, not just to the current sub-directory. You simply use the full path name in the MKDIR command.

For example, suppose that you are in the \TEXT\IN-HOUSE sub-directory and you want to add a sub-directory to \PROGRAMS called GAMES. You do not need to change your sub-directory with the CHDIR command; simply give the command:

```
B>MKDIR \PROGRAMS\GAMES
```

This specifies exactly where you want the new sub-directory.

Understanding the DIR
And TREE Command Listings

Now that you know more about sub-directories, it will be easy to understand the DIR command listing that you get when a disk has sub-directories. The following is an example of the DIR listing, taken from the \TEXT sub-directory in Figure 4-1.

```
B>CD \TEXT

B>DIR

  Volume in drive B has no label
  Directory of  B:\text
  .            <DIR>        2-11-84   10:54a
  ..           <DIR>        2-11-84   10:54a
  CLIENTS      <DIR>        4-07-84    9:12p
  IN-HOUSE     <DIR>        6-30-84    3:41a
  OTHER        <DIR>        3-28-84    7:17p
  MESSAGE  TXT        91   11-19-84    3:29p
        6 File(s)     303104 bytes free
```

There is only one file on this sub-directory, MESSAGE.TXT. The DIR command does not list files in other sub-directories, even those below the current one.

The second line gives the name of the sub-directory that the directory listing is for. Notice that there are five lines that have <DIR> on them; these are entries for sub-directories, not files. You probably recognize the .. (double-dot) as the parent, and CLIENTS, IN-HOUSE, and OTHER as the three children. MS-DOS also includes a . (dot) directory, which is the name for the current sub-directory; there is really no use for this entry.

You may wonder why the last line reports six files, when you can only see one that is not a directory. This is because MS-DOS stores all of the internal information about parent and child sub-directories as file entries in each directory. Thus, it counts each entry—for child sub-directories as well as for dot and double-dot—as files. You see these entries when you use the DIR command; however, since you cannot treat these entries as files, you cannot rename or copy them.

The root directory does not have a dot or double-dot directory entry in it:

```
B>CHDIR \

B>DIR

  Volume in drive B has no label
  Directory of  B:\

  PROGRAMS     <DIR>        2-11-84   10:54a
  OTHER        <DIR>        2-11-84   10:54a
  TEXT         <DIR>        2-11-84   10:54a
  AUTOEXEC BAT        91   11-19-83    3:29p
        4 File(s)     303104 bytes free
```

The TREE command (which is an IBM-specific command) can help you figure out what your tree looks like without having to give the CHDIR and

DIR commands for each sub-directory. Here is the first part of the output for the TREE command for the tree in Figure 4-1:

```
B>A:TREE /F

DIRECTORY PATH LISTING FOR VOLUME ??????????

Path: \PROGRAMS
Sub-directories:   SYSTEM
                   WP
Files:             None

Path: \PROGRAMS\SYSTEM
Sub-directories:   None
Files:             FORMAT   .COM

Path: \PROGRAMS\WP
Sub-directories:   None
Files:             TEXTP    .COM

Path: \OTHER
Sub-directories:   None
Files:             USAGE    .RPT

Path: \TEXT
Sub-directories:   CLIENTS
                   IN-HOUSE
                   OTHER
Files:             MESSAGE .TXT

             .
             .
             .
```

Remember from Chapter 3 that TREE is an external command. Unlike CHDIR and RMDIR, both of which are internal commands, you must direct MS-DOS to the drive containing your system disk before it can execute the TREE command. Without the /F argument, TREE will list only sub-directories, not files.

Using RMDIR
To Remove Sub-Directories

Removing sub-directories is as easy as adding them, except that you should first be sure that the sub-directory is empty. The command you use to remove sub-directories is the RMDIR command.

Fortunately, MS-DOS will not let you use RMDIR on a sub-directory that contains files; it will simply give you an error message. MS-DOS does not let you remove your current sub-directory since it would not know which sub-directory to put you in. This would be akin to pulling the rug out from under your own feet.

Using the RMDIR command is just like using the MKDIR command: you can give either a relative or absolute path name.

Remember that you added the GAMES sub-directory to \PROGRAMS earlier in this chapter. You can remove this sub-directory in the same way that you made it. Assuming that it is empty, enter the command

```
B>RMDIR \PROGRAMS\GAMES
```

If a sub-directory has files in it when you use the RMDIR command, you will get a somewhat vague error message:

```
B>RMDIR SMITH
Invalid path, not directory,
or directory not empty
```

In fact, this is the same error message that you will get if you misspell the name of the sub-directory that you want to remove.

One special warning: if you give the name of a sub-directory to the ERASE command instead of a file specifier, it will erase all of the files in that sub-directory after asking, "Are you sure?" This is unfortunate, since you may have files and sub-directories with similar names.

For example, enter the command

```
B>ERASE SMITH
Are you sure? Y
```

This erases all the files in the SMITH sub-directory, although the sub-directory itself remains on the disk. The only way to remove a sub-directory is with the RMDIR command.

Finding Programs
With the PATH Command

Now that you know how to use paths, you may wonder how to tell MS-DOS about files that are on different paths. Actually, telling MS-DOS about different paths is quite easy with the PATH command; telling other programs about them is much harder.

Normally, MS-DOS looks only on the default directory (or sub-directory) of the default disk when you give an external command. That is why you had to include the A: drive in the command line when you entered the TREE command in the earlier example.

The PATH command performs a function similar to including the drive name: it gives MS-DOS a place to look for external commands. The PATH list can be thought of as an extended search list because it gives MS-DOS a list of places to search for commands. This is one nice benefit of having paths: you can tell MS-DOS to look in many different places on the disk for the commands that you give on the command line. It is fairly easy to tell MS-DOS that you have stored your programs on many different paths, and even on paths on different disks.

But why would you want to store programs in different sub-directories? You may have noticed that the PROGRAMS sub-directory in Figure 4-1 would be a logical place to put programs. Its two children, SYSTEM and WP, give an easy way to separate the dozens of programs that you may have: SYSTEM could hold all of MS-DOS's external commands, and WP could hold your word processing program. Of course, as you work, you want all of the programs in these two directories to be available, regardless of which of the tree's sub-directories you are in.

MS-DOS's search order (which is set with the PATH command) makes managing your program files easier. The description of the PATH command in Chapter 3 explained that the command's argument is a list of the sub-directory names separated by semicolons. Remember that regardless of the list of sub-directories you specify in the PATH command, MS-DOS will always look on the current sub-directory first.

For instance, you can give MS-DOS the following search order:

- Look on the default sub-directory
- Then look on \PROGRAMS\SYSTEM
- Then look on \PROGRAMS\WP.

To do this, you would give the command

```
B>PATH \PROGRAMS\SYSTEM;\PROGRAMS\WP
```

Notice that the default here is B:.

It is important to remember that MS-DOS needs to know on which disk it should look for the commands. If you don't tell it, as in the last example, it will only look on the default disk. No harm is done by explicitly including the disk name with each path name in the PATH command.

If you gave the PATH command (from the previous example) and the default disk was A:, MS-DOS will look for the \PROGRAMS\SYSTEM and \PROGRAMS\WP paths on A:, which is not what you want. Instead, the command should have been given as

```
B>PATH B:\PROGRAMS\SYSTEM;B:\PROGRAMS\WP
```

This ensures that MS-DOS always looks on the correct disk. If you omit the drive name in any of the paths, MS-DOS will only look on the default drive for those paths.

Finding Files With Path Names

As long as you give an explicit path name, MS-DOS will have no problem finding files in any sub-directory. The PATH command only affects how MS-DOS looks for external commands given on the command line. The PATH command does not affect how MS-DOS looks for other files.

In the previous example, MS-DOS will only find program files in the two sub-directories you specified on the command line. Thus, if your default sub-directory is \OTHER and the file you want, SALES.MEM, is in the \TEXT\IN-HOUSE sub-directory, you will get an error message when you give the command

```
B>TYPE SALES.MEM
File not found
```

MS-DOS will only find this file if there is a file called SALES.MEM in the OTHER sub-directory (the default sub-directory).

To tell MS-DOS commands how to find other files, give the files' path name with the file name.

The correct TYPE command from the previous example is

```
B>TYPE \TEXT\IN-HOUSE\SALES.MEM
```

The two MS-DOS commands that cannot look on other sub-directories are the FOR and EXIST batch commands. (It is not clear why Microsoft left these out.) This means that commands like COPY, ERASE, and RENAME can all find files whether or not they are on your default path.

Unfortunately, about half of the application programs available for MS-DOS do not work with files that are not on your default sub-directory. For example, if you gave a word processing program a path name for a file you wanted to edit, it might not be able to understand what you want. This unfortunate situation is mostly due to oversights by the people who write and maintain application programs. Many of these programs were first written for MS-DOS version 1, which did not include paths. After the newer versions appeared, the programs were not updated because the companies felt it was too expensive (or too difficult) to make the necessary changes to include path names. As a result, there is little you can do if you have an application program that does not use sub-directories.

The only way around this is to put the application program in the same sub-directory with all of the files that it uses. This means that you may have many copies of identical files and programs on your disks. If this restriction forces you to copy files from one sub-directory to another just to run the program, you can (and should) complain to the software manufacturer about their lack of compatibility with MS-DOS version 2.

REDIRECTING I/O

Another capability that Microsoft added to version 2 of MS-DOS is *redirected I/O*. Redirected I/O is the ability to reroute a program's input or output from one I/O device to another. With redirected I/O, you can instruct a program that normally reads information from the keyboard to read it from a file instead, or you might tell a program that normally writes information on the screen to write it to a file instead. Redirected I/O can save you a great deal of typing and screen watching.

You redirect input when you tell MS-DOS that every time a program is waiting for keyboard input, MS-DOS should instead give it input from a file. Output redirection, on the other hand, is when you tell MS-DOS to put a character into a file whenever the program wants to put a character on the screen. Figure 4-2 shows how these redirections look.

You may have noticed that three of the commands in Chapter 3 (MORE, SORT, and FIND) required a less than sign (<) before a file name. This strange addition to the argument tells MS-DOS that these commands are using redirected input (a greater than sign (>) indicates redirected output). You can also redirect input and output to and from a device. Simply give the device name instead of a file name on the command line.

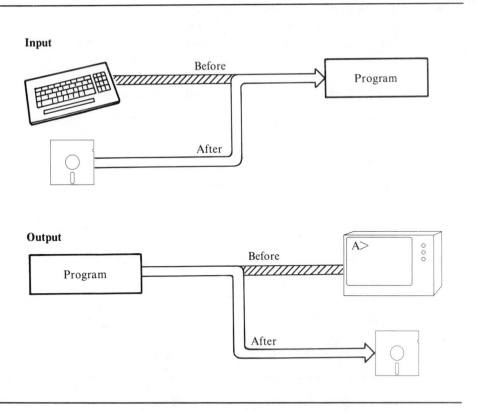

Figure 4-2. Redirected I/O

Redirected Input

Redirected input can save you a lot of time if you normally have to type in the same information each time you run a program. By using redirected input, you can put your usual responses in a file and tell MS-DOS to read that file instead of the keyboard.

To tell MS-DOS which file you want it to read from, put a less than sign (<) in front of the file name. The less than sign was chosen to indicate that the input "comes from" the file, since it resembles an arrow pointing from the file toward the command name. (This is the same method used in other operating systems like UNIX.)

Suppose that you have an inventory report-generating program called SUPERINV that asks you two questions: what file to write the report to and what file to use as a data base. Each time you run the program, you always type in the same two answers: INVEN.RPT and INVEN.DAT. Of course, since the program asks you these questions and expects you to type the answers at the keyboard, you can't run the program from a batch file unless you sit at the console until both questions have been answered.

However, with redirected input you can create a file with your two responses in it and tell MS-DOS to read the file when the program asks for keyboard input. Your file (which might be called INV.INP) would look like this:

```
INV.INP

INVEN.RPT
INVEN.DAT
```

The command you give to use this file instead of the keyboard is

```
A>SUPERINV <INV.INP

What file would you like to write the report to: INVEN.RPT

What file would you like to use as the main data file:

INVEN.DAT
```

Notice that MS-DOS typed the responses for you. You can now incorporate this command in a batch file, and the program will no longer require you to use the keyboard when it runs.

There are some disadvantages to using redirected input, and these require some extra preparation. You must be sure you have answered every question your program asks every time it asks you for information. If it asks a question you did not expect, the results can be disastrous. If there is a line in the input file that was meant as an answer to a particular question, but a different question is asked, the program will get the wrong answer. For instance, if you had put "YES" in the input file because you thought the program was going to ask, "Should I start now?", but it instead asked, "Should I erase the file?", you could lose valuable information.

Another disadvantage is that once you have redirected input to come from a file, you can no longer enter data from the keyboard. If there are no more answers left in the input file and the program asks another question, it will wait forever for more input, and you will have to reboot your computer. This is a very serious drawback to using redirected input: if you use it to answer the first set of questions from the file, all answers that the program might ask must be answered from the file until the program is complete.

These considerations limit the usefulness of redirected input. With care, however, many simple programs can work with redirected input.

Redirected Output

The most common reason for using output redirection is to study the information a program will put out at a later time. Another use for output redirection is to save the output of a program in a file that can later be edited with a word processor. In fact, most of the examples in this book were saved that way.

For example, imagine you had to study the data from a program that types out a huge quantity of information on the screen. Normally, you would have to watch the screen and save the information by manually writing it all down. This would be a time-consuming task. Instead, you can redirect the output to a file that you could scan later.

To tell MS-DOS that everything that usually appears on the screen should instead go to a file, you give the greater than sign ($>$) and the file name. The greater than sign indicates "goes to"; you can remember that because it resembles an arrowhead pointing toward the file name.

Redirecting output is useful for some MS-DOS commands that give you voluminous information. For example, the CHKDSK command with the /V argument usually displays many screens of information as it runs. Instead of having to watch it carefully, you can send all of this information to a file that you can later scan with a text editor.

For instance, to send the information that would normally appear on the screen to the file CHKOUT.TXT, give the command

```
A>CHKDSK /V >CHKOUT.TXT

A>
```

Once the information is in the CHKOUT.TXT file, you can print it on a printer or view it with the TYPE command or a word processor.

If the file that you are redirecting information to already exists, the > tells MS-DOS to erase it and replace it with the new data. You can, however, use two greater than signs (>>) if you want to add text to the end of an existing file.

For instance, to make a file called BC-DIR that has the information the DIR command typed out for B: and C:, give the commands

```
A>DIR B: >BC-DIR

A>DIR C: >>BC-DIR
```

The first command starts a new file, and the second command adds the text to the end of this file.

A disadvantage to using output redirection is that no text appears on your screen until the program is finished. Therefore you won't know if the program asks you a question and is waiting for you to type something. Thus, output redirection is only useful for programs that don't ask you questions as they run.

PIPES

A third advanced feature of MS-DOS is pipes. A *pipe* is a way of connecting two programs so the output of one program becomes the input of the next. All the information that the first program would have printed on the screen is instead sent as input to the second program, replacing keyboard input. It is similar to redirecting the output of the first program to a file and then using that file as redirected input for the second program.

The method you use to pipe two programs together is very simple: put a vertical bar (|) between the two programs on a single command line. You can use any number of arguments in each command, but the two commands to be connected must be separated by the vertical bar.

Unfortunately, this concept has very limited use with MS-DOS, since very few programs produce the exact input that is necessary to run another program. Generally, only special utility programs (like the SORT and FIND commands) are useful with pipes. The remainder of this section gives examples of piping commands together.

You can connect the FIND command with the DIR command to get useful information about the files on your disk. To find files that were last updated on a particular date (11-27-83, in this example), you can pipe the output of the DIR command into the FIND command:

```
A>DIR | FIND "11-27-83"
HARDQUES DOC      1076  11-27-83    9:33p
NEWHARD  LET      1384  11-27-83    9:31p
```

You can also use this method to find the names of the sub-directories since you know that the less than sign will only appear on lines with the sub-directory names:

```
A>DIR | FIND "<"

.              <DIR>      12-06-83    6:06p
..             <DIR>      12-06-83    6:06p
STEIN          <DIR>      12-06-83    6:07p
SMITH          <DIR>      12-06-83    6:09p
```

This leads to a novel way of getting a directory of your files that ignores the sub-directories:

```
A>DIR | FIND /V "<"
 Volume in drive A has no label
 Directory of  A:\text\clients

MAILLIST BAS       689   9-14-83     9:08a
HARDQUES DOC      1076  11-27-83     9:33p
NEWHARD  LET      1384  11-27-83     9:31p
MAILLIST DAT        89  12-05-83     9:48p
SALES    84         28  11-09-83    12:22p
%PIPE1   $$$         0   2-27-84     3:45p
%PIPE2   $$$         0   2-27-84     3:45p
        11 File(s)      317440 bytes free
```

Remember, from the description of the FIND command in Chapter 3, that the /V argument in the FIND command causes the command to output the lines that do not contain the string (in this case, "<").

Notice the two files at the end of the directory listing in the example. These are created by MS-DOS when you use pipes. They are only temporary, and they are erased when the last command in a list of pipes is finished. Unfortunately, they show up in directory listings that you run with pipes.

The SORT command can also be used with the DIR command. Remember, however, that the SORT command sorts by ASCII sequence, which is often impractical.

For example, to sort the files in a directory by their extension, use the SORT command with the /+9 argument. (Remember from Chapter 3 that the SORT command will sort the lines starting with the left column unless you give it a column number to start on.)

```
A>DIR ¦ SORT /+9

.                <DIR>        12-06-83     6:06p
..               <DIR>        12-06-83     6:06p
STEIN            <DIR>        12-06-83     6:07p
SMITH            <DIR>        12-06-83     6:09p
%PIPE1   $$$          0       2-27-84      3:45p
%PIPE2   $$$          0       2-27-84      3:45p
SALES    84          28      11-09-83     12:22p
MAILLIST BAS        689       9-14-83      9:08a
MAILLIST DAT         89      12-05-83      9:48p
HARDQUES DOC       1076      11-27-83      9:33p
NEWHARD  LET       1384      11-27-83      9:31p
        11 File(s)     317440 bytes free
      Volume in drive A has no label
      Directory of  A:\text\clients
```

Since a blank precedes normal alphabetic or numeric characters, the sub-directory entries are listed first.

You can link many commands together as long as the output of one is always usable as the input of the other.

For example, a single line can be used to list in sorted order all of the files (not sub-directories) in a directory, not including the pipe temporary files:

```
A>DIR ¦ FIND /V "<" ¦ FIND /V "e" ¦ FIND "-" ¦ FIND /V "%PIPE" ¦ SORT
HARDQUES DOC      1076  11-27-83    9:33p
MAILLIST BAS       689   9-14-83    9:08a
MAILLIST DAT        89  12-05-83    9:48p
NEWHARD  LET      1384  11-27-83    9:31p
SALES    84         28  11-09-83   12:22p
```

In this example, successive FIND commands are used to weed out the lines you don't want to display. Briefly, FIND / V "<" eliminates the sub-directory entries; FIND / V "e" eliminates the lines containing the label and the number of files (since both these lines contain at least one lowercase "e"); FIND "-" eliminates blank lines (since they don't contain dashes as does each line with a file name); and FIND / V "%PIPE" eliminates the temporary pipe files. Then the final SORT command sorts the lines by file name and file type. Remember that the output from each FIND command is the directory listing minus the lines that the FIND command took out.

EDITING MS-DOS COMMAND LINES

The advanced commands discussed so far in this chapter are all new to version 2 of MS-DOS. The last MS-DOS feature discussed in this topic is a practical tool that is also present in version 1. This feature is the use of special keys for editing command lines.

Whenever you type a command, MS-DOS saves it in a *template*, which is a special area of memory that MS-DOS uses for command editing. If you want to repeat the last command that you gave MS-DOS, or if you want to give a command that is similar to the last command, you can tell MS-DOS to get a copy of that command and allow you to edit it with special keys. Unfortunately, these keys are not always useful, since MS-DOS sometimes "forgets" the meaning of the keys.

Table 4-1 shows the keys that you can use to edit this template and the meaning of each key. These keys match those of the IBM PC and similar computers. Since all keyboards are not alike, the key names for your computer's keys may be different from the ones given here.

The key that you will use most often is the F3 key. You use this key to copy the command line from the template.

Table 4-1. The Command Editing Keys

Key	Meaning
F1	Copy next character from the template (same as → key)
F2x	Copy all characters up to (but not including) the x character from the template
F3	Copy the remaining characters from the template
F4x	Disregard all characters up to (but not including) the x character from the template
F5	Copy the current line into the template and begin editing again
DEL	Disregard the next character in the template
INS	Start insert mode; all characters typed up to the next editing key are inserted
BACKSPACE	Move back one character (same as ← key)
ESCAPE	Discard the current line and begin editing again

For example, assume that you gave the command

```
A>DIT
Bad command or file name
```

You intended the program name to be DIR, not DIT. MS-DOS tries to find the program called DIT and fails. Now instead of having to type out the command line again, you can simply press the F3 key:

```
A>DIT
```

MS-DOS copies the template (the last command) onto the command line for you and leaves the cursor at the end of the line. You then press the BACKSPACE key once, erasing the T:

```
A>DI
```

Now simply type the R to produce the command you wanted.

The other editing keys are also easy to use. For example, if the last command you gave was TYPE C:ACCNTS.RPT and you meant to type the file on B: instead, you would press the F1 key five times, type B, and then press the F3 key. This would produce the line you wanted. You should experiment with these keys for a while until you become comfortable with them.

One problem with the editing keys is that sometimes MS-DOS "forgets" them. The reason that this happens is too technical to dwell upon here, but you will notice immediately if they have been forgotten, since pressing them produces no result.

5

HANDLING EMERGENCIES

Some Typical Disasters
Taking Care of Disks
Avoiding Disasters by Making Backups
What to Do About Error Messages
Recovering From Disasters

Every operating system can fail at different times for different reasons. Some operating systems, such as MS-DOS, provide a few recovery capabilities for the various hazards of computer use. Others, such as CP/M, give the user virtually no help in an emergency. Whether disasters are caused by human error, hardware failure, software bugs, or power failures, they can cause the loss of many weeks' worth of work. However, such losses can be prevented by exercising a small amount of extra caution. This chapter alerts you to the potential hazards and gives you hints on how to avoid them.

SOME TYPICAL DISASTERS

The more you use computers, the more you depend on their reliability. Unfortunately, computer reliability is based on hundreds of factors working together successfully. The breakdown of any of these factors can cause serious problems. The severity of the resulting disaster is a combination of the amount of information or work that is lost and, of course, the amount that can be recovered.

Some of the errors you are likely to encounter are:

- *Bad disk.* Disk errors are the most frustrating problems with almost any computer, since they cannot be avoided and can cause large amounts of data to be lost. Even with excellent disk-handling practices, a small error on the disk can make the whole disk unreadable.

- *Accidentally erased file.* Unfortunately, there is no "un-erase" command in MS-DOS. Some utility packages allow you to unerase files under certain circumstances (usually, if you have not written to the disk since the file was erased). The ERASE command isn't the only dangerous command in MS-DOS; you can accidentally destroy a file with the COPY command if you copy to a disk that already has a file with the same name on it. Of course, formatting a disk that has important information on it can also be disastrous.

- *Frozen program.* Your computer may seem to stop dead while it is executing an application program (such as word processing or accounting): the screen doesn't change, the disks don't move (or they simply keep spinning), and pressing keys does not change anything. These problems are almost always due to a bug in the program or to the failure of the program to anticipate all of your responses. Usually, the worst damage this causes is when you lose the work you put in since you ran the program.

- *Hardware failure.* Although most computer hardware is very reliable, it can sometimes stop working. When this happens, it is often very difficult to determine exactly what part is not working. Most computers have only a few moving parts (such as the disk drives), and finding problems with these is usually easier than determining if a chip burned out or finding a short circuit on a circuit board.

- *Power failure.* A power failure or even a short power glitch while you are running a program may cause you to lose the work you have just done. It can also cause major damage to the files on your disk if you were writing to the disk at the time or if the disk drive head was positioned over an important part of the disk.

There are, of course, a multitude of other errors that can cause you serious hardship. This chapter describes both the normal preventive measures you should take to obviate the worst disaster (losing all of your data) and some of the common problems that come up and how to recover from them.

TAKING CARE OF DISKS

One of the best ways of preventing disaster is to take care of your disks. It is far better to prevent damage than to have to recover from it. Here are some tips:

- Never touch the exposed portions of a floppy diskette. Because your fingers are always covered with a thin layer of natural oils (not to mention dust and particles from the environment), even a single touch can render a large amount of data inaccessible to MS-DOS. Always put a diskette back in its paper sleeve whenever it is not in a disk drive.

- Do not lay floppy disks on the top of your computer where they can be damaged by the occasional intense magnetic waves that are often found around power supplies. Since the information on your disk is stored magnetically, a strong magnetic source could obliterate data on your diskette. Be sure to avoid all other seemingly innocent magnets (such as the ones that hold paper on a typing easel).

- Do not leave disks out in the sun or near heat sources like radiators, water heaters, and lamps. The plastics in the disk are sensitive to heat and may warp.

- Do not write on the outside label of a floppy diskette with anything but a soft felt-tipped marker. Pencils and ball-point pens can dent the surface of the magnetic media, and this can cause errors when MS-DOS reads or writes data.

- When you move a computer that has a hard disk, always lift it. Never slide it, since the rubber feet cause strong vibrations when you slide the computer across a surface. This vibration can cause damage to the drive heads and the magnetic media.

There are, of course, many more precautions that you can take to help prevent damage to your disks. You should read your computer's hardware manual carefully, paying special attention to the sections on warnings and pre-cautions.

AVOIDING DISASTERS BY MAKING BACKUPS

Another important way of averting disaster is to back up your disks regularly. Computer *crashes* (failures to work) can occur despite the best precautions. If you make regular copies of your data and program disks, however, they will cause only limited damage.

Almost every computer professional stresses the importance of regularly copying data onto another disk, known as making a *backup disk*. The disk should be stored in a safe location. Safety is, of course, relative: if your office floods or burns down and your backup disk is in the office, it obviously won't be much help to you. However, for most situations simply backing up your file is usually an adequate precaution. The process of backing up files is sometimes also called *archiving*.

You must decide what files you need to back up, how often you should make backup copies, and what backup method to use. The first two decisions can be made fairly simply: back up every file on your computer at least once, and back up every file that changes as often as you can afford the time to do so. The last decision, what backup method to use, depends on your computer's hardware.

Choosing a Backup Method

The backup method you use will depend on the hardware in your system. Most MS-DOS computers have only floppy and hard disk drives; others also have tape drives. A summary of the methods suggested in this section is given in Table 5-1.

Table 5-1. Methods for Backing Up Data

Source to be backed up	Destination for backup	Suggested method
Floppy	Floppy	DISKCOPY or COPY commands
Hard disk	Floppy	COPY command or utility from computer vendor
Hard disk	Tape	Utility from tape drive vendor

If your system has only floppy diskettes, the DISKCOPY command is a fast and easy way to copy full diskettes. The DISKCOPY command can make a complete copy of each of your diskettes, and it is very simple to use. Refer to Chapter 3 for a complete description of the command.

After you have made several backup copies of a particular diskette, you will begin to have many diskettes with backup copies. Since it is both costly and confusing to keep many copies of the same file on several diskettes, you must decide how long to keep each of the backup copies.

One good method for controlling your backups is to keep two incremental sets of backup diskettes marked X and Y. You would then alternate between the two sets of diskettes when you perform your current backup. For instance, if your last backup was to the X diskettes, then your next backup will be to the Y diskettes. This ensures that if both the master and backup diskettes somehow are destroyed, you will still have a slightly older version of the diskette.

If you are only changing a few of the files on a floppy diskette, it is not necessary to copy the whole diskette with the DISKCOPY command. Instead, you can just use the COPY command to copy those few files that have been changed. A quick way to check which files need backing up is to look at the dates and times of the last update with the DIR command. To make sure that the copy you are working on is always the most current, you should keep a record of when you last backed up every file.

Other commands besides COPY and DISKCOPY are available for backing up hard disks. Many hard disk computers come with a backup program to copy files from the hard disk to floppies. For instance, IBM supplies two programs, BACKUP and RESTORE. IBM users should note, however, that these programs are not easy to use. You can lose information if you do not use the exact diskettes IBM instructs you to use. If you do not have a special program to copy from the hard disk, you should use the COPY command to copy any files that you have changed since the last backup.

Some hard disk systems, such as those from Tecmar and Xcomp, have disks that you can remove (called *removable media*). If your system has two of these, you can back one disk onto another by using DISKCOPY or an equivalent command supplied with the disk drives. Even if you regularly back up your hard disk files, remember to back up files you create on floppy disks also.

Streaming tape drives are another method of backing up hard disks. Streaming tape drives use large cassettes or reel-to-reel tapes and can store data much more accurately than small cassette decks. Streaming tape drives are extremely fast, and they allow you to back up a large amount of data onto one tape. For instance, many tape drives are able to back up an entire 10 megabyte hard disk in less than 5 minutes. If you have a streaming tape drive for your computer, it probably came with a program that will back up a variety of disk types to the tape drive.

Every data and text file should be backed up whenever possible. For example, if you constantly use a set of data files for your accounting system, you should back up the files twice a day. In this way, you will lose only half a day's work if a file is lost or corrupted. If you only update the files once a week, you will lose a week's worth of work. Of course, if you never back up the data, you can possibly lose your business.

Some files never change. For instance, a file may be a letter you wrote and have already sent. There is no reason to back up such files more than once. You only need to back up files that have changed since the last time you backed them up.

Backing Up Application Software

Most of the software that you buy or that comes with your computer is distributed on diskettes. Since diskettes wear out or become damaged, you should always make a complete copy of each original software diskette (the *master*) before you use your software. You should then store the master in a safe place and use the copy instead. If your working copy should later become unreadable because of wear or mishandling, you can simply copy the master again. You should put a write-protect tab on the master disk unless your software instructions tell you not to.

Software manufacturers usually include instructions for backing up the master diskette. If instructions are not included, try the COPY or DISK-COPY command described in Chapter 3. It is likely that you will find that you cannot copy the disk: the commands will report errors such as "Sector not found." Most software manufacturers use copy-protection to prevent you from copying the diskette. They do this to limit the number of illegal copies of their software that are made. Many of these manufacturers include backup copies of the software when you buy the package, and others will send you backup copies for a fee.

What should you do if your software diskette is copy-protected and you cannot obtain a backup copy? You must be sure that your original diskette never fails, or you won't be able to use the software. Since all diskettes fail at some time, however, this situation is hardly desirable. The following section shows one method you can use if you cannot get an adequate backup copy of your application software.

Copying Copy-Protected Diskettes

A number of programs are on the market that allow you to make copies of copy-protected software diskettes. If you own any copy-protected software, a disk-copying program can provide you with insurance against disaster.

Of course, you should not use one of these programs to make copies of software that otherwise might be sold. Such an action is illegal, in the same way that it is illegal to copy a book on a photocopier instead of buying it in the store. In fact, since copying software is easier and less expensive than copying a book, illegitimate copying is much more harmful to software vendors than it is to book publishers.

One popular program is *Copy II PC* from Central Point Software. It backs up more than 100 protected programs and is very easy to use. Acting as a replacement for the DISKCOPY command, *Copy II PC* even automatically verifies the copied disk. It also includes a utility to check the speed of your disk drives. Other similar programs are *SafeCopy* from Computer Shack, Inc., *PC Duplicator* from Logical Systems, and *Savior* from Omega Micro-Ware, Inc. Some of the disk programs listed later in this chapter also copy-protect disks.

You should do a bit of research before buying a disk-copying program to make sure the program can copy the software product that you need to back up and that you can use it with your computer system. Most of these products only work on the IBM PC.

WHAT TO DO ABOUT ERROR MESSAGES

Backing up disks provides you with "insurance" against losing too much valuable data. Another form of insurance is the ability to recognize error messages, because if you understand a problem as it is occurring, you may be able to correct it before it is too late.

Error messages can appear for a wide variety of reasons involving both hardware and software. The causes for some hardware failures are obvious: coffee spilled on a diskette or in the computer, or a broken disk drive. Most of the time, however, it is not obvious why an error has occurred. Many application programs give mysterious error messages, if they give any at all; MS-DOS's error messages are usually easier to recognize.

If you understand the error messages you get, you can prevent mistakes from recurring. This is because error messages often help you understand the correct way to do what you wanted to do. If the error was caused by something out of your control, messages often tell you how to recover from the problem.

Understanding MS-DOS Error Messages

MS-DOS's error messages are often better than those given by other operating systems, but they can still befuddle you if you aren't familiar with them. Everyone gets error messages because of simple typing errors in commands or arguments. Don't be alarmed if you get one.

Table 5-2 lists the common MS-DOS error messages, their probable causes, and possible solutions. This list is far from exhaustive; there are dozens of error messages you can receive. Some commands (especially CHKDSK) have numerous error messages that, while important, probably are unintelligible to anyone except an advanced programmer. However, this list should help you recognize some of the errors that are common in using MS-DOS. Many of MS-DOS's disk error messages listed in the table ask you the question

```
Abort, Retry, Ignore?
```

This means that MS-DOS is giving you another chance to read from, or write to, a disk. You type in the first letter of one of the three choices. "Abort" indicates that you do not want to try writing or reading that disk again. "Retry" means that you think that MS-DOS might be successful if it tries again (for instance, if you left the drive door open). "Ignore" tells MS-DOS to forget what it was trying; this almost always causes the same result as "Abort," since it is rare that a program can recover properly without having written or read the information it meant to.

With some effort, it is almost always possible to understand MS-DOS's error messages and determine what you need to do to recover from the errors. When you come across these errors, you should remember what caused them, and try to prevent them in the future. You can get disk error messages from both MS-DOS and application programs.

Application Program Error Messages

Many application programs' error messages are harder to understand than MS-DOS's. If you cannot understand them, you will also have trouble recovering from the problems they describe. When you look for answers in your manual, you may find the causes of the error are very rarely explained.

Table 5-2. Common Error Messages and Their Solutions

Error messages	Probable cause	Possible solution
Bad command or file name	MS-DOS could not find the command you gave on the command line.	Check that you typed the command name correctly. If it is an external command, be sure that the command file for that command is on the default disk.
Bad floppy diskette	MS-DOS is trying to format a diskette with a write-protect tab on it, or the diskette is not rotating correctly in its jacket.	Check for the write-protect tab. If it is not there, throw out the diskette so that it doesn't cause problems later.
Disk error reading (or writing) drive x	MS-DOS cannot read information off of the drive.	This might be caused by a large number of different problems. There may be a bad sector, or the disk directory may be out of order. Try running the CHKDSK program on the disk.
Duplicate file name or File not found	You have tried to rename a file to a file name that already exists on the disk, or you tried to re-name a file that is not on the disk.	Choose a different name, or check that you typed the name you intended.
Error reading FAT 1 (or FAT 2)	The File Allocation Table for your disk is corrupted.	This is a serious error. Use the COPY command to copy as many files as you can from the disk, and then discard it (if it is a floppy diskette) or reformat it (if it is a hard disk).

Table 5-2. Common Error Message and Their Solutions (*continued*)

Error Messages	Probable cause	Possible Solution
File allocation table bad, drive x	The File Allocation Table for your disk is corrupted.	This is the same as "Error reading FAT 1 (or FAT 2)."
File cannot be copied to itself	COPY cannot copy a file on top of itself.	Give COPY a destination name different than the source name, or use the same name on a different disk.
File not found	One of the files listed in a command could not be found.	Check that the file exists, that you spelled the name correctly, and that you gave the command arguments in the correct order.
Invalid directory	You have named a sub-directory that does not exist.	Check that the path exists and that you have spelled each name in the path correctly.
Not ready error reading (or writing) drive x	The drive door is not shut or there is no diskette in the drive.	Check the drive, and be sure that the diskette is oriented properly.
Write protect error writing drive x	MS-DOS cannot write on a disk that is write-protected.	First check if you really meant to write on that disk. If so, remove the write-protect tab.

Some error messages are more obscure than others, often containing unintelligible numbers and letters (such as "Error 43: interrupt exception at 4AC2").

Most software comes with documentation; good documentation should list all the error messages you can encounter. Unfortunately, many popular programs have manuals with skimpy or nonexistent error message definitions, so you may have to try to figure out what an error message means by yourself. If you find yourself in that situation, here are some pointers:

- *Read the error message carefully before panicking.* For example, the message "FATAL ERROR 12: Cannot write file on B:" may at first seem terrible, but it may only be the software author's way of telling you to close the drive door on B:. If an error message tells you that it can't do something on a disk drive, be sure that the drive is ready and that the proper disk is in the drive. If the program is trying to write a file on a disk, be sure that the disk is not write-protected and that it is not full.

- *Write it down.* Whenever you see an unfamiliar error message on your screen, write it down exactly as it appears. If the error turns out to be severe, you will have to get further help from your computer vendor, who will need the complete error message in order to figure out what went wrong.

- *Read your manual.* There may be a chapter or appendix in your software manual on error messages; if not, you may find the information you need in some other relevant chapter. For instance, if your word processor gives a message like "Can't find WRITE.OVR", read the chapter on installation to find where it is looking for the file. A quick rereading of the first two chapters and the appendixes of a manual clears up most common errors.

- *Ask someone else who uses your computer or software.* Other people who are familiar with the program may have experienced the same problem. If they haven't, they may at least be able to guess its cause.

  Since the error may mean that you have lost hours' worth of work, your anger and frustration might cause you to ignore a reasonable solution. Take a break and come back to it later; a clear mind always helps with problems that can often be logically solved.

- *Call the dealer who sold you the software.* If the error happened when you gave an MS-DOS command and it is not explained in your computer manual or in this book, call your computer dealer (see the section later in this chapter on "Who to Call for Help"). He or she is probably familiar with most common errors.

RECOVERING FROM DISASTERS

Now that you have learned some ways of preventing disasters and diagnosing problems, you are less likely to fall victim to computer disasters. Problems can't always be avoided, however, and you should also know how to recover from those that appear during normal computer use. This section explains the methods you can use to restore data that has become unreadable and the best way to get help with other problems.

Recovering Bad Disks

Most operating systems don't provide a way for you to recover data from an unreadable or damaged disk. This is unfortunate, since disk damage is a common problem. MS-DOS provides a few simple commands to aid you in recovering a bad disk; however, some disk problems require more technical solutions. In these more serious cases, some of the utilities listed in the next section can help. Unfortunately, to use these utilities you must have a greater technical knowledge than the MS-DOS commands require.

If the disk you want to use has unreadable areas, the first decision that you need to make is whether it is worthwhile to save it. For example, if there is only one file on the disk and you still have a copy of the file, it is probably easier simply to throw the disk out than to try to recover it.

More often than not, the disk has valuable data. If this is the case, MS-DOS has two commands to recover from bad disks. These commands are CHKDSK, used with the /F argument, and RECOVER. The difference between them has to do with the files they attempt to recover: CHKDSK is used for recovering files whose directory entries contain incorrect information, and RECOVER is for recovering files in bad sectors.

You may get a message that MS-DOS cannot read part of your disk (such as "Disk error reading B:"). To recover from this message, first try using the CHKDSK command. If this command indicates disk errors, give the command again with the /F argument. If the screen messages do not say that the disk is fixed, then try the RECOVER command.

Some errors are more serious, rendering the entire disk unusable. If this is the case, the CHKDSK and RECOVER commands won't be of any use. For example, the message "Disk error reading FAT 1" followed by "Disk error reading FAT 2" indicates that your file allocation table is so badly corrupted that MS-DOS can't figure out what to do. The *file allocation table* is the part of your directory that tells MS-DOS where each part of each file resides on the disk. If a portion of a table is bad, any files in that portion are unreadable.

In most cases of bad file allocation tables, however, you can still read most of the files from the disk, but you probably cannot write to the disk. After transferring as many files as you can with the COPY command, you should throw out the diskette. If the FAT error occurs on your hard disk, reformat the disk.

Although MS-DOS provides you with the CHKDSK /F and RECOVER commands, they are woefully inadequate when a serious error occurs. In the next section, you will see that some programs are available that can recover large amounts of lost work.

Disk-Saving Utilities

When the commands supplied with MS-DOS don't do enough, you can buy programs from other vendors that help recover unreadable disks. When you shop for utilities, you should note that some programs are very little more than file "un-erasers," while others are suites of programs that let you look at the bytes on the disk, analyze bad files, and more.

The main drawback of these packages is that they assume you have a fair amount of technical background to understand the information. However, if your time is important to you, you should buy at least one of the packages and have it on hand in case of a disk failure. You may be able to use the utility with the documentation, or you can ask for outside help.

Of the many packages on the market, the *Norton Utilities* from Peter Norton is the most comprehensive and easiest to use. The extensive documentation is well written and informative, and the programs allow you to unerase some accidentally deleted files. They also allow you to perform the disk modification necessary for most recoveries in cases where disk damage has occurred. Peter Norton is one of the better-known people in the IBM PC world, because of the usefulness of these utilities as well as his excellent books. *Disk Mechanic* from MLI Microsystems is a similar package aimed at a more technical market. The package includes a utility for backing up copy-protected disks.

These two utility packages only work on the IBM PC. If you have another MS-DOS system, ask your dealer if any of the packages are available for your system. The addresses for the manufacturers of these products are given in Appendix E.

Where to Find Help

When all else fails, you can call the store that sold you the computer or software. Explaining a computer problem over the phone can be very difficult. Therefore, before you call your dealer, put yourself in his or her shoes, and imagine what information will be needed to understand the problem. Write everything down, even if you are sure of all the facts. If nothing else, it will make the dealer more confident that you have a well thought-out reason for calling.

When you do need help, first determine whom you should contact. If you are running an application program, call the dealer who sold it to you. If it is a hardware error that you can't fix, call your hardware dealer. If the error appears to be in MS-DOS (which is exceptionally rare), call your hardware dealer if the operating system came with the computer. Calling your dealer is usually more effective than contacting the software or the hardware manufacturers, since their first reaction is usually to tell you to call your dealer.

Your best bet is to do as much as you can by yourself. If you keep current backups, even with a major problem you will not lose much work. Most people start keeping backups after their first disaster; those who start keeping backups before their first hardware or software failure will certainly lose less work than those who wait.

6

APPLICATION PROGRAMS FOR MS-DOS

The Current MS-DOS Software Market
How to Buy Software
Word Processing Software
Spreadsheets
Data Base Management Systems
Integrated Software
Accounting Programs
Project-Planning Programs
Graphics Programs
Communications Software
Computer-Aided Learning
Programs That Enhance MS-DOS
Games and Entertainment
Programming Languages
Other Programs

Thousands of software programs are available for MS-DOS. This chapter discusses many of these programs and describes the myriad of things you can do with software that runs on an MS-DOS computer.

- Understand the many types of software that are available and know what tasks your computer can do with them.

- Know the good and bad points of a few software packages in each specialized group so you can compare a package with others on the market.

- Avoid such disappointments as exorbitant prices and poor documentation when buying software.

- Choose from the many general packages on the market that solve your business problems.

This chapter only covers buying software; Appendix D provides information you will need for buying hardware.

The main goal of this chapter is to help you as a consumer by comparing many software programs. Specific prices aren't listed, since each program's price can vary so much. You should, of course, always check the prices of competing software so you can compare your needs with the cost of buying the software. You can easily find general price ranges by looking at the ads in computer magazines like the ones listed in Chapter 7.

Figure 6-1 lists the main types of software that are discussed in this chapter. The sections are presented in order of importance to the average reader. You may want to skim the software discussions that do not relate to you (instead of skipping them), in case you later become interested in the subjects they discuss.

Word processing software

Spreadsheets

Data base management systems

Integrated software

Accounting programs

Project-planning programs

Graphics programs

Communications software

Computer-aided learning

Programs that enhance MS-DOS

Games and entertainment

Programming languages

Other programs

Figure 6-1. Overview of Chapter 6

The names of software packages and their manufacturers are listed throughout the chapter. For an alphabetical list of these names and addresses (and those in Chapter 5), see Appendix E.

THE CURRENT MS-DOS SOFTWARE MARKET

Most of the nongame software being written for microcomputers is for MS-DOS users. Companies that were constrained by the limitations of other operating systems like CP/M are now using the expanded capabilities of MS-DOS to create better programs. New packages are introduced every day, and many packages that run on other operating systems are being converted to MS-DOS.

Unfortunately, the MS-DOS software market is still dominated by the IBM PC. This means that more than half of the MS-DOS programs available will run only on IBM PCs or PC look-alikes (computers that are internally similar to the IBM PC). The result is that many MS-DOS computers cannot run some of the best software programs.

With only a few minor additions, most MS-DOS software designed for the IBM PC can run on most other MS-DOS computers. However, software companies do not make these additions or give help to anyone other than IBM owners. Thus, if you don't own an IBM (or a look-alike), you must always check the compatibility of the software with your computer.

HOW TO BUY SOFTWARE

As you read this chapter, you will discover many interesting software packages. However, it is not recommended that you simply call your computer dealer and order a program that looks interesting. There are many factors that you should consider before you buy a particular piece of software:

- *Cost in dollars.* Some software packages cost less than $100, and others cost well over $1000. The majority of MS-DOS software, except for games and most educational programs, costs between $250 and $600 per package (although some good software is free).

- *Cost in time.* This refers to the time spent learning to use the software. If you are already familiar with the general concept behind a package, you can learn to use it faster than if the subject were new. You can learn the basics of some packages in an hour or two; however, five to ten hours is a more likely estimate for learning sophisticated packages. For instance, programs that always list all of the possible commands on the screen take much less time to learn than ones that do not.

- *Competition.* Almost every software package on the market has at least one competitor (some have dozens). You should always try to find a few competing packages to compare with the one you are interested in.

- *Dealer support.* This refers to the amount of responsibility a dealer is willing to take for a program. Support is important because you will probably want to ask questions about how to use the package. If the sales staff seems knowledgeable, it is likely that they will be able to help you when you have questions. Remember that the dealer, not the software manufacturer, is expected to help you.

- *Reputation of the manufacturer.* Some software companies have good track records for writing bug-free, easy-to-use software. Your dealer should know which companies have better software. Other important considerations are how long a program has been available and how well the software manufacturer will help your dealer help you.

- *System requirements.* Some programs require a great deal of RAM, while others require a color monitor or a special peripheral. Be sure that a program works with your configuration of computer before you buy it, especially if you own a non-IBM computer.

- *Software manuals.* The documentation for a program should be easy to read and should explain all the problems you might encounter. Many manufacturers let you buy the manuals without the programs so you can read them before buying the software.

- *How much training is available.* Many stores and training specialists have set up courses to teach about popular software products. Some stores even include this training at no additional cost when you purchase their software. Many popular software packages have on-screen tutorials that train you how to use the software.

Once you have decided which software program to buy, you need to decide where to purchase it. The simplest method is to find out whether your computer dealer carries the software. If so, you might wish to buy it there. This method may not be the best, however; the store may sell the software at full list price, while other sources may discount it. Your dealer might also be unfamiliar with the product or may not have the software in stock. (It often takes weeks for dealers to get software delivered.)

You have two major choices if you decide to shop around: buying software from a computer dealer or a specialty store, or buying from a mail-order firm. Almost every computer store carries some software, although it is usually limited to a few best-selling titles. Stores that specialize in software often carry hundreds of titles; they are also a good source of information on what competition a particular product has. Mail-order firms vary widely in quality, but they have the general advantage of low prices and plentiful stock.

There are, of course, pros and cons for each choice. Retail dealers usually charge more for software and often do not stock as wide a variety as mail-order houses. On the other hand, retail stores, especially software-only stores, usually give better customer service than mail-order stores. At retail stores, you may have an opportunity to try a number of competing products (such as a few similar word processors). Mail-order firms also have advantages, however. In addition to lower prices, some mail-order firms have good or even excellent customer service (since most software questions can be answered over the phone). Table 6-1 summarizes the advantages and disadvantages of these three types of stores.

Some software is not available either in retail stores or through standard mail-order houses. If a manufacturer is too small to get shelf space in the normal outlets, it may sell the product through mail order. Usually, the only way to find out about these products is by reading ads in magazines. Buying software this way is risky unless you have read favorable reviews or know someone who has the product.

If you are willing to pay to try a software program, you may be able to rent it from a software rental firm. The rental fee is usually a percentage of the cost of the package, and you are often allowed to use it for about two weeks. If you decide to buy the package from the rental firm, the fee will often be credited toward the purchase.

Despite your best efforts, you may buy an application program that you do not like. Unless the manufacturer of that package has such a policy, it is

Table 6-1.   Comparison of Benefits of Different Software Dealers

Consideration	Computer Store	Software Store	Mail-Order
Price (in general)	Highest	Middle	Lowest
Service after purchase	Good, if they are familiar with the product	Best	Usually fairly poor (often involves a toll call)
Selection of competing products	Fair (often only carry top-sellers)	Very good, often very helpful when deciding between packages	Best, although not very helpful for shopping
Training available	Good	Good	Usually none

unlikely that any dealer will let you return software if you are not satisfied. One of the unfortunate facts of life in the computer industry is that you may have to buy more than one package of a particular type of software in order to get the one that is right for you. Careful shopping can greatly reduce your chances of making a mistake.

Public Domain Software and Shareware

Public domain software is software that is not copyrighted and can be freely copied. There are thousands of public domain programs, many of which are extremely useful. For instance, some of these programs help you transfer files between incompatible application packages (such as from one spreadsheet program to another), teach you how to program, or are examples of how to use BASIC to perform common tasks. There are also hundreds of games available for free.

The easiest way to find out about these programs is to join a local computer user group. There are groups specifically for the IBM PC and IBM look-alikes. Most of these groups have librarians who have complete collections of public domain software. They will often copy the programs you want if you bring your own diskettes, or sell you the diskettes with the programs already copied on them. The magazines listed in Chapter 7 often have lists of local user groups. Many computer stores can also provide this information.

Shareware is an interesting alternative to the traditional method of buying software. Many of the shareware programs are well written and easy to use; some are much better than the corresponding regular software or public domain software. Shareware is software that you get for free, and if you like it, you send its makers a voluntary contribution. You can get copies of shareware programs from user's groups or from friends. This concept is radically different from the typical software sales. Anyone can give out copies of the software, and you are under no obligation to pay the developers. However, since you did not pay for the software, you cannot expect support from the authors.

Often the people who write shareware include the source code (the programming instructions) with the software. If you are a programmer and you improve the product, the software writers ask that you send them the improvements so that they can share them with others. In this way, many people contribute time to improving the source code, making the resulting programs usually bug-free.

Although the shareware concept is new, it is catching on. In this chapter, you will find descriptions of three good shareware programs: PC-Write for word processing, PC-FILE for data base management, and PC-TALK for communications. If you have a friend who has these programs, be sure to get copies. If you like them, send the suggested contribution to the authors; if not, you have not lost anything in the transaction.

WORD PROCESSING SOFTWARE

Word processing software lets you type and save any sort of text (memos, letters, reports, and books) and print it on a printer. Most business people find word processing the most useful kind of application program. Once you try it, you will find word processing an extremely valuable tool on your computer. Even if you bought your computer to run some other application packages, you should still have a good word processor.

As word processing programs become more common, more people are realizing the tremendous difference between using a word processor and a typewriter. With a word processor, revising text is extremely easy, restructuring a letter or memo is very fast, and saving text on disk means you never need to retype it. This first section covers some important fundamentals of using a word processing program.

How Word Processing Works

It is probably easy for you to imagine a program that displays the characters on the screen as you type in characters from your keyboard. Except for the screen, the program acts like a normal typewriter. You can also imagine that as you type the characters, the program saves the characters in a file; later you can give a command to print the file on the printer. So far, this description fits a memory typewriter: once you type something, you can always print it.

However, the similarity ends when you want to change what you have typed. With a word processor, you can easily add or delete words, sentences, and paragraphs. You can also move sentences and paragraphs around in the text file you have created. In making these changes, your program is allowing you to *edit* your text. Another feature of a word processor is that you can design your document to have a particular format (automatic page numbering, indentions, italics, and so on) when you print it out on paper.

Just as you gave MS-DOS commands earlier in this book, you give a word processing program commands to tell it what you want to do and where. With most programs, you use a combination of keystrokes to give these commands (such as to move forward or backward in the text, to delete, to insert, and so forth). Most MS-DOS computers have special keys on the keyboard that make word processing easier.

The letters, chapters, or reports you write on a word processor are kept in files like the ones discussed in Chapter 2. If you are entering a new file, you tell the program that you want to enter text and then begin typing. If you are editing text you have already written, you tell the program the name of the file you want to edit and where the text is that you want to edit (such as the first line or the second sentence in the fourth paragraph). When the program takes you there, you can make your changes. In fact, you move through the whole file this way, changing old text or adding new. One of the nice features of editing is that you can move back and forth through a file at will; you are not constrained to going only from the beginning to the end.

You should save your work on disk periodically as you are writing and then save it again when you are done editing or entering the file. If you want, you can print out this new file. After you have used word processing software to edit text, you may never want to go back to using a typewriter.

A good word processing program (called a *screen-oriented editor*) lets you see a full screen of lines. This feature is one of the main reasons why a word processing program is useful to you, even if you don't use it to word process. When you want to edit a file with MS-DOS's EDLIN command, you will only see one line in your file at a time; in comparison, word processing programs allow you to see at least 15 lines so you can evaluate the line in the context of its surroundings.

Most word processing programs show you on the screen how your text will look on the page. Such programs are often referred to as "see-what-you-get" programs. Other programs show you only the contents of your file on the screen. With these others, you will not see the format of your text until you print your file on the printer. You use formatting commands to tell the printer how to print your text.

Generally, the more powerful the word processor, the more things you can do with its *formatting commands*. There are many types of formatting commands. Some let you do simple, typical things (such as setting the left and right margins, numbering pages, or indenting a paragraph), while others are more sophisticated. Such commands, for instance, may do such things as automatically indenting a list, centering section titles, putting a specific heading at the top of every page, or automatically boldfacing or underlining a group of words.

There are advantages to both methods: if you want to see on the screen exactly how a document will look, then the "see-what-you-get" programs will be best for you. However, this feature limits the type of formatting commands that the software can offer. Neither is inherently better; they are just different. You should choose which kind of program to use based on your needs.

How important are formatting commands? For writing short documents, you do not need the sophisticated print-formatting features of many word processors. You should be more concerned with the editing capabilities. On the other hand, the more sophisticated the formatting commands, the better your reports and longer documents will look. If your documents are longer (for instance, if you write manuals or books), the more advanced formatting features could make your job much easier. For instance, features that automatically number the headings or generate a table of contents are very important with long documents.

What to Look for in a Word Processor

Word processing programs are available in a very wide price range. The prices generally fall into two groups: under $100 and between $250 and $600. Curiously, you cannot assume that a more expensive word processing package will be easier to use and have more abilities than a cheaper version. Some inexpensive word processors have more features than some expensive ones. The most important criteria are, first, whether a package is easy to learn and use, and second, whether it can do all the things you need it to do.

If a word processor is important to your job, you should make your selection carefully. First, thoroughly assess your needs; most business people use word processors to write, edit, and format letters, memos, and reports. Then try out several programs. The best way to do this is to bring a sample of your work to a retail store. If you write a lot of letters, try typing them using several different programs. How easy is it to produce the exact letter you want? You should take notes on each program and compare them.

The following are some questions to consider when you begin your search for the best program:

- How easy is it to enter, change, format, and print your text? You probably want to avoid programs that require you to memorize complicated sequences of keystrokes to give the editing commands.

- Can the word processor work with your printer? Some printers can switch printing styles (called *fonts*), use proportional spacing, or create superscripts and subscripts. However, you can only use these features if your word processor knows about the type of printer you have. Most word processors can only work with a few types of printers; if the one you buy doesn't know about your printer, it won't use the special features.

- Does the program include a mailing list feature? Many programs allow you to use a mailing list file with a letter to produce a mass mailing by inserting the name and address at the top of each letter.

- Does the program have features for advanced users? Many people who use a word processor regularly become very proficient with the program. Many packages have advanced features that, although too complicated for beginning users, give advanced users a great deal more flexibility. An example of these features is the ability to perform many commands at the same time.

- How easy is it to learn? Some programs come with well-written documentation, on-screen help menus, and templates or command reference cards to help you pick up the system as soon as possible. Other programs have poor documentation, awkward keystrokes for commands, and other features that prevent you from becoming comfortable with the program.

The best way to determine how easy a word processor is to learn is through word of mouth. If you can, ask someone who has learned to use the word processor, or ask your dealer. It is probably worth your time to attend a local computer user's group meeting and ask other people what they recommend. However, be warned that this is a controversial subject; asking people which word processor to buy produces the same kind of subjective judgments as asking about religious preference or favorite cars would.

Magazines are another good source of information, especially if they contain reviews of the program you are interested in. These articles often have comparison charts that show you the features of each word processor reviewed. Chapter 7 lists some books that give complete introductions to word processing as well as magazines that have product reviews. If you are inexperienced, you probably should select an easy-to-use word processor over one with more features. If you have already learned one word processor, however, another one should be fairly easy to learn.

You should be sure that the package you buy is a word processor, not just a text editor (unless you are sure you want the latter). There is a big difference between the two: text editors cannot format text and are used by programmers (since programs do not need formatting) or by people who have a separate text-formatting package. Most of the word processors discussed in this section have both editing and formatting capabilities.

A few word processing packages include *spelling check* programs. A spelling checker examines each word in your text file, looks it up in its dictionary, and tells you which ones it does not recognize. It then lets you decide if you misspelled the word or if the program is just not familiar with the word (for instance, acronyms and proper names). As you might imagine, each file might have many words that are not in the program's dictionary; thus, it is especially important to get a spelling checker program that lets you easily update the dictionary. These programs are described later in this section.

The remainder of this section will present a sampling of word processing programs, text editors and formatters, and spelling checkers currently on the market. It will start by looking at alternatives that are available if you don't wish to purchase a word processing program.

What Is Available for Free

MS-DOS comes with a weak text editor called EDLIN. Frankly, it is hardly worth considering EDLIN if you want to write or edit more than a few lines of text. It can be used, but it is difficult to learn and does extremely little for you. If your computer manufacturer included a word processing package with your computer, you should probably ignore EDLIN altogether.

The main difficulty in using EDLIN is that it is a *line editor*; that is, it does not let you look at a screenful of information, only at a single line. Thus, you can't move around the file easily, since EDLIN always moves to the beginning of the line. EDLIN also has no text-formatting capabilities.

If you can't spend the money to buy a professional word processing system (some are only $50), there is a fairly good free alternative to EDLIN. *PC-Write*, a shareware package from Quicksoft, has many of the features found in programs that cost $200 to $500 (see the discussion of shareware programs earlier in this chapter). The requested contribution for PC-Write is $75, for which you receive a printed copy of the manual, the source program (written in Pascal), and a telephone number if you need help.

PC-Write has fairly good editing and formatting capabilities. You can use it to edit any text file, and it includes limited print-formatting capabilities. The editor uses the IBM PC's function keys instead of control keys for editing text. It has an interesting array of advanced features, including split-screen editing. The documentation, which is included on disk, is not well written, but you can certainly pick up the basics from reading the first few chapters.

Other public domain word processors are available, but none of them equals PC-Write in abilities or completeness. Even the worst of these are often better than EDLIN.

Word Processing Programs on the Market

This section provides a broad overview of the market by describing a few of the available programs. There are more than 50 word processing packages for MS-DOS, and new ones appear every month. As a result, it is very likely that you can find one that closely meets your needs.

One of the easiest packages to use is *Volkswriter*, from Lifetree Software. Instead of a long manual describing how to use the editor, most of the instructions are given in a few files. To learn the system, you read the files and try each editing command as it is presented. The text formatting is, unfortunately, inadequate for much more than letters. However, the package is very popular with beginners because it is inexpensive, has many editing features, and provides a gentle introduction to using word processors. *Volkswriter deluxe* has more features for advanced users, but it costs more.

Another easy-to-learn package is *Super Writer*, from Sorcim. The program comes with full instructions in one manual, as well as a supplementary manual called *10 Minutes to Super Writer* that teaches you to create, edit, and print a letter in 10 minutes. Although some of the prompts are not very clear, a help screen is available for each prompt. Those who have used Sorcim's popular spreadsheet program SuperCalc will recognize most of the prompts. Another very useful feature of SuperWriter is the document history, which keeps track of who created a document and when it was last updated. This can be quite important in an office where many people work on a document.

WordVision, from Bruce & James Program Publishers, is a much more complete word processing package than Volkswriter or SuperWriter. The manual is very easy to follow, although it takes a long time to begin any useful word processing. The package includes small adhesive tabs that you are supposed to stick on the keys on your keyboard; unfortunately, these tabs make the keyboard seem cluttered. You can also send for key caps that are semipermanent and easier to use. Although many programs purport to show you on the screen exactly what your output will look like, WordVision does this better than any other program. Its use of color also makes certain features easier to see. For instance, boldface text is highlighted in a different color on the screen than regular text (on monochrome monitors, this is displayed as a different level of highlight).

If you decide that you don't need to see your formatted document immediately, *The Final Word*, from Mark of the Unicorn, is an excellent package. The text-editing commands are easier to remember than any other package's, and the expanded memory capabilities of MS-DOS are used to their fullest. It is fairly easy to use the formatting commands to do advanced reports and manuals, but the documentation for the formatting commands is not very explicit. *Perfect Writer*, from Perfect Software, has many of the same features as The Final Word, but they are easier to use in The Final Word.

PFS: Write, from Software Publishing Corp., has an interesting advantage over many packages: it allows you to merge business graphics from the PFS:Graph program into your text. Graphics can make your output much more interesting and can facilitate report production. PFS:Write has an unfortunate limitation, however. Each file that you edit must be fairly small. This forces you to join many small files together if you are writing a long document.

PeachText 5000, from Peachtree Software, is a word processor that lets you format text for printing, but doesn't show the page format on the screen. Many users swear by PeachText, but others feel that the program often makes incorrect assumptions about what they want. For instance, most of the safety measures in the package require you to give two sets of keystrokes, one to give an editing command and another to confirm that you want to perform the command. In addition, the manual does not provide full explanations of how to use the formatting features. This makes them very hard to figure out.

MultiMate, from Softword Systems, makes your MS-DOS computer resemble an advanced word processor. In fact, if you are familiar with Wang word processors, you will feel quite comfortable with MultiMate. Features like global format lines (areas of text that describe the document format) are identical to those in the Wang word processor.

WordPerfect, from Satellite Software International, has a multitude of both editing and formatting features. It is able to edit two documents at once, but not on the same screen. The formatter allows you to put multiple columns of text on the page and have many lines in your headers and footers. This package is quite complete, and although the manual is not written for the beginning user, you should be able to use many of the commands immediately.

Benchmark, from Metasoft, is one of the most difficult packages to learn. You are forced to go through a great deal of preparation before you can even run the program. The large number of technical choices you are presented with during installation may intimidate beginning users. The program has some interesting features, such as a built-in calculator, that are not found in most word processors. However, the poorly written documentation may make it difficult to take advantage of these features.

Some programs burden you with help messages and informative displays. *VisiWord*, from VisiCorp, is one of these. The on-screen messages and the well-written manual are great while you are learning, and they provide plenty of support for infrequent users. But once you learn the system, you may find that the messages get in the way. One big advantage of VisiWord over many other word processing packages is the ease with which you can use it to format tables with numbers.

Microsoft Word, or simply *Word*, is probably the most powerful word processing system available under MS-DOS. It is easy to learn, but you may be overwhelmed by the number of advanced features. Word allows you to use a *mouse*, which is a hand-held device that you use to move an arrow on the screen. The mouse points to choices on the command menu, a word (or group of words) to move or delete, or simply the location where you want to start entering text. Some typists complain that using a mouse is tiring, since the hand has to leave the keyboard in order to move it. You can use Word without the mouse, however.

Microsoft Word uses "glossaries," which are collections of rules about your text that you store on disk. For example, you can tell Word that each time it sees a title, it should center the line and print it in boldface characters. Then all you need do is mark a line as a title and Word will format it. In fact, you can have many glossaries with different rules. There are many other advanced features that make Microsoft Word an excellent choice for a full-functioned word processor.

Textra, from Ann Arbor Software, is one of the better low-priced word processing packages. It has many of the features of larger packages (such as previewing the formatted text) and a very good on-line tutorial that teaches the product in a simple way.

WordStar, from MicroPro, is one of the best-selling programs. It was one of the first full-screen microcomputer editors. Many software dealers find it easy to sell because of the common name recognition. However, it is not as easy to use as many of the other programs listed here. Its commands are easy to forget, and some people who use it every day still find it necessary to keep a copy of the command reference handy.

On the positive side, there are more than a dozen books available on learning WordStar, and there are more WordStar training courses than there are for any other word processing program. With WordStar, all of your current editing choices are displayed on the screen. Some find this feature inconvenient because the menu takes up almost a third of your usable text area. If you want "the industry standard," WordStar is it. Remember, though, that there are many other programs, and some of these may be better for your purposes, easier to learn, and less expensive.

Other popular MS-DOS word processing packages include *Palantir*, from Designer Software, *WordPlus*, from Professional Software, *Easy Writer*, from Information Unlimited Software, *XyWrite II*, from Xyquest, *Readi-Writer*, from ReadiWare Systems, and *Blue*, from Symmetric Software.

Text Editors and Formatters

Although there is a wide selection of word processors, you may have special circumstances and want to use a text editor and a text formatter separately. These specialized editors and formatters frequently have outstanding features that are not available in word processing programs. (Remember that word processing packages have both a text editor and formatter combined into one program.)

For advanced users, *VEDIT*, from CompuView, is an excellent text editor. You can program VEDIT to perform a group of editing tasks in one command. For instance, you can tell VEDIT to search for the next occurrence of a word and to change it one way if it is at the end of a sentence, but another way if it isn't. There are many features of VEDIT that resemble TECO, a powerful editor that runs on mainframe computers.

Another good editor is *MINCE*, from Mark of the Unicorn Company (the same people who make The Final Word). MINCE has a number of editing features that are not available anywhere else, and this allows you to work with very large files. In fact, MINCE was used to write most of this book. The Mark of the Unicorn also makes a text formatter called *SCRIBBLE*.

Text formatters allow you to edit the text you are formatting with any text editor. A very good text formatter that works with any text editor is *Micro-Script*, from MicroType. It has most of the features that other formatters have and additional features for multicolumn text, lists, footnotes, and automatic table of contents and index generation. The program can use the special printing commands that are available on a wide variety of printers.

Other good editors include *Edit Tool*, from Amerisoft, *PMATE*, from Phoenix Software Associates, *Edix*, from Emerging Technology, and *KEDIT*, from Mansfield Software Group. Other good formatters include *ProScript*, from SoftCraft, and *TypeGraph*, from Soft Lab.

Spelling Checkers

Most spelling programs operate the same way: you run them, they choose the words that they don't recognize, and you tell the program whether to add the word to its dictionary or to correct your text. These programs can save a great deal of time for everyone who is not a top-notch speller. Even if you do spell well already, these programs will help you correct typographical errors because they catch anything that is not in their dictionaries.

When evaluating spelling checkers, the most important factors are the ease of use and accuracy. A large number of words in the dictionary is usually not important if the program lets you add words easily. Most people use fewer than 5000 words in all of their writing, and almost every spelling checker available has at least 25,000 words in its dictionary. Some spelling checkers can be run with your word processing program so that you can edit and check spelling easily.

The WORD Plus, from Oasis Systems, is a very good spelling checker. It is easy to use and has some novel features. When the program finds a word it does not recognize, it shows you the word; if you think the correct spelling is close to what you had, the program will look for similar words in the dictionary. Thus, you can use it to help you find the right word without knowing the right spelling.

Another good spelling checker is *MicroSpell*, from Trigram Systems. Like The WORD Plus, MicroSpell looks for similar words, but it may not find the correct one quite as often. That is because it uses a method of checking called *stem processing*, which assumes that common prefixes and suffixes added to a word are always correct. Thus, a stem-processing spelling checker would say that "untree" and "radioer" are valid words.

SPREADSHEETS

Spreadsheet programs can take much of the credit for making microcomputers popular with small businesses. Until VisiCalc, from VisiCorp, was first released, the business uses for personal computers were limited almost exclusively to word processing. (Data base management, discussed later in this chapter, had not been introduced, and business software was just beginning to be developed.) The microcomputer became a much more viable tool for businesses when a program was developed to model a company's growth and coordinate income and expenses. This made the computer look much like an accountant's graph paper.

The basic idea behind a spreadsheet package is very simple: the screen is divided into rectangular *cells*, similar to the boxes on an accountant's balance sheet. Figure 6-2 shows a sample spreadsheet. The columns are marked with letters, and the rows are marked with numbers. Cells are named by the column and row that they are in. For example, the number 110201 is in cell B4.

Each cell can contain one of three types of information: numbers, equations, or text.

- *Numbers.* This can be the number of dollars earned by a department for the year, the number of parts in an inventory, the amount of time spent on a project, or virtually any other number. These numbers are fixed; that is, they are data that you enter. For instance, in Figure 6-2, the number in cell B4 represents the number of dollars earned in 1981 on hardware sales.

- *Equations.* Equations relate other cells to each other. For instance, cell B13 in Figure 6-2 contains the equation B4+B7+B10. By adding the contents of those three cells, it produces a total revenue for 1981. In the same way, the cells in column F contain equations that project probable

	A	B	C	D	E	F
1		1981	1982	1983	1984	1985
2						estim.
3						
4	Hardware	110201	124933	121640	145283	148910
5	sales					
6						
7	Software	48270	65391	86922	94280	97640
8	sales					
9						
10	Rentals	0	0	15900	32740	46000
11						
12						
13	Total	158471	190324	224462	272303	292550
14	revenue					

Figure 6-2. A sample spreadsheet, showing numbers and labels (the equations are not shown)

sales for 1985 on the basis of sales growth in previous years. The equations are not displayed in the spreadsheet, although you can see them when you move the cursor to the cell itself. Otherwise, only the results of the equation are displayed.

Equations can use many mathematical functions. For example, a cell might contain an equation that determines what percentage of the company's earnings were contributed by an individual department.

- *Text.* Text is usually used for labels on the spreadsheet to explain what the numbers represent. An example is the word Rentals in cell A10.

The beauty of the spreadsheet programs is that they allow you to change numbers and equations and then see the results. (These are called *what-if* calculations.) For instance, if you wanted to see what would happen if the sales pattern shown in Figure 6-2 were shifted to concentrate more on rentals, you might change the numbers in the 1984 column and see how this affects the 1985 column. Or you could change the equations you used in the 1985 column and see how the projected earnings change.

Spreadsheet programs have numerous applications as a general-purpose tool for modeling with numbers. Aside from giving you an easier way to guess the future, they also provide a sophisticated method for tracking a company's cash flow. After looking at the various ways that money enters and leaves a company, a manager can look at possible strategies for maximizing profits.

Spreadsheets are also used for modeling engineering problems or for almost any task that requires equations.

Most spreadsheet programs perform identical tasks. The main differences between them are how easy they are to learn and use and the number of additional features that they provide. Some spreadsheets can use more of the memory in your computer than others and thus give you more cells to use. Almost every integrated software package contains a spreadsheet program.

It is hard to judge which features make a spreadsheet package worth buying. The ability to sort rows or columns is the most interesting difference between packages, although advertisements for packages with this feature overstate its usefulness. (Sorting is useful if you have a long list of numbers and want to see quickly which are highest and lowest.) You should purchase a spreadsheet based on how easy it is to learn and use. The fact that many dealers offer training classes for particular spreadsheets is probably a good enough reason to choose one manufacturer over another.

Of the spreadsheet packages that are not integrated with other software, *VisiCalc* is the most popular. *Multiplan*, from Microsoft, is similar. It has a better user interface, and the manual provides many useful examples. *Micro-Plan*, from Chang Laboratories, has many advanced features, including a programming mode. *CalcStar*, from MicroPro, has the advantage of using WordStar-like commands so you can get used to it fairly quickly if you are familiar with WordStar. There are dozens of other MS-DOS spreadsheet programs on the market. Many of them have almost indistinguishable names, and many include "calc" somewhere in the name. Be sure you buy the one you intend to.

DATA BASE MANAGEMENT SYSTEMS

A *data base management system (DBMS)* is a program that organizes information, extracts selected information, allows you to add new information, and updates the information already in the computer. A DBMS can help you keep track of inventory, general ledger, customer names and addresses, and so forth. You might also use the DBMS to get information out of your data base (such as a list of all overdue accounts sorted by amount owed).

How a DBMS Works

A *data base* is a collection of information that is stored in your computer. Each data base has a *structure*, which is the basic pattern or format in which your information is stored. The structure defines what types of information

Table 6-2.   Structure of a Customer Data Base

Field	Type	Notes
Customer ID	Number	Always 4 digits
Company	Text	Maximum length 20 characters
Contact's name	Text	Maximum length 25 characters
Address	Text	Maximum length 25 characters
City	Text	Maximum length 15 characters
State	Text	Maximum length 2 characters
ZIP code	Number	Always 5 digits
Telephone	Text	Always in form ###-###-####
Sales rep's name	Text	Maximum length 25 characters
Balance	Number	Shown in reports as dollars

you can store (names, addresses, part numbers, and so on), and whether information is text or numerical values. For example, if you keep a data base of customers, the structure of the data base might look like Table 6-2.

The information in the structure is contained in *fields* and *records*. Fields are pieces of information that have a particular purpose in the data set. For example, an entry for a name is a field, an address is a field, and so on. The structure defines the characteristics of each field.

A group of related fields is called a record, and each record has a set of values for its fields. A good analogy is a card catalog in a library. The catalog itself is the data set, each card is a record, and each similar piece of information (such as the author's name or the book title) is a field.

Figure 6-3 shows a record from the data base defined in Table 6-2. Each field appears in the record exactly once. You do not need to fill in each field of

Customer ID: 4120
Company: Phil's Stationery
Contact's name: Tim Schmidt
Address: 2311 W. Palm Ave.
City: Ashville
State: CA
Zip code: 94766
Telephone: 415-555-8110
Sales rep's name: Dale Byers
Balance: $45193.12

Figure 6-3.   A record from a customer data base

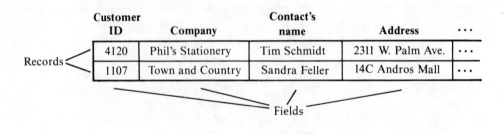

Figure 6-4. Schematic view of a data base

a record. Figure 6-4 shows a schematic view of what a data base looks like. As you can see, each record conforms to the overall organization of the data base.

The DBMS stores your data base in a file on your disk. You use the DBMS to change records or to add new records to the data base. For example, assume that Phil's Stationery changes its phone number. You would use your DBMS to find the appropriate record, and then change the phone number listed in the files.

Changing and adding records is fine, but the main reason you use a DBMS is to get information out of your data base. A good DBMS allows you to see information based on almost any criteria you set. Some of the requests that you might make of your DBMS are

- List all companies that have a ZIP code beginning with 902.

- Type out mailing labels on the printer for all of Sharon Thompson's clients.

- List all clients who owe you money, sorting by the amount owed and showing the total amount owed.

- List all clients who have been added to the data base in the last month.

A DBMS is very helpful for doing an on-the-spot analysis of information, such as giving totals for numeric quantities. Another task it can perform well is sifting through information. For instance, you may want to look at the record for a company, but all you remember about it is that its name starts with the letter *P* and it is located in San Francisco. Your DBMS can simultaneously find records that match these two criteria.

You can imagine that it might take a long time for a DBMS to search

Table 6-3. Structure of an Orders Data Base

Field	Type	Notes
Order number	Number	Always 6 digits
Customer ID	Number	Always 4 digits
Order date	Text	Always in form ##/##/##
Part ordered	Number	Always 5 digits; part number
Quantity	Number	Up to 4 digits
Price	Number	Shown in reports as dollars

through a very large data file for specific information. To speed up the searching, almost all DBMS on the market use *keyed fields*. When you define a structure, you tell the DBMS which fields you think you will commonly use for searching (in the example, company name and location are good guesses). The DBMS then keeps this information in a special file of keys which it uses to find records quickly.

One highly touted feature of some systems is called *relational processing*. This feature allows a DBMS to relate two data bases to each other based on specific fields. This is useful because it is common to have more than one data base on your computer, each with a distinct structure although certain fields are the same. A true relational system allows you to relate many files at once.

To see how relational processing works, look at Table 6-3. It shows a data base of the orders for a company. Notice that the structure has a customer number just like the one in Table 6-2.

With relational processing, you could find out the name of every customer that ordered part 33100 this month even though neither of the two data sets contained all the necessary information. You would first ask the orders data base to find every order for part number 33100 made this month, and then use the customer data base to list out all the customers whose IDs were found in the first request. This relationship between the two data sets is shown in Figure 6-5.

There are many other areas where a relational DBMS can make life much easier. For example, you can easily answer questions like, "Of the companies that owe more than $2500, which ones have outstanding orders?" even if the orders data base is separate from the accounting data base.

By now, you may have thought of many other ways you could use a DBMS. You may wonder how easy it is to use them. Unfortunately, it takes at least five hours to learn how to use a good data base management system. The easier ones often have limitations on their usefulness.

Customers:

Customer ID	Company	Contact's name	Address	...
4120	Phil's Stationery	Tim Schmidt	2311 W. Palm Ave.	...
1107	Town and Country	Sandra Feller	14C Andros Mall	...

Orders:

Order number	Customer ID	Order Date	Part ordered	Quantity	Price
451552	1107	07/12/84	33011	144	422.00
451553	2832	07/12/84	18000	1	7.12

Figure 6-5.   The relation between the customer and orders data sets

What to Look for in a DBMS

Just as there are dozens of word processing programs on the market, there are also dozens of DBMSs, many of which have similar features. Like word processors, each DBMS is usually advertised as being easier to learn and more powerful than its competitors. However, any DBMS is inherently harder to use than a word processor; in fact, most people use them less than they expected because they are so difficult.

Using a DBMS is often like using a programming language that knows about fields, records, and files. This means that whoever is going to be setting up your data bases and applications should have some knowledge of programming or be willing to learn about it. A great deal of learning won't be necessary to set up a DBMS. In fact, a reasonable manual should give you everything you need. Some DBMSs do not require that you use any programming at all; instead, you use fairly straightforward menus to input data and produce reports.

The main criterion for choosing a DBMS is your intended use for it. If you use many large data bases and write complicated reports, you should buy an advanced DBMS and expect to spend a great deal of time (at least 40 hours) learning the system and writing the DBMS programs for your application. However, remember that the more complicated the data base system, the more likely it is to sit on the shelf gathering dust. On the other hand, if your needs are fairly simple, a DBMS that does not require programming would probably suit your purposes.

If you are performing fairly standard accounting functions (such as general ledger or inventory), you should probably buy an accounting package. The applications required by most small businesses are usually available in pre-programmed accounting packages. The advantages of these packages are that you don't have to program them and that they come with complete manuals so you don't need to explain to someone else how to use your system. Accounting packages are discussed later in this chapter.

Most other criteria that are important for choosing a DBMS (such as processing speed and the ability to handle large files) are very hard to judge. Be sure to do your own research, since it is exceptionally difficult to make a good decision based on advertising. Most major DBMSs have been reviewed in the magazines listed in Chapter 7. The best way to choose a DBMS is to ask someone you trust which one he or she uses and to try a few programs with it.

Some of the other important features to ask about before you buy a DBMS are

- Ease of setting up a data input screen.
- Ease of getting reports.
- Relational features (such as how many files can be related and how easy it is to specify the relations).
- Keyed field access.
- On-line help.

It is often hard to compare these features, so getting advice from experienced users is important.

If you are a novice, the amount of training and help available is very important, since these programs are significantly harder to use than most other types of software. Unfortunately, there are very few sources for this type of help. Check your local computer stores and user groups. Some computer consultants offer informal classes and help sessions. The availability of such services may be an important factor in your decision to buy a particular DBMS.

Some DBMS Packages

This section highlights a few different types of DBMS programs so you can determine what is important to you. Remember that your best sources of information are other MS-DOS users and your computer store.

The best known DBMS on the market is *dBASE II*, from Ashton-Tate. Like WordStar, this package is popular despite the fact that many of its competitors are easier to use, faster, and have more features. However, since dBASE II is so popular on MS-DOS (as well as CP/M), most computer stores are more familiar with it than others.

dBASE II is most useful for programmers who are writing DBMS applications. Even though Ashton-Tate tries to sell the program to beginning users, some programming knowledge is important to take full advantage of the software. Other limitations are a limited number of internal storage areas (which hinders programming) and a relatively slow processing speed. dBASE II is advertised as a relational DBMS. Note, however, that it can relate only two files at a time, while other programs let you relate any number of files.

Ashton-Tate has worked hard to improve the documentation of dBASE II, but with only partial success. The manual is good for programmers, but may be difficult for beginners. dBASE II comes with a tutorial program, although the tutorial will quickly leave a novice behind.

R:base Series 4000, from Microrim, is similar to dBASE II in its programmer orientation, but it has many advantages. It runs significantly faster, has a better user interface with many menus and screens of explanation, and its manuals are easier to understand. R:base provides ample on-line help, and it helps a beginning programmer through many of the necessary commands. R:base also permits you to have files with many more records than in dBASE II, and lets you open as many as 40 data files at one time. Even though R:base has many features that dBASE II lacks, dBASE II's popularity means that a much larger number of dBASE II users, dealers, and training consultants are available for dBASE II than for R:base.

If you are not going to do a large amount of work, your best choice is a DBMS that is easy to learn and use. *Infoscope,* from Microstuf, lets you enter and retrieve data easily. It also has many novel features that make it popular. For instance, Infoscope "stacks" files so you can see the relationship between your data bases. When you look at information in a file, a portion of the file is shown on the screen. If you look at a different file, that file is laid over the previous one; if you want to see the first file again, you can "lift" it to the top of the stack. Other useful features of Infoscope are the use of color (on computers that have color monitors) to differentiate the data bases, a friendly command interface, help screens with much more information than other DBMSs, and extremely fast searching and sorting.

Infoscope also has some drawbacks. For instance, the size of the data bases is limited, and so is the length of the records. However, for the job that it performs, it is an excellent program and is also much less expensive than most other DBMSs.

An excellent nonprogramming DBMS, *PC-FILE* from Jim Button, is a shareware program. (The suggested contribution is $35.) PC-FILE allows you to set up simple data bases very easily. The program is written in BASIC, so you may be able to modify it yourself if you know BASIC. PC-FILE has a number of useful features that let it work with other commercial programs, although the documentation is not very complete.

As you can see, a wide range of features and options is available for the DBMS. This discussion has only described a few of the DBMSs; there are many others. The programmable ones include *T.I.M*, from Innovative Software, *DB Master*, from Stoneware, *DataKeep*, from Mathtech, *Knowledge-Man*, from Micro Data Base Systems, and *RL-1*, from ABW. Packages like *PFS:File*, from Software Publishing Corporation, *InfoStar*, from MicroPro, and *Data Design*, from Insoft, do not require programming skills and are often much more appropriate for beginning users.

INTEGRATED SOFTWARE

An *integrated software* package contains a few application programs that can share information. Generally, integrated software contains at least a spreadsheet, a data base management system, and graphics operations (discussed later in this chapter), but they often contain other programs, such as word processing, communications, project planning, and business accounting. The main idea behind integrated software is that since each part of the program can use each other part's data, you do not need to spend a great deal of time transferring data from one to another.

Integrated software offers several benefits. You can easily pass information between applications. For instance, you might be able to graph the statistics derived in your spreadsheet. In addition, your interaction with each part of the software is similar, since the same command structure is usually used for the whole program. There are price advantages, too, since integrated software allows you to buy most of the application programs you need for your computer in one package.

Remember that you can buy the applications you need separately, but you may not be able to transfer information from one program's files to another's. In addition, although integrated software often costs more than individual packages, the cost is less than the combined price of the separate packages.

There are a few good integrated programs on the market, but dozens of fair or poor ones. Before you buy integrated software, consider your needs carefully and look for software that fulfills them and is easy to use. You should ask the following questions when you consider integrated software:

- Are the individual programs good? The convenience of combining many programs into one is quickly negated if the individual programs do not work well. Make sure that the programs you will use most are right for your needs.

- Is the package really integrated, or is it simply a group of vaguely related software? An easy way to determine this is to check if your interaction with each program in the package really is similar. For instance, check if the function keys have a similar meaning in each program.

- Can you really pass information from program to program? Some integrated packages require that you run special utility programs before using data from one part of the program with another. Programs like this are just like using unrelated software, since most unintegrated software comes with programs that allow you to use other popular software.

- Do you really need all the programs in the package? If you only run two types of programs, integration will probably be of no use to you. However, if it is important that several of your programs use the same data, integrated software is a good idea.

One of the first popular software packages for MS-DOS was *1-2-3*, developed by Lotus Development Corporation. 1-2-3 is a combination of a spreadsheet program, a data base management system, and business graphics. The product was an instant success, and other software companies have rushed to copy it, thus starting an integrated software "revolution." A new product from Lotus, called *Symphony*, has all of 1-2-3's features and also includes telephone communications and word processing.

Of the integrated packages, 1-2-3 is still one of the best. Its manual is well written and easy to use, making it perfect for the beginning user. 1-2-3 lets you perform complicated tasks by simply pressing one or two keys. In addition, many companies offer 1-2-3 courses.

Another excellent integrated package is *SuperCalc3*, developed by Sorcim. This package offers the same benefits as 1-2-3, but its business graphics are superior. If you are familiar with older versions of SuperCalc, you know that Sorcim's spreadsheet is very good and has a great deal of power. The manual for SuperCalc3 is not as well written as Lotus's, but *10 Minutes to SuperCalc* provides an excellent introduction to using the program.

Some other popular packages include *Context MBA*, from Context Management Systems, *Framework*, from Ashton-Tate, *InteSoft*, from Schuchardt Software Systems, *The Creator*, from Software Technology for Computers, *IT*, from Martin Marietta, *Number Cruncher*, from Pyramid Data, and *Open Access*, from Software Products International. There are dozens of other integrated programs.

ACCOUNTING PROGRAMS

Most small businesses that purchase an MS-DOS computer expect to use it for accounting. There are accounting programs for every type of accounting function. Unfortunately, choosing accounting programs is more difficult than choosing other application programs, since people from different departments are often involved with computerizing the accounting process.

Accounting programs are like preprogrammed DBMSs. Common accounting functions like accounts payable and inventory require a set of data, procedures for entering data, and a method for reporting on data in the data set. Although you can do this with a DBMS, accounting packages are easier to use because all of the programming has been done for you.

Most accounting packages are used to take in business data and give reports such as monthly and quarterly summaries, cash on hand, and so forth. The most common accounting functions are general ledger, accounts receivable and payable, and inventory. Every program has a slightly different way of performing each of these tasks. Accounting programs vary in both the way in which they take your business data and the kind of report they produce.

Accounting packages may be difficult to use at first. Since you didn't write them yourself, they may not exactly suit your needs. This may not sound like a serious hindrance, since with a word processor, you usually become used to such differences and make adjustments in your typing style. In an accounting package, however, the differences between what the program does with your data and how you usually arrange it may be extremely difficult to get used to. Almost everyone will agree that the best way to describe the first week (or first year) with a new accounting program is "frustrating." But in the long run, your books will be more organized and easier to use.

Accounting packages are usually more expensive than other software, often costing from $500 to $5000, depending on the number of accounting tasks they perform. Fortunately, computer stores are often willing to let you try them before you buy. This is good, since each program handles data in a different way. Before you buy the program, you should be sure that you (or the person who will use the program most) are comfortable with the type of interaction required. Many programs allow you to customize the way you put information into the program, as well as the way in which the program displays the results.

If you have an accountant or bookkeeper, ask for his or her opinion before you buy a program. Many small companies often computerize their accounting system without consulting the people who work with the figures the most. The cost of including these people in the decision process is easily justified if the end result will be less time spent on the books. Accountants often can tell whether a particular accounting package meets the needs of the company. In fact, it is often useful to bring a sample of your data and reports when you shop for accounting software.

Some accountants know other people who use MS-DOS computers and may know about some good programs. You can also ask someone who has tried several packages which one to choose and why. Computer magazines, such as those described in Chapter 7, often have good reviews of accounting packages often written by accountants.

Even though there is a great variety of packages, you may have truly special needs that no program can satisfy. In this case, your best bet is to hire a consultant to write a program that meets your needs. This is not as unusual or expensive as it sounds. In fact, the consultant may have already written a similar program that can be modified slightly for you. Note, though, that one accounting program written by a consultant can cost as much as three or four packaged programs. Many companies hire a consultant who is familiar with many of the packages on the market to help them decide which one to buy.

Faced with what may seem to be dozens of identical packages, it may be tempting to simply pick one made by a well-known manufacturer. Resist the temptation. Hasty decisions are usually a poor strategy, and this is especially true with accounting packages. Once you put all your records into one system, it is very expensive to change to another.

Some features that you should look for when you shop for an accounting package are

- Customizable input screens
- Customizable reports
- Interfaces to popular data base management systems
- Availability and cost of new versions of the programs
- Seminars given by the manufacturer for accountants
- Amount of support that the dealer gets from the manufacturer
- Recommendations from major accounting firms.

The Structured Systems Group is well known for having one of the first and easiest sets of packages with excellent customer support. Information Unlimited Software's *Easy Business* series covers a very wide range of applications. *Solomon*, from Computech Group, is one of the favorite packages for accountants, since users can specify the format of the reports it puts out. This program is also easy to learn. The *RealWorld* series, from MicroBusiness

Software, and *Desktop Accountant*, from Rocky Mountain Software Systems, are also quite popular.

PROJECT-PLANNING PROGRAMS

Computers are very good at organizing lists, especially long lists. If your job involves project planning, you know how difficult it is to organize individual tasks in the order in which they will be performed. Fortunately, there is very good MS-DOS software to do this.

The biggest headache in project planning is establishing an order of precedence, which determines whether other sub-tasks need to be done before the current sub-task, or whether these tasks rely on the current one being completed first. For instance, if you are building a house, you must build the frame before installing the walls; thus, the wall installers are not needed until the frame builders are finished.

If every job were performed one task at a time, you would simply have a one-dimensional list of tasks with each task performed after the other. However, many preparatory tasks for different jobs can be performed at the same time. In the house example, even though the wall installers do not need to show up before the frame builders are finished, the wall materials can be delivered and cut to size while the frame is being built. In this way, it *is* important to perform unrelated tasks at the same time. Figure 6-6 shows an

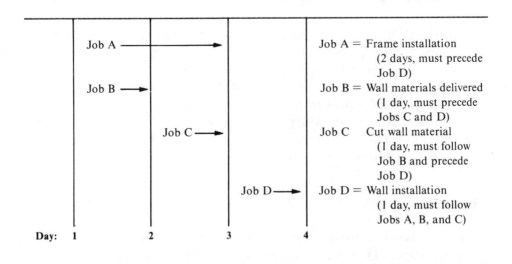

Figure 6-6. Sample output of project-planning software package

example of the type of output a project-planning program might produce.

Project-planning software helps you organize a myriad of sub-tasks so you can plan a large job. You describe each sub-task of the project and list all of the other sub-tasks that need to be completed before the sub-task is begun. Once the program is given all of the input, it shows you how to organize the project, indicating which tasks can be performed simultaneously and the elapsed time of the whole job.

One huge advantage of project-planning software is the ability to perform what-if calculations. For example, you can easily project what will happen if a certain job is not finished on time. You can adjust numbers and revise predictions as a project progresses in real life.

Many project-planning packages even help you estimate job costs. For instance, if you input the cost of a worker's hours for each job, you can calculate total costs for the job's duration. If the materials differ in cost at different times, you can include this factor in your calculations.

Both of the popular MS-DOS planning packages, *MicroGANTT*, from Earth Data, and *Project Scheduler*, from Scitor, use the Gantt method, one popular management tool for planning. Project Scheduler has many interesting features, such as built-in holiday tables and the ability to read VisiCalc and SuperCalc files. MicroGANTT allows you to make output files that can be read by spreadsheet packages. *Project Management System*, from Peachtree Software, performs similar functions.

GRAPHICS PROGRAMS

Most MS-DOS computers can display black-and-white graphics on their monitors, and many can also display in color. Every computer that has either a serial or a parallel port can be connected to external graphics devices that can often be used with programs that produce graphics. Two of the most common graphics devices are *plotters* and *dot-matrix printers*. A plotter is a device that draws pictures with pens, based on instructions from the computer, while a dot-matrix printer is a printer that can print many individual dots, much like the dots on your computer's screen.

Business Graphics

Business graphics software displays numeric data in bar charts, pie charts, and line graphs. The saying that a picture is worth a thousand words is often used to describe business graphics. However, business graphics programs are more useful as a method of summarizing long reports than as a way of presenting information in a new light. Being able to reduce a set of numbers to a pie chart may allow you to see the relation between the numbers, but it can also obscure their magnitude.

There are many factors to consider in choosing a business graphics package. The most important question is whether it can produce graphics on your hardware. For instance, many packages only work if you have a monitor (almost all that run on the IBM PC require both a color adapter and a monitor); others only work on graphic printers (such as an Epson) or plotters. Some computers and some add-on color graphics adapters offer higher resolution than the standard IBM color adapter card.

Another important consideration in choosing a package is how easy it is to input data. Many packages can read data that is produced by other application programs like spreadsheets and DBMSs. Others require that you type in the numbers manually. Although it is usually easy to figure out how to get the

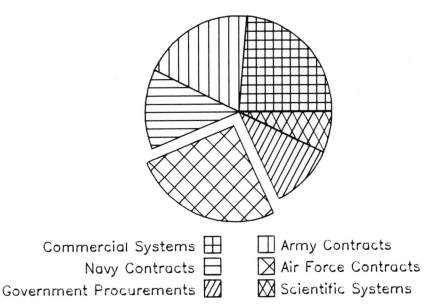

Acme Scientific Sales, 1983

Commercial Systems ⊞   ▯ Army Contracts
Navy Contracts ⊟   ⊠ Air Force Contracts
Government Procurements ▨   ⊠ Scientific Systems

Figure 6-7. A sample pie chart

data to the graphics program, it may still be time consuming to do so.

If you want other people to see the graphics you produce, be sure to get a package that can work with either a printer or a plotter. Even with the best graphics, the printers are slow and usually do not produce good business graphics. Many manufacturers sell low-cost plotters that produce much better results. Most plotters can produce multicolored output on either paper or transparent overhead slides. You do not need to have screen graphics capabilities in order to use a graphics printer or a plotter. In fact, you can buy a two-pen color plotter for less than a color monitor and adapter.

Before you buy a business graphics package, be sure that the package offers enough different charts for your different types of data. Pie charts (shown in Figure 6-7) and bar charts (shown in Figure 6-8) are only useful for showing one-dimensional data, such as the sales of different departments in one year.

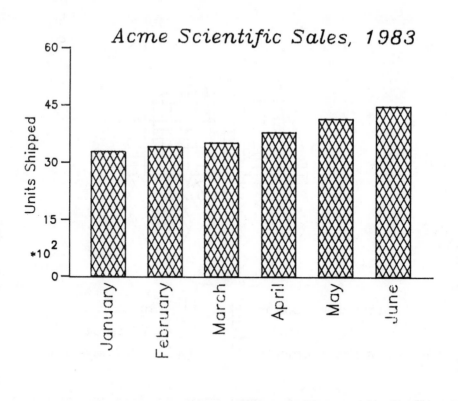

Figure 6-8. A sample bar chart

One-dimensional data is common, but you usually do not need graphics to see the relation between the numbers. Most graphics packages draw one or both of these types of charts.

Two-dimensional data is shown with line drawings, stacked or clustered bar charts, or with three-dimensional bar charts. This is where business graphics become more useful; it is not as easy to see differences when you are comparing data with different relationships at the same time. Two-dimensional data shows the relationship between items based on two different criteria. For example, the comparison of the sales of different departments over many years uses two-dimensional data: the first dimension is the different departments, and the second dimension is the different years. These charts easily allow you to compare the departments against each other in a given year and against themselves over many years.

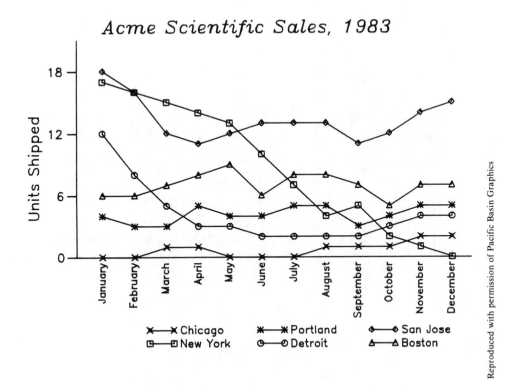

Figure 6-9. A sample line chart

Figures 6-9, 6-10, 6-11, and 6-12 show a line chart, a stacked bar chart, a clustered bar chart, and a three-dimensional bar chart respectively. Even though they look quite different, they all allow you to compare two types of data at once.

An inexpensive and easy-to-use graphics package is *PCcrayon*, from PCsoftware. It produces charts from one- and two-dimensional data and can make a variety of charts on your color screen. It can also copy the contents of the screen onto a dot-matrix printer. The business graphics are only one part of the package, however; you can also use the program to draw pictures using colors and text. It is a versatile package, although its manual does not explain all its features.

PBG 100, from Pacific Basin Graphics, produces all types of charts on monitors, printers, and plotters. The software runs under CP/M and UNIX, as well as MS-DOS, so that a company running different operating systems

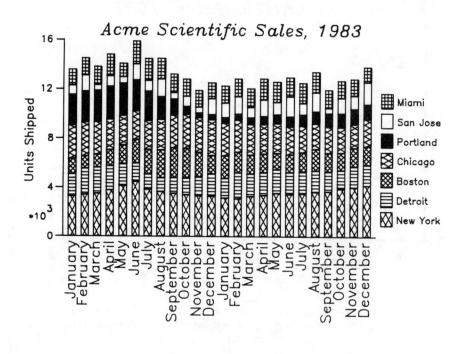

Figure 6-10. A stacked bar chart

can use the software on all of its computers. The figures in this section were all produced with PBG 100 and a pen plotter.

GSS-Chart, from Graphic Software Systems, is a more sophisticated package. It can display charts on devices from many different manufacturers since GSS supplies graphic software to many hardware companies. The user interface for GSS-Chart may provide too much help for persons familiar with the program, but the output is quite good.

EnerGraphics, from EnerTronics, is another high-quality program that lets you display charts on the screen or print them on a graphics printer. You can also use EnerGraphics to create sophisticated two- and three-dimensional drawings (such as engineering renderings) and other functions. Another good package is *Grafox*, from Fox & Geller. There are also dozens of public domain programs that perform business graphics.

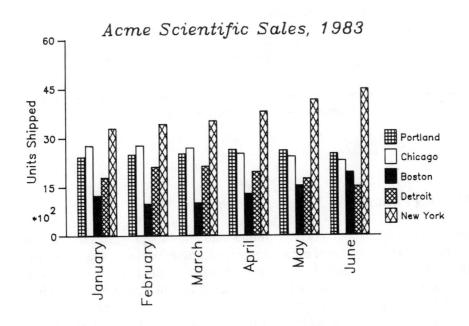

Figure 6-11. A clustered bar chart

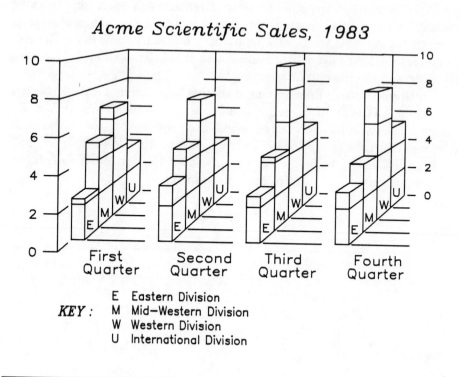

Figure 6-12. A three-dimensional bar chart

Drawing Pictures

Of course, you can do many other things with graphics programs in addition to business graphics. There are a number of graphics packages that allow you to draw pictures instead of graphically displaying data. Like a word processor, once you have drawn a picture, you use the graphics program to edit it to your exact specifications. You can usually produce "slide shows," which are sets of images you create with the programs. Some even let you perform a bit of animation. PCcrayon and EnerGraphics both perform these functions.

One of the most novel approaches to drawing is used by *4-Point Graphics*, from IMSI. This package has a unique method for capturing an image and reproducing it on other areas of the screen. For example, you can draw a company logo once and then quickly put it in many places around a picture. You can also store images in files and build a collection of pictures. Although the manual is difficult to follow, 4-Point Graphics is one of the easiest drawing programs to use.

Another interesting drawing program is *PC-DRAW*, from Micrografix. PC-DRAW uses symbols to build flowcharts, electrical diagrams, and other pictures that use symbols. Although creating symbols takes some patience, once you have your symbols, creating pictures with them is quite easy.

On the more expensive end of the graphics market, *EASEL*, from Time Arts, Inc., is a wonderful product. It is designed for graphic artists and can be used for screen-oriented or video production. Most input is done with a digitizing pen (a special input device for drawing on a pad and having the drawing transferred instantly to the screen). EASEL allows you to use special hardware to get very high-resolution color pictures with many MS-DOS computers.

Other drawing products are *Mantis*, from Suttle Enterprises, *Ultradraw*, from Ultragraphics Systems, *Lenipen*, from Duncan-Atwell Computerized Technologies (which allows you to use a light pen to draw images), and *TELIgraph*, from Microtaure.

Computer-Aided Design

If you are an architect or are interested in using your computer for design or drafting, there are a number of products you can use. These packages provide such sophisticated features as three-dimensional drawing and are written specifically for the needs of designers. However, they often cost five to ten times more than the graphics packages just described. Of course, none of these packages are as sophisticated as the professional systems that cost around $50,000. But they offer a less expensive way for you to begin designing with your computer.

AutoCAD, from Autodesk, Inc., is an excellent package that lets you edit your drawings with a mouse. You can create two-dimensional room and building plans as well as other drawings (such as organizational charts). *MicroCAD*, from Computer Aided Design, is similar but gives you much more flexibility, since you can draw three-dimensional plans. MicroCAD's perspective drawing is a great help to architects in designing exteriors because it allows you to view a building's plans from all angles. Other design packages are *Drawing Processor*, from BG Graphics, and *CADPLAN*, from Personal CAD Systems.

COMMUNICATIONS SOFTWARE

A common hardware addition to microcomputers is a *modem*. A modem allows you to communicate with other computers through normal telephone lines. A few computers come with modems as standard features. Modems allow you to use a vast number of information services (such as large data bases and user groups) that are available on other people's computers.

How does a modem work? The process is actually quite simple. With modems, the telephone company's lines become a very long cable between computers. In the same way that your computer sends characters to your printer through a cable, a modem sends characters through the phone line to another modem on another computer. Unfortunately, most modems do not allow you to communicate very rapidly. Most commonly, they transmit 30 characters per second (300 baud) or 120 characters per second (1200 baud).

You need more than a modem to exchange data with other computers; you also need communications software to tell the modem how to send the information. The following are tasks that communications software can perform:

- In its simple form, communications software connects your terminal directly to the other computer. This is called *terminal emulation*. For instance, if you connect with a mainframe, the communications software will send every character you type to the other computer and print every character the other computer types on your screen. There are many companies that will let you access information on their mainframe computers if you have a communications program and a modem.

- Communications software also allows you to send text files back and forth between computers. For example, you can send a report file over the phone lines to someone else who has a computer and modem. Sending a text file with the communications program is faster and more accurate than retyping the file and sending it.

- Some programs even allow you to send programs through the phone lines. In order to do this, both people need to either run the same communications programs or have two programs that use the same method for transmitting and receiving program files. Since programs are like files with special characters, most communications programs that allow you to send and receive text files also let you send and receive programs.

- Some modems are capable of dialing your phone for you (a feature called *auto-dialing*), but they need software to provide the right commands.

Many communications programs will let you store phone numbers internally so the program does the dialing. This makes using the modem even easier: you simply tell your communications program to dial a certain computer.

Almost every communications program can perform the terminal emulation and text file transfer, and most can perform program transfer and auto-dialing.

The other features that you should look for in communications software are ease of use (most are quite simple) and compatibility with other programs. Unfortunately, the latter is difficult to determine. You should know what *communications protocol* (the method that computers use to be sure that the correct data was sent) is used by the computers you call, since your communications software must use the same protocol. You don't need to know what the protocols do, just the name of the protocols. Two of the more common protocols are XON/XOFF (pronounced ex-on-ex-off), also known as "CONTROL-Q/CONTROL-S," and MODEM7, a protocol that is used almost exclusively by microcomputers. Communications programs often cost between $50 and $200.

Several communications packages on the market have enough features for both beginning and advanced users. *PC-TALK*, from Headlands Press, is an excellent communications package. It is very easy to use, although the manual is not clearly written. PC-TALK can communicate with either the XON/XOFF or MODEM7 protocols, and it can store numbers and dial from a directory of saved phone numbers. Like PC-Write, PC-TALK is shareware, which means that you can get a copy for free. (The requested contribution is $35 if you decide you want to use it.) The distribution diskette contains the source code in BASIC. Thus, if you know how to program in BASIC, you can alter the program.

Another very nice product is *Crosstalk XVI*, from Microstuf. Crosstalk has been one of the best-selling communications programs on both CP/M and MS-DOS for years because of its capabilities and ease of use. The manual is excellent, and the program also provides on-screen help. An especially useful feature is its ability to store commands in a file and then tell Crosstalk to use that file (this is similar to MS-DOS's batch files). Microstuf also sells *Transporter*, which allows you to send and receive files while you are away from your computer (such as overnight, when the phone rates are low).

Other popular programs are *Asynchronous Communications Support*, from IBM, *Micro Link II*, from Digital Marketing, *LYNC*, from International Software Alliance, *ReadiTerm*, from ReadiWare, and *Ascom*, from Dynamic Microprocessor Associates.

COMPUTER-AIDED LEARNING

Most people like to learn from reading books or from listening to a speaker; this is probably due to the way they were taught in school. Books and printed material are still the commonest ways to learn about computers (after all, you are reading a book right now). However, computers are also a valuable medium for learning. Many companies have experimented with computer-aided learning for many years, and computer-based educational software is often good.

Computers can be used to teach noncomputer subjects. In fact, many training companies are using computer-aided instruction for a wide variety of fields from auto repair to nursing. The programs discussed in the next section teach only about MS-DOS; the following section looks at other teaching programs.

Learning About Computers

Computer programs provide an ideal method for learning about computers and software because they are *interactive*: you type in information, and they respond. On the simplest level, this interaction is the computer equivalent of turning the page. When you have finished reading the text on the screen, you press a key to display more information. A more advanced interaction takes place when the computer asks you a question and then does what you want based on your answer. For instance, if the computer asks a test question and you get it wrong, it can repeat the information that you did not learn.

There are many drawbacks to learning from computers, however. They are relatively inefficient. Most of the programs that teach you MS-DOS only scratch the surface, yet they may need 5 floppy disks of storage space. Another problem is that you cannot use these programs as an easy reference like a book or a magazine. You may be restricted to forward progress through the disk and not be able to backtrack to recheck a point. In addition, many programs allow little or no experimentation with commands they don't discuss.

A good training program must keep the users' attention, ensure that they understand each point before they progress to the next, and allow them to try examples of what they are learning. Otherwise, there are no advantages over the traditional book or classroom education.

Since computer education is very popular, there are many computer tutorials on the market. These tutorials cover many topics, from how to use operating systems (such as MS-DOS) to learning to program. They range in quality and price, and you should definitely try one out before you buy it.

PC Tutor, from Comprehensive Software, is a good example of a well-written, inexpensive program that presents an overview of MS-DOS with plenty of interaction. Another good package is *How To Use Your IBM PC*, from Cdex Corporation. This program slowly takes you through a limited range of topics. *Teach Yourself MS-DOS*, from ATI, is much less interesting because of its limited interaction and poor use of the screen.

Creative Learning Programs

The tutorial programs discussed in the last section resemble textbooks with a bit of interaction, some flashy screen graphics, and occasional sound. There are other educational programs for adults that use completely different teaching methods. Although they seem like games, the purpose is to learn, not win. These programs resemble strategy games because they have a goal that you attain by using your mental skills.

Knoware, from the company of the same name, is a package that teaches business people what their computer can do for them. The game introduces some common computer functions (such as programming, spreadsheets, financial decision making, and DBMS) while giving you a reasonable goal: to become head of the board and a millionaire. To get more money and higher job ratings, you have to learn about the salient subjects and perform tasks. The program emphasizes applied learning rather than rote memorization. The tasks are interesting, and you can ask for help at any time.

Millionaire, from Blue Chip Software, is a game that is also a very realistic stock market simulation. The idea behind the game is to teach you how to work with stocks and bonds and take a loss gracefully without going off the deep end. Since the stocks in an industry group often move together, you buy, call, and put options as the program flashes financial news. You can even borrow money to buy stock, if you dare.

Many people are frustrated with their computer, not because it can't do enough, but because they can't type well enough to give it commands. *MasterType*, from Lightning Software, is a fun way to learn how to type. It uses good teaching techniques and works on both color and monochrome displays.

The *FriendlyWare PC Introductory Set*, from FriendlySoft, is a good introduction to computers for beginners. It includes a well-written manual, learning games, fun games, and a very good description of how a BASIC program is written.

A number of educational games are available for children. Often, however, these are neither educational nor fun. One exception to this rule is *In Search of the Most Amazing Thing*, from Spinnaker Software. This game teaches children how to take notes, read a map, bargain, and get help making decisions. The game is much more complex than others, although each part is simple enough for most ten-year-olds. Spinnaker also makes *Delta Drawing*, an innovative package that teaches geometry and programming. It is similar to, but easier and more fun than, the Logo language.

PROGRAMS THAT ENHANCE MS-DOS

Many products can make using MS-DOS easier or more efficient. These products are called *shells*, since they surround MS-DOS with a "protective shell." Instead of giving commands to MS-DOS, you give commands to these products, and they interpret the commands for MS-DOS.

There are basically two types of shells: programs that make it easier to give commands to MS-DOS, and programs that allow MS-DOS to run more than one job, thus making it multitasking or multiuser. The first type of shell eliminates the need to remember all of the syntax of all of the possible MS-DOS commands (although using Chapter 3 of this book should make that easier). The second type, multijob shells, attempts to make MS-DOS more flexible. Many application programs do not work with them, however.

Programs That Hide the A> Prompt

The goal of some shell programs is to prevent you from entering MS-DOS commands directly. You don't need to remember what to do when you see the A> prompt, because you rarely see it. These programs change the way you interact with MS-DOS on the assumption that you do not want to remember MS-DOS commands. This is probably true; it is never convenient to have to look up the syntax of a command or search a book for a way to do something. However, as you learned in the first few chapters, there are relatively few commands that you use regularly, and learning these commands is fairly easy.

Shell programs place the user at a disadvantage because no program can predict all of someone's needs. A shell program may be sufficient for most of your needs, but there are situations where you really need to give an MS-DOS command, and a shell program may get in the way.

The most sophisticated software of this type are programs that use a portion of your screen to help you make choices. For example, *visuALL*, from Trillian, uses the concept of the *pop-up window* to make it easier to

APPLICATION PROGRAMS FOR MS-DOS **241**

interact with the operating system and your programs. With visuALL, you use a mouse or your function keys to move up and down a menu of choices (such as the MS-DOS commands). If you want to work with files, visuALL lets you select the files with the same method. This eliminates most of the memorization involved with both MS-DOS commands and your application programs.

Another excellent program is *DESQ*, from Quarterdeck Software. DESQ is similar to visuALL in its use of the screen; however, DESQ lets you see several different programs on the screen at the same time. You can even move information from one screen to another. Another though less sophisticated shell is *1Dir*, from Bourbaki.

POWER, from Computing!, does not make it easier to give commands, but it does simplify the task of handling directories. For instance, when you give the ERASE command, POWER shows you a sorted list of all the files on the disk and puts a number in front of each. You can then specify which files you want to erase by giving the numbers, not the names. This is especially useful for any MS-DOS commands that require file names.

Multiuser and Multitasking Programs

Until Microsoft comes out with another version of MS-DOS that is either multitasking or multiuser (or both), it's probably safe to say that non-MS-DOS enhancement products will not work with any great reliability. There are many such programs, but none work with all MS-DOS software. The greatest obstacle to the effectiveness of these programs is application software that uses nonstandard MS-DOS features. An example of this is programs that are written specifically for the IBM PC. Such programs may not run on other MS-DOS computers.

Another general problem with these programs is that some computers are not fast enough to make multiuser or multitasking software practical. For example, because the IBM PC has a fairly slow CPU, putting many users on it will make the system run very slowly. (This is not true on MS-DOS computers with very fast CPUs, such as the Radio Shack Model 2000.)

The market for MS-DOS software is changing because of MS-DOS improvements and hardware manufacturers' search for the perfect niche in the MS-DOS market. No programs are listed in this section since the viability of any of these products will be radically changed by an announcement of a new version of MS-DOS or an enhancement like Windows. The best way to keep up with what is available is to read the magazines that cater to the MS-DOS market.

GAMES AND ENTERTAINMENT

Since MS-DOS is usually run on business computers, Microsoft did not provide extensive game capabilities. As an operating system, MS-DOS does not support graphics; any graphics that a program displays must be tailored to each computer. However, this has not deterred software companies that make games from converting them to MS-DOS.

Like many of the programs in this chapter, most games require an IBM PC or a very accurate work-alike computer. Most game manufacturers have chosen to write games that run only on an IBM PC or work-alikes, ignoring the rest of the MS-DOS market. In fact, most of the arcade games listed in this section require the IBM PC to have a color graphics adapter, not a monochrome screen. (Some of the games listed in this section are not really MS-DOS games, since they contain their own operating system, but are listed here anyway.)

There is a wide variety of types of games. The games discussed in this section are categorized into arcade games and thinking games. Many people do not like arcade action games because of their violence or their repetitive nature. However, it is easy to avoid the shoot-'em-up (or eat-'em-up) arcade games. If you are not interested in arcade games, you may still find some of the thinking games interesting.

If you are new to computer action games, keep the following points in mind:

- Don't judge a game by its cover. The flashy art on the package may look great, but remember that it is less expensive to produce a brilliant package than to hire good programmers. Good graphics programmers are more expensive than good graphic artists.

- Don't expect more than what you have seen at the video arcades. (In fact, you should probably expect a great deal less.) If you don't like any of the games at the arcades, you definitely won't like the arcade games available for the IBM PC. Most of the MS-DOS arcade games are conceptual copies of the video arcade games.

- Expect to add a joystick to your computer. Many of the arcade games that require speed and agility are extremely hard to play without a joystick. Using cursor control keys can be very difficult with these games.

- Test a game before you buy it, if possible. However, most computer stores will not allow you to play games in the store — especially on their business computers.

- If you want good action games, you may find that your best bet is to buy an inexpensive home computer (such as an Apple, Atari, or Commodore). If this is a practical option for you, you'll probably be much happier with the results.

Arcade-Type Games

Most of the arcade games that run with MS-DOS are not terribly exciting, but they are popular. Examples of popular games that have been adapted to the IBM PC are *Burger Time*, from Mattel Electronics (a direct adaptation of the arcade version), *Styx*, from Windmill Software (a clone of QIX; very good), *Digger*, also from Windmill (a fair imitation of DigDug), *PC-MAN*, from Orion Software (you can guess what this is a copy of), and *J-Bird*, also from Orion (a good imitation of Q-Bert).

Other arcade-like games are *St. Hippolyte's Wall*, from XOR (an interesting man versus wall game), *Mousekattack*, from Sierra On-Line (a humorous twist on the standard maze game), *Lasercycle*, from Brady (yet another wall-chase game), and *Night Stalker*, from Mattel (lots of shoot and run). Penguin Software, Electronic Arts, Broderbund, and Datasoft also make excellent series of games for the IBM PC. *The PC Arcade*, from FriendlySoft, is an interesting mix of action games and strategy games; they all can be run on both graphics and text-only monitors.

Some skill games are also good learning tools. Many of the flight simulation packages (such as the one from Microsoft) make you pay attention to the numerous dials and lights a small aircraft normally has and respond using controls like those in a real airplane. Although you don't get points as you normally do with games, the object is to take off and land without crashing.

One innovative arcade game is *Night Mission Pinball*, from subLogic. Although there are other pinball simulations, this package lets you design your own playing field: you can add bumpers or targets or simply move them around for better play. This makes an interesting design program more than just an arcade game.

Thinking Games

It is hard to compare the thinking games with anything familiar. Some games are described as "interactive fiction," while others are "learning games." They are similar to stories that you can participate in by describing where the main character goes and what he or she does.

By far the most interesting of the nonarcade games are adventure games. In an adventure game, you solve mysteries and acquire treasures by using words to move through an environment. For instance, if the program tells you that you are near a cave and you say that you want to enter the cave, the program will then tell you what you find there. You can do many things (acquire treasure, slay dragons, and so on), but the object of the game is to solve a mystery or to reach a goal.

In the adventure-game world, the games from Infocom are considered some of the most interesting (these include the *Zork* series, *Planetfall*, and *Starcross*). The scenarios vary from dungeon-and-dragon fantasy to science fiction to standard detective stories. Infocom games are known for their humor and intriguing twists. Your interaction with the game is surprisingly realistic because you can ask questions and give lists of orders in English.

Another interesting game in the adventure and mystery genre is *Mystrix*, from Insoft. This game is like an interactive detective book where you have choices about how you collect clues. Some adventure games display pictures as you move through the fantasy world. Sierra On-Line's *Ulysses and the Golden Fleece* has an absorbing plot (the well-known legend) and very good graphics.

If you like word games, there is an excellent adaptation of the standard *Jotto,* from Word Associates. Insoft makes two word-oriented games, *Wordtrix* (similar to Boggle) and *Quotrix* (a quotation guessing game). Computer Advanced Ideas also has similar games.

If you like strategy games, you may like *Pits and Stones*, from Orion Software. This is a direct adaptation of the classic Oh-wah-ree game, and its animation is very good on both color and monochrome screens. You can play against another person or the computer, who is a very tough opponent. *Edo,* from XOR Software, is a unique strategy game with similarities to the Japanese game Go; it is hard not to become addicted to this game. Bluebush has an excellent version of chess that most people will find very challenging.

PROGRAMMING LANGUAGES

This book has stressed that you do not need to learn how to program in order to use your MS-DOS computer. This is because most of the applications you are likely to want have already been written. However, if you feel inclined, you can gain a great deal by learning to use different computer languages. Learning a computer language like BASIC can benefit you in several ways:

- You will gain a better understanding of how your computer performs tasks.

- You will begin to appreciate how complicated it is to program a large package like a word processor.

- You will better understand the relationship between different components of your computer (such as the keyboard and the CPU).

It is important to remember that you do not need to learn anything about computer languages in order to use your computer. Many people in the computer field advocate learning a computer language, but many others feel that this is counterproductive for most beginning users. Most people who learn computer languages never write more than one or two small programs with them. If you are not interested in learning more about computer languages, feel free to skip the next section.

Learning a Computer Language

Every major computer language has been transferred to MS-DOS computers. One of the first languages for microcomputers, BASIC, is still the most popular language used with MS-DOS. In fact, most computer manufacturers include a copy of Microsoft's BASIC (often called GWBASIC or BASICA) with MS-DOS. Other languages that are available include FORTRAN, COBOL, Pascal, and *assembly language* (also known as machine language). If you have never learned a computer language, you should probably learn BASIC first.

If you learned to program in BASIC on another computer, you will have no problem learning GWBASIC. Some "computer jocks" may tell you that BASIC isn't really a useful language. However, considering how many games, accounting packages, communications packages, and word processors have been written in BASIC, it is difficult to take this claim literally. It might be argued that some other language is better for programming, but not that BASIC isn't useful.

The easiest way to learn BASIC is to read a book that lets you try the examples as you learn. Be sure you read a book that is tailored for GWBASIC users, since there are many dialects of the BASIC language. Most of these books have short examples that you type in as you read so that you can check your progress.

If you decide to learn a different language, you should concentrate on one of the so-called "high-level" languages like FORTRAN or COBOL. Even though these languages are not as useful for programming, there are many good instructional books for them (see Chapter 7). After you learn one language, learning a second one takes relatively little time.

Of the languages, assembly language is by far the hardest to learn. This is unfortunate, because when you understand the concepts behind assembly language programming, you understand most of what makes your computer work. It is also extremely difficult to program in assembly language.

If you decide to program in a language other than GWBASIC, you will have a very wide selection. This section lists many of your choices and gives the names of their manufacturers. Although there are dozens of manufacturers that are not listed, almost every language is.

Most of the languages listed here are *compilers*, that is, languages that convert your program into machine instructions your computer understands. Some of the languages are *interpreters*, which act as translators between your program and the computer. The difference between the two is that compilers produce files that can be run like commands (they have file extensions EXE and COM, like MS-DOS's external commands), while interpreters produce files that can only be run while you run the interpreter. Compiled programs also run faster than interpreted programs. For example, GWBASIC is an interpreter, not a compiler.

BASIC

Most of the popular BASIC packages are interpreters rather than compilers. BASIC interpreters are available from people other than Microsoft. These other versions of BASIC often have features that GWBASIC does not. If you are writing large programs, *Waterloo microBASIC*, from Watsoft, is easier to use. Digital Research offers *CBASIC-86*, which is similar to its popular version of BASIC on CP/M. Also offered is *Personal Basic*, which is easier to use than GWBASIC because it checks your commands as you type them in. *metaBASIC*, from Software 128, is another good version of BASIC.

Microsoft, SuperSoft, and Digital Research also offer BASIC compilers. These compilers make programs that run much faster than interpreters, but they often have limitations that the interpreters do not (such as error handling that is more difficult to understand).

Since GWBASIC is so popular, there are many other products you can buy that help you program with GWBASIC. *Active Trace*, from Awareco, is a set of utilities that helps you find problems in your BASIC programs. It is very easy to use, and the manual is humorously written. There are many similar "cross-reference" programs available, but this one is better organized and more useful than most.

Another excellent package is the *BASIC Development System*, from Softool Systems. This package allows you to run your programs one command at a time so it is much easier to find programming mistakes. It includes other functions that are helpful in writing and revising programs.

Generally, you should use a BASIC interpreter for a while before you buy a compiler (with BASIC, you should also note that compilers are more expensive than interpreters). If you are using the IBM BASIC compiler on an IBM PC and have an 8087 chip in your computer (an uncommon add-on chip), you can use *87 BASIC*, from MicroWare, which makes the compiler use the 8087 for much faster math processing.

The C Language

The C language is rapidly becoming one of the most popular computer programming languages. Although not as easy to learn as BASIC, it has many features that make it generally better for writing programs. For instance, it is relatively easy to write coherent programs in C. Unfortunately, some aspects of the language, such as its way of handling strings of characters, still make it very hard to use.

All of the C packages listed here are compilers. In general, C compilers are much less expensive than BASIC compilers. Since there is a well-established standard for what a C compiler should do, converting C programs written for other operating systems to MS-DOS should be much easier than converting BASIC programs.

One of the best values in C compilers is the *DeSmet C* package, from C Ware Corporation. The compiler produces very fast and small programs, and it is extremely close to the commonly accepted "Kernighan and Ritchie" standard for C compilers. DeSmet C is also less expensive than most other C compilers. The software comes with a very good, inexpensive editor (which was also used to write part of this book). C Ware also offers the same C compiler for CP/M-86.

Another well-respected C compiler is *C86*, from Computer Innovations. This package includes source code for most of the internal routines, so that advanced users can reconfigure the package to meet their own needs. The latest version features an *optimizing compiler*, which knows how to make your programs run faster (and take up less disk space).

Usually, it is very hard to have a compiler run a program one step at a time; this is usually only possible with an interpreter. However, c-systems has developed a C compiler and debugger (called *c-window*) that allows you to do this. This advanced feature makes writing large programs much easier, since you can find your mistakes much more quickly.

Other companies with MS-DOS C compilers are Microsoft, Digital

Research, Vandata, Telecon, Mark Williams Co., Lifeboat Associates, and SuperSoft.

Since C is so popular, several manufacturers are offering packages that make working with C even easier. For instance, the *Entry System for Programmers (ESP)*, from Bellesoft, makes editing in C much easier because it knows about the structure of the C language. For example, when you type in the name of a function, ESP knows what kind of arguments that function takes, automatically includes the parentheses for the function, and tells you what is expected.

There are also many sets of "C tools," which are sub-programs to incorporate into your C programs. A good package, simply called *C Tools,* comes from XOR; it includes routines to do graphics, sound, and input on the IBM PC.

Pascal

Pascal is another popular language that is used in a variety of programming areas. It has many features that make it easy to use, but the programs that it produces are often larger and slower than C programs. Its main advantage is that when you write Pascal programs, you can easily see the structure of what you have written; this usually leads to better programs. Many good Pascal compilers and interpreters exist, including those from Digital Research, Microsoft, and Watsoft. Modula, from Logitech, is a new language that is similar to Pascal.

FORTRAN

FORTRAN is the language that scientists began using in the 1960s. It has few advantages over other languages available for MS-DOS, since its best features were used by the developers of new programming languages. However, if you already program in FORTRAN, you might not want to spend time learning another language. There are many FORTRAN compilers for MS-DOS, including those from Microsoft and SuperSoft.

COBOL

COBOL is like FORTRAN. It is an older language that has been superseded by faster, easier-to-use languages. However, COBOL programs are even harder to write than FORTRAN programs, since you often have to write many more lines of program to produce the same result. Since so many programs are written in COBOL, it appears that it will stay for a while at least. mbp has an excellent COBOL compiler that gives you many features that COBOL on mainframes leave out. Other companies supporting COBOL for MS-DOS include Digital Research, Microsoft, and Ryan-McFarland.

Logo

Logo is a language that is currently very popular as a means of teaching children how to program. The merits of using Logo with children is a hotly debated topic. Logo is an easy-to-learn language that lets students discover programming ideas by themselves. Logo uses a graphic "turtle," which draws lines on the screen as it moves, based on your programming instructions. It is much easier to draw pictures and patterns with Logo than with other languages.

There are many different versions of Logo available. *PC Logo*, from Harvard Associates, is a very complete package with an extensive manual. Although it may be too advanced for young children, it is more comprehensive than others. *Waterloo Logo* comes with a very short manual, which means that the user has to do more experimenting. However, Waterloo Logo lets you experiment with sound (PC Logo doesn't), which makes it more interesting than strictly using visuals.

FORTH

People who program in FORTH swear by it; they say that it is the language of the future and that everyone should learn it. FORTH uses a completely different method (syntax) for giving commands and is often incomprehensible to most programmers; most users find that it is often hard to learn to use FORTH. FORTH programs often run faster than programs in other languages, and they often take up less RAM space. If you choose to learn FORTH, there are a number of good books on the subject.

Many versions of FORTH can be used with MS-DOS. One of the best is *PC/FORTH*, from Laboratory Microsystems. The program is easy to set up, and the documentation is excellent. (This is important for a language like FORTH, since it is often very hard to figure out how to use it.) Other popular MS-DOS FORTHs are from Quest Research, Satellite Software International, and Mountain View Press.

Ada

In 1983, the Department of Defense officially sanctioned Ada as the language it will use to develop programs. Ada is similar to Pascal, but has much more rigorous rules for how you write programs. Although a casual user probably won't be interested in it, RR Software has developed a subset of Ada called *Janus/Ada* for MS-DOS. This package is very well documented, although the myriad of programming rules in Ada will scare off most programmers.

Pilot

Pilot is an interesting language, in that it is not used to write programs. Instead, it is used to write tutorials. It is for teachers to use in putting together computerized class materials. *PC/Pilot* is easy to use and available from Washington Computer Services.

APL

If you have problems that involve mathematical matrices, APL is the best language for programming the solutions. Its syntax is even more bizarre than FORTH's, requiring you to use different symbols on your keyboard and screen than the standard alphabet. However, the inconvenience of learning a strange language is compensated by the superb matrix handling that APL gives you. The most popular APL package for the IBM PC is *APL*Plus/PC,* from STSC. This is a complete APL, and it comes with a number of well-written manuals.

LISP

Artificial intelligence (AI) is becoming a popular research subject, especially among Japanese computer manufacturers. In fact, some of these manufacturers, such as Fujitsu, are implementing the results of American AI research much faster than are American firms. Many programs that use AI are becoming available to microcomputer users. The language used most by artificial intelligence researchers is LISP. Like FORTH and APL, LISP has a nontraditional programming format that scares off most beginning users. The current AI theory is that LISP does a good job of modeling many human thought processes.

Norell Data Systems makes a very good LISP interpreter, with a fairly good manual. LISP is available from a number of other manufacturers, including Microsoft and Soft Warehouse.

OTHER PROGRAMS

Many programs do not fit into neatly defined categories. Yet some of these programs are more interesting and useful than many that are listed in the preceding sections. This section explores the most important of these programs.

Data Security Programs

Data security is a very big problem with personal computers. Many companies have data (such as customer lists and manufacturing reports) that could help competing companies put them out of business. If you transmit sensitive data over phone lines, or even on diskette, there is still a chance that your data can be intercepted. In these cases, you need a method of *encrypting* the data (making it unreadable to outsiders). The encryption method supported by the National Bureau of Standards is called Data Encryption Standard (DES). Note, however, that many security experts question the long-term usefulness of the DES and feel that it may even be insecure today.

DATASAFE, from IMSI, is a simple program that allows you to use the DES without adding any special hardware to your system. You simply run the program on a file that you want encrypted. The program is very fast, converting about 1K of text per second. The manual includes a good discussion of security. To decrypt the message, you give the program the encrypted file and the secret code that you used to encrypt it.

Another excellent encryption technique, called *public-key*, is becoming popular, despite (or because of) the government's disapproval. This method allows a great deal more flexibility in how you transmit messages and does not require that any secret codes be transmitted. *Crypt Master*, from Digital Signature, uses the public-key system.

Statistics Programs

Many companies collect data on their clients, but often do very little data analysis, due to lack of software. However, there are good statistics programs available for MS-DOS that are fairly easy to use. One of these, *ABSTAT* from

Anderson-Bell, is good for producing statistical reports and has an excellent help facility built into the software. *MathStat,* from MPR/Mathematica, has a very good manual that explains all of the statistics that the program produces, as well as their applications. Another statistics package is *Micro-Stat* from ECOsoft.

Keyboard Enhancers

Many application packages ignore their users' learning curves. For instance, when you first start, you may need to think about each command as you give it, but after a while, pressing the same keys every time becomes very boring. *ProKey*, from RoseSoft, allows you to redefine the keys on your keyboard so that pressing one key will have the same effect as pressing many. (This is called *reconfiguring* your keys.) ProKey saves an immense amount of typing and makes it easier to use almost any application program. For example, if your word processor requires you to press four different sets of keys every time you want to do one function, ProKey can make one of the keys on your keyboard send out all four sets.

ProKey is also a great boon for people with physical disabilities, since it simplifies the keystrokes they need to use. For instance, it allows them to avoid pressing the CONTROL key at the same time as other keys. *SmartKey II,* from Heritage Software, is similar to ProKey but does not have as many features.

Formula Solving

If you work with mathematical formulas, you will love *TK!Solver*, from Software Arts. This innovative program (from the people who originally developed VisiCalc) allows you to enter equations and variables and then let the computer do the algebra to find the unknowns. For instance, you can give a complicated fluid dynamics equation and some of the variables and ask for the solution; TK!Solver will tell you what it needs in order to find the answer. It will also convert the units in your equations for you.

Personal Productivity

Dayflo (from Dayflo Software) is an interesting cross between a word processing system and a DBMS. You use Dayflo to enter memos, letters, customer lists, and so on. Like a DBMS, Dayflo keeps track of fields such as name and telephone number so that you can ask to see all information entered about a particular person. It will then show you each item pertaining to that person, even though the data comes from different document areas to your disk. This means that you do not have to keep track of which data bases do what: Dayflo looks at them all at once.

If you write outlines before you start writing a report or memo, *Think Tank*, from Living Videotext, Inc., will help you organize your thoughts. As you prepare an outline with Think Tank, you can focus on one particular level of information or exclude all lower levels. This helps you plan better, since you are not confined to preparing your outline sequentially. It can also be used as a low-level word processor, since you can add paragraphs to your outline and extract those paragraphs later.

Software Tools

There are packages that give you a number of the little programs that you always wanted, such as one that moves columns in a text file, or one that counts words in a file. An excellent example of these are the *Software Tools* from Carousel Microtools. This set includes many text file tools, as well as other utilities that help you manage your files and directories.

Tax Preparation

When you are not using your computer for company business, you can certainly use it for your own. *Micro-Tax* (from Microcomputer Taxsystems, Inc.) is a very popular program for preparing personal income taxes and for helping you plan future taxes. It is well documented, and it has all of the applicable tax laws built into the program. It even prints IRS-approved forms. Although it is intended for tax preparers, it is also useful for individuals with complicated tax needs.

Programming Aids

Most people who program in assembly language have learned to live with *DEBUG*, the symbolic debugger that comes with MS-DOS. However, there is an excellent package called *CodeSmith-86,* from Visual Age, that gives you many more functions than DEBUG, as well as incorporating the best features of a screen-oriented editor. CodeSmith-86 makes debugging much easier.

7

READING MORE
ABOUT MS-DOS

Computer Magazines
Computer Books

One of the best ways to continue learning about your computer and MS-DOS is to read books and magazines. When you look for books and magazines about computers, you will notice there are dozens to choose from. This chapter tells you how to save time and money building a reference collection.

The publishing industry has outdone itself putting out books for the computer market. There are generally two categories of books: trade paperbacks, which are usually under $8, and specialty books, which are often $15 to $25. Magazines include everything from *Popular Computing*, which lightly covers the whole range of personal computers, to *BYTE*, which is very technical and often is more than 700 pages long.

It is almost as easy to get "burned out" on computer publications as it is on computers themselves. With so many books to choose from (and so many that are out of date) and magazines to subscribe to (many of which may not cover your interests), you might give up in despair. This chapter will help you concentrate your money and time on the right publications.

COMPUTER MAGAZINES

Computer magazines have an inherent advantage over books: because they are usually current, changes in the marketplace are quickly reflected in their content. The plethora of ads can help you quickly learn what is available. On

BYTE
70 Main Street
Peterborough, NH 03458

InfoWorld
1060 Marsh Road
Menlo Park, CA 94025

PC Magazine
One Park Avenue
New York, NY 10016

PC Tech Journal
The World Trade Center, Suite 211
Baltimore, MD 21202

PC World
555 De Haro Street
San Francisco, CA 94107

Personal Computer Age
1981 Locust Street
Pasadena, CA 91107

Popular Computing
70 Main Street
Peterborough, NH 03458

Programmer's Journal
2765 Potter Street
Eugene, OR 97405

Softalk for the IBM PC
Box 60
North Hollywood, CA 91603

Figure 7-1. Magazine names and addresses

the other hand, computer magazines can certainly be intimidating because of the amount of information in each issue.

There are over 50 magazines for microcomputers, many of which cover the entire microcomputer field. Of the numerous magazines for the IBM PC and the PCjr, some are for novices and others are for advanced computer users. Most of the IBM PC magazines are equally appropriate for people with PC look-alikes. However, if your MS-DOS computer is not very compatible with the PC, there isn't much in these magazines that would interest you. Figure 7-1 lists the names and addresses of the magazines discussed in this section.

Some of the general microcomputer magazines contain information that is interesting and important for MS-DOS users. For example, information about the trends in the microcomputer industry is important because it will certainly affect the future of MS-DOS computers.

A good strategy for staying informed is to subscribe to one or two of the IBM-related magazines (especially if you own an IBM-compatible computer) and one of the general microcomputer magazines. Remember, you are under no obligation to read everything in these magazines; in fact, you will probably find that many of the articles are neither relevant nor interesting.

IBM PC Magazines

Of the many IBM PC magazines, three stand out as especially informative. They are *Softalk, PC World,* and *PC Magazine.* Each has a different style and different content. You should probably buy one issue of each, skim through them, and pick one to subscribe to.

Softalk for the IBM Personal Computer (there is also *Softalk for the Apple*) is a wonderful magazine that does not take itself too seriously. If you own an IBM PC, you can get your first year's subscription free simply by sending the publisher your PC's serial number. *Softalk* has fewer pages and about half of the circulation of the other two, but it has a much friendlier tone. Every month, there are contests that challenge your creativity, an inside look at a leading software company, and excellent columns for both beginners and experts. The letters to the editor are also interesting, more so than in many microcomputer magazines.

PC World has a wider following than *Softalk*. Most of its articles are well written, and many have easy-to-follow examples. Although it has fewer pages than *PC Magazine, PC World*'s circulation is about the same. Generally, this magazine hits the widest range of readers, although it has fewer articles for beginners than the other two. Still, *PC World* has established a reputation as an innovative and exciting magazine, due to its willingness to try new ideas. For example, *PC World* was the first magazine to include a demonstration diskette in one of its issues, as a promotion for one of its advertisers.

PC Magazine has been around longer than the other PC magazines, and its size shows it. The sheer bulk of the magazine (often more than 500 pages per issue), much of it ads, makes it very useful for people who are interested in finding new information by reading ads. *PC Magazine*'s articles are more likely to be written for beginners than are *PC World*'s articles; as a result, they may not cover their subjects in as much depth as those in *Softalk* or *PC World*. Some of the regular columns are excellent (such as the columns aimed at different professions), and the magazine carries many product reviews each month. (These reviews, however, are sometimes less critical than are the reviews in other magazines.)

Other IBM PC magazines include

- *Personal Computer Age,* a magazine for beginners.
- *PC Tech Journal,* a magazine directed only at advanced users and published by the same people who make *PC Magazine.*
- *Programmer's Journal,* another advanced user's magazine.

The magazines you receive when you join local user groups are often very good. These magazines usually contain news and informative articles. User groups also provide a good opportunity to ask about which magazines you might be interested in subscribing to.

General Microcomputer Magazines

Three of the most popular microcomputer magazines are *BYTE*, *Popular Computing*, and *InfoWorld*. If you are only interested in your MS-DOS computer and not in any of the other developments in the microcomputer industry, these may not be as relevant as the magazines mentioned in the last section. However, the more involved you become with the computer world, the more you will need to follow the general trends.

BYTE is similar to *PC Magazine* in its length and its wealth of ads. *BYTE* is the premiere magazine for the microcomputer trade. Many of the articles are quite informative, but they rarely break any news because of the minimum four-month lead time for publishing articles. In addition, many of the articles are for advanced users only, since this is *BYTE*'s primary audience; however, *BYTE* has many articles and columns for intermediate users and people who just want to follow the microcomputer industry. *BYTE* often covers the technical details behind major new products better than other magazines.

Popular Computing is published by the same people as *BYTE,* but it is aimed more toward the beginning user. The articles are often introductory, and very few of them discuss products that don't relate to the microcomputer user. Although there are fewer ads in *Popular Computing,* the quality of its articles make it a very good buy. This magazine emphasizes applications of using microcomputers in business.

InfoWorld is the industry's weekly newspaper. As such, it is one of the best sources of news about developments in the microcomputer industry. Close to half of *InfoWorld* is devoted to news and columns, and the other half to product reviews and longer articles about the status of a particular field (such as computer graphics or the use of computers in schools). The reviews are very informative and include a quick reference scorecard. Most of *InfoWorld* is aimed toward a wide audience, and many of the articles and columns deal with the social impact of the microcomputer revolution.

There are, of course, many other magazines that deal with microcomputers. If you want to get a feel for them, you should look for a magazine rack with a large number of computer titles, and buy one or two new titles every month. One of the best places to look for a good computer magazine retailer is near a university or an industrial park.

A new type of IBM PC magazine is available on diskettes. These magazines usually have articles and programs that you can use. This new format has some advantages (you don't need to type in programs covered in the magazine, and you can often search for a particular subject). However, you may find these diskette magazines hard to read since you must use your computer screen.

Remember that reading magazines is time-consuming, especially since they often cover the same current topics. It is probably wise to give yourself a time allowance for magazine reading, and if you find yourself going over the limit, start skimming more.

Getting the Most Out of Computer Magazines

Computer magazines are so different from other magazines that many people often feel overwhelmed by them. If you are familiar with the different features that computer magazines have, you can usually get more of the important information out of them with less trouble. For example, many people spend between five and ten hours with each month's issue of *BYTE* and often end up exhausted; some planning can make your reading time much more useful.

You may be accustomed to ignoring the advertisements in most of the magazines you read. If you're interested in getting the most out of computer magazines, you should break this habit since there is a great deal of important information in the ads. Often, in fact, the number of advertising pages equals or exceeds the number of text pages. Ads are the best place to find out about both new products and improvements on older products.

Ads are also a good way to determine the approximate price you should pay for a particular piece of software or hardware. For instance, many discount houses list the prices of hundreds of products, making price shopping very easy. As always, you can't believe everything you read in the ads. Hardware and software manufacturers have an understandable tendency to overstate the usefulness or value of their products; fortunately, most magazines review many of the products you see advertised, so you can often find out more about a product from a less biased source.

If a local magazine store carries computer magazines, it often receives them one to two weeks before people with mail subscriptions. If it is important to get your information early, you should consider purchasing your magazines from a store. However, this is often significantly more expensive than subscriptions.

When you get a magazine, you may want to remove all of the advertising cards that are attached to the magazine; this often makes turning the pages easier and helps keep the magazine open when you are reading an article. It is also usually helpful to have a pencil and a piece of paper handy for taking notes as you skim the issue.

Instead of reading the magazine page by page, some people prefer to read the interesting articles and columns separately from the advertising. Some people like to read the ads before the articles so that they find out what is new first; others prefer to get the information out of the articles before being barraged with the ads.

You can often look at all the ads in a magazine, even those as hefty as *BYTE* or *PC Magazine,* in a few minutes. After a few issues of scanning ads, you will probably recognize the ads that you saw in the last issue and skip over them quickly. If an ad looks interesting, read it and mark down the company, product, and page number, so that you can find it again later.

Most magazines have an advertiser's index near the back of the magazine. This is especially useful if you remember the name of the company that makes a product, but don't remember where in the magazine you saw its ad. Some magazines also have reader service cards, which you can use to get more information after reading an ad (the reader service number is often listed in the advertiser's index). The reader service card is provided as a service to the manufacturer; unfortunately, many advertisers do not respond to requests on the card or take months to do so. However, almost every manufacturer will respond to a letter or even a post card. (This might be a terrific use for your word processor.)

Most magazines also have a "New Products" section, which is really advertising, not editorial. Magazines usually reprint what is sent to them for this section and often do not charge the manufacturers for this space. This is sometimes a good place to find descriptive information on a product.

You can often tell from the table of contents which articles you want to read. You will also probably find that you will want to read some of the regular columns that appear in every issue, either because they cover material that you find useful or because the columnist writes well. You will also probably find columns or regular features that are of no use to you; feel free to skip them. For instance, the letters to the editor are generally not very useful, although they sometimes contain important clarifications of previous articles.

Many magazines publish articles from companies which are essentially just advertising their products. Before you read an article, look at the occupation and employer of the author. This can save you from reading a glowing article about a product, only to find at the end that it was written by the product's manufacturer or by someone who has a vested interest in the product.

COMPUTER BOOKS

Books are, potentially, much better reference sources than are magazines because they can develop individual subjects in far greater depth. Although some magazines have monthly columns on specific topics, it might take a year for the column to present as much material as a book might cover in one chapter. If you dislike ads, you will find it easier to read books without being distracted.

The microcomputer industry is changing rapidly, however; and like the products they describe, most microcomputer books have only a limited period of usefulness before they become outdated. Considering that MS-DOS did not even exist five years before this book was published, it is quite conceivable that in another five years someone might think this book quaint for having talked about the "advanced features" of version 2 of MS-DOS. However, most books are meant to be read and used as references for many years.

Computer books are more expensive than other paperbacks, just as computer magazines are more expensive than many other monthlies. When you are figuring out how much you will spend, a rough guess is that one book will cost about three-quarters as much as a subscription to one magazine. If you are a careful reader who likes to read a great deal on one subject, you should probably buy more books than magazines; if you prefer a smattering of information on a large number of subjects, you will probably be happier subscribing to more magazines.

As with computer magazines, it is easy to feel overwhelmed when trying to select books that will help you use your computer. Many are on the market, but you should make your selection carefully. The following two sections describe a few of the better books written for MS-DOS (or the IBM PC) and about computers and software in general.

Books About MS-DOS and the IBM PC

Your IBM PC Made Easy by Jonathan Sachs (Osborne/ McGraw-Hill, 1983) provides a very complete overview of much of what you need to know about your IBM PC. Sachs covers both hardware and software and gives plenty of examples of how to use MS-DOS's commands. There is an excellent section on the internal hardware in the PC, how to care for it, and what to do in case of problems.

Peter Norton is a well-known author who writes many articles for the

PC-related magazines. Two of his books, *Inside the IBM PC: Access to Advanced Features and Programming* and *MS-DOS and PC-DOS: User's Guide* (Robert J. Brady Co., 1983) are good guides to using your IBM PC. The first book is by far the best technical reference for the PC; it has excellent charts and tables, and it covers a number of interesting topics missed in other advanced books. The second book is too technical for some readers, although it has a wealth of information and fairly humorous cartoons. It also has a marvelous glossary.

Another good general book on the IBM PC is *IBM Personal Computer Handbook,* edited by Dzintar Dravnieks and many others (And/Or Press, 1983). This is a collection of articles from many authors, as well as a good listing of resources for the PC.

If you want a reference set that is organized in alphabetical order, try the *Reference Encyclopedia For the IBM Personal Computer* by Karen and Gary Phillips (Ashton-Tate, 1983). This two-volume set is an excellent reference source, and you can find almost anything in it, including information about hundreds of software packages and peripherals.

For beginners, *Your IBM Personal Computer: Use, Applications, and BASIC* by David Cortesi (CBS College Publishing, 1982) has some good discussions about what computers are and what they can do for you. The book is not up-to-date, however.

Other Useful Books

There are many books that do not relate directly to MS-DOS or the IBM PC but are still very useful. Some provide general information about computers and the microcomputer industry; others cover important application programs. These books may prove more valuable to you than the books listed previously because they give you an in-depth look at the background of the field.

For people who are interested in the social impact that computers have on their lives, as well as the lives of everyone else, the book *Computer Power and Human Reason: From Judgement to Calculation* by Joseph Weizenbaum (W. H. Freeman, 1976) is an excellent discussion of a number of social topics. The topics include personal involvement with computers and how much computers can really do. Weizenbaum is now famous for his knowledge, and the book is easily understood.

If you want to know more about word processing, Peter McWilliams's *The Word Processing Book, Questions and Answers on Word Processing* and *Word Processing on the IBM Personal Computer* (all from Prelude Press) are good sources of information. Although McWilliams's style is often folksy, he gives good practical information, and his analogies often clear up difficult concepts.

Data Base Management Systems: A Guide to Microcomputer Software by David Kruglinski (Osborne/McGraw-Hill, 1983) has an excellent description of various DBMS and how they work. Although the software described in the book is for CP/M, much of his material is still useful for the MS-DOS user.

Probably the most practical book on buying and owning a small computer is *Computer Wimp* by John Bear (Ten Speed Press, 1983). It is full of wonderful anecdotes, advice, notable quotes, and good sense; its blatant irreverence for hardware and software manufacturers is refreshing. It is an excellent book to give to someone who is looking for a computer.

A

COMMAND REFERENCE

Table A-1 lists the MS-DOS commands in alphabetical order. It also gives the functional group within which each command is listed from Chapter 3. Table A-2 lists all of the syntax and arguments for the commands.

Table A-1. Alphabetical Listing of MS-DOS Commands

Command	Internal	External	Description	Functional group
ASSIGN		*	Changes the letters assigned to disks	System Settings
BACKUP		*	Makes backup copies of the hard disk	Disk Maintenance
BREAK	*		Causes MS-DOS to check for user interrupts more often	System Settings
CHDIR	*		Changes default sub-directory	Path Maintenance
CHKDSK		*	Examines and repairs disks	Disk Maintenance
CLS	*		Clears the screen	Other Commands
COMMAND		*	Runs another program	Batch Files
COMP		*	Compares files	File Maintenance
COPY	*		Makes copies of files	File Maintenance
CTTY	*		Changes the console to a serial port	System Settings

Table A-1. Alphabetical Listing of MS-DOS Commands (*continued*)

Command	Internal	External	Description	Functional group
DATE	*		Sets the date	System Settings
DEBUG		*	Examines and changes binary files	Programming Tools
DIR	*		Displays the list of files on a disk	Disk Maintenance
DISKCOMP		*	Compares two diskettes	Disk Maintenance
DISKCOPY		*	Copies an entire diskette	Disk Maintenance
ECHO	*		Prints a message on the screen	Batch Files
EDLIN		*	Edits text files	File Maintenance
ERASE	*		Removes files from a disk	File Maintenance
EXE2BIN		*	Converts EXE files to COM files	Programming Tools
FDISK		*	Performs maintenance on the IBM PC/XT	Disk Maintenance
FIND		*	Searches for text in a file	Other Commands
FOR	*		Repeats a command for many choices	Batch Files
FORMAT		*	Prepares a disk for MS-DOS	Disk Maintenance
GOTO	*		Jumps to a different part of a batch file	Batch Files
GRAPHICS		*	Allows you to print graphics screens	Other Commands
IF	*		Executes commands based on a decision	Batch Files
LINK		*	Combines object files	Programming Tools
MKDIR	*		Adds sub-directories to a disk	Path Maintenance
MODE		*	Changes communication parameters	System Settings
MORE		*	Displays a file on the screen with pauses	File Output
PATH	*		Changes command search list	Path Maintenance

Table A-1. Alphabetical Listing of MS-DOS Commands (*continued*)

Command	Internal	External	Description	Functional group
PAUSE	*		Waits for a key to be pressed	Batch Files
PRINT		*	Prints a file on the printer	File Output
PROMPT	*		Changes the MS-DOS prompt	System Settings
RECOVER		*	Repairs files with bad sectors	Disk Maintenance
REM	*		Puts a note in a batch file	Batch Files
RENAME	*		Gives files new names	File Maintenance
RESTORE		*	Makes copies of backed-up files	Disk Maintenance
RMDIR	*		Removes sub-directories from a disk	Path Maintenance
SET	*		Changes environment strings	System Settings
SHIFT	*		Moves the command line arguments	Batch Files
SORT		*	Sorts a text file	Other Commands
SYS		*	Puts the system files and boot tracks on a diskette	Disk Maintenance
TIME	*		Sets the time	System Settings
TREE		*	Prints out list of sub-directories	Path Maintenance
TYPE	*		Displays a file on the screen	File Output
VER	*		Displays the MS-DOS version number	System Settings
VERIFY	*		Tells MS-DOS to double-check when it writes on disks	System Settings
VOL	*		Displays the label of a disk	System Settings

Table A-2.   Syntax and Arguments for MS-DOS Commands

Command	Syntax and Arguments
ASSIGN	ASSIGN [*d1*=*d2* . . .]
BACKUP	BACKUP *filespec d:*
BREAK	BREAK [{ON | OFF}]
CHDIR	CHDIR [[*d:*]*path*] CHDIR [*d:*]
CHKDSK	CHKDSK [*d:*] [/F] [/V] CHKDSK *filespec*
CLS	CLS
COMMAND	COMMAND /C *command*
COMP	COMP [*filespec1 filespec2*]

COPY	COPY [{/A | /B}] *filespec1* [{/A | /B}]
	   {*d:* | *filespec2*} [{/A | /B}] [/V]
	COPY [{/A | /B}] *filespec1a* [{/A | /B}]
	   [+ *filespec1b*] [{/A | /B}] . . . [/V]
	   {*d:* | *filespec2*} [{/A | /B}] [/V]
	COPY {*filespec1* | *device1*} {*filespec2* | *device2*}

CTTY	CTTY *device*
DATE	DATE [*mm-dd-yy*]
DEBUG	DEBUG [*filespec*] [*params*]
DIR	DIR [{*d:* | *filespec*}] [/P] [/W]
DISKCOMP	DISKCOMP [*d1:*] [*d2:*] [/1] [/8]
DISKCOPY	DISKCOPY [*d1:*] [*d2:*] [/1]
ECHO	ECHO [{ON | OFF | *message*}]
EDLIN	EDLIN *filespec* [/B]
ERASE	ERASE *filespec*
EXE2BIN	EXE2BIN *filespec* [*filespec*]
FDISK	FDISK
FIND	FIND [/V] [/C] [/N] "*string*" [*filespec* . . .]
FOR	FOR %%*varname* IN (*list*) DO *command* FOR %%*varname* IN (*filespec*) DO *command*
FORMAT	FORMAT [*d:*] [/S] [/1] [/8] [/V] [/B]
GOTO	GOTO *label*
GRAPHICS	GRAPHICS
IF	IF [NOT] *condition command*

Table A-2.   Syntax and Arguments for MS-DOS Commands (*continued*)

Command	Syntax and Arguments
LINK	LINK
	LINK @*filespec*
MKDIR	MKDIR [*d:*]*path*
MODE	MODE LPT*n*: [*linewidth*] [,[*linesize*] [,P]]
	MODE *screenwidth* [, {R | L} [,T]]
	MODE COM*n*: *baud* [*,parity* [*,databits* [*,stopbits* [,P]]]]
	MODE LPT*n*:= COM*n*
MORE	MORE <*filespec*
PATH	PATH [*d:*]*path*[;[*d:*]*path* . . .]
PAUSE	PAUSE
PRINT	PRINT [*filespec* [/T] [/C] [/P] . . .]
PROMPT	PROMPT [*prompt-string*]
RECOVER	RECOVER *filespec*
	RECOVER *d:*
REM	REM *comment*
RENAME	RENAME *filespec1 filename2* [*.ext2*]
RESTORE	RESTORE *filespec d:*
RMDIR	RMDIR [*d:*]*path*
SET	SET [*varname*=[*string*]]
SHIFT	SHIFT
SORT	SORT [/R] [/+*n*] <*filespec*
SYS	SYS *d:*
TIME	TIME [*hh:mm:ss.xx*]
TREE	TREE [*d:*] [/F]
TYPE	TYPE *filespec*
VER	VER
VERIFY	VERIFY [{ON | OFF}]
VOL	VOL [*d:*]

B

DIFFERENCES BETWEEN
MS-DOS VERSIONS

Each new version of MS-DOS includes more commands and features than previous versions; this is the major difference among successive releases. Each new version of MS-DOS is compatible with older versions. Thus, almost all programs that work with version 1 of MS-DOS work with version 2; however, the reverse is often not true. (The few times when programs written for version 1 do not work are usually due to mistakes made by the software manufacturer.)

Another difference between versions is the amount of memory each requires. Version 2 uses more RAM because it is larger than version 1. If you find that programs that work with version 1 run out of memory in version 2, you will probably have to buy more memory for your computer. This can be a problem with computers that do not allow you to add memory banks. Therefore, check the memory requirements of your programs for each version of MS-DOS.

Minor updates are often made within a version of MS-DOS. These updates are reflected in the part of the version number to the right of the decimal point. For example, version 1.1 is a newer release of version 1.0, and version 2.1 is a newer release of version 2.0. The updates are used to correct bugs or deficiencies in the operating system; no new commands or internal features are added to these updates.

NEW FEATURES IN VERSION 2

The following are the new features of MS-DOS version 2:

- Tree-structured directories (described in Chapter 4).
- Input and output redirection and the use of pipes (covered in Chapter 4).

- Volume labels on disks (see the FORMAT command in Chapter 3).
- The ability to use hard disks (version 1 was not able to use them).
- Other internal technical features, including installable device drivers (which allow hardware manufacturers to add peripherals to your computer), resident application programs (which stay in RAM), and a configuration file that gives MS-DOS additional information when you boot your computer.
- The ability on some computers (like the IBM PC) to increase the number of sectors per track on a diskette from 8 to 9. This means that version 2 diskettes written with 9 sectors per track cannot be read by computers running version 1.

NEW COMMANDS AND ENHANCEMENTS IN VERSION 2

Table B-1 lists the version 1 commands that were revised for version 2. This table does not include enhancements that simply reflect the features of the new command programs listed in Table B-2 (for instance, the TYPE command's ability to use path names in the file specification).

Table B-2 lists the commands added to version 2 of MS-DOS and gives a brief description of their functions. All of these commands are described in full in Chapter 3.

Table B-1.   Commands Revised in Version 2

Command	Added Features
CHKDSK	More methods for saving lost data. The /F option was added so the command does not automatically try to fix a damaged disk.
COMP	The ability to compare multiple files.
DIR	Displays the volume name, the sub-directories, and the amount of space left on the disk.
FORMAT	The ability to put a volume label on a disk with the /V option.

Table B-2. Commands Added to Version 2

Command	Description
ASSIGN	Changes the letters assigned to disks
BACKUP	Makes backup copies of the hard disk
BREAK	Causes MS-DOS to check for user interrupts more often
CHDIR	Changes default sub-directory
CLS	Clears the screen
CTTY	Changes the console to a serial port
ECHO	Prints a message on the screen
FOR	Repeats a command for many choices
GOTO	Jumps to a different part of a batch file
IF	Executes commands based on a decision
MKDIR	Adds sub-directories to a disk
PATH	Changes the command search list
PRINT	Prints a file on the printer
PROMPT	Changes the MS-DOS prompt
RECOVER	Repairs files with bad sectors
RESTORE	Makes copies of backed-up files
RMDIR	Removes sub-directories from a disk
SET	Changes environment strings
SHIFT	Moves the command line arguments
TREE	Prints out a list of sub-directories
VER	Displays the MS-DOS version number
VERIFY	Tells MS-DOS to double-check when it writes on disks
VOL	Displays the label of a disk

NEW FEATURES IN VERSION 3

The following are the new features of MS-DOS version 3:

- The ability to specify a path for finding MS-DOS external commands and application programs.

- User selection of keyboard layout and date/time configuration by country.
- New commands to set and display file attributes and disk labels.
- Use of ASCII characters greater than 128 in the SORT command.
- Internal technical features, including file-sharing support and selectable number of files and drives accessible.

NEW COMMANDS AND ENHANCEMENTS
IN VERSION 3

Table B-3 lists the version 1 and version 2 commands that were revised for version 3. Table B-4 lists the commands added to version 3 of MS-DOS and gives a brief description of their functions.

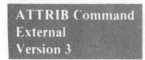

ATTRIB Command
External
Version 3

The ATTRIB command lets you check and set the read-only attribute of files.

Table B-3. Commands Revised in Version 3

Command	Added Features
BACKUP	Makes backup copies from either hard disk or floppy disk to either hard disk or floppy disk.
DATE	Accepts dates in mm-dd-yy, dd-mm-yy, or yy-mm-dd format.
FORMAT	Formats high-capacity drives on IBM PC ATs with the /4 argument.
GRAPHICS	Supports more models of IBM printers.
RESTORE	Restores backup copies from either hard disk or floppy disk to either hard disk or floppy disk.
SORT	Sorts foreign characters whose ASCII values are above 127 in the same sequence as normal letters.

Table B-4.   Commands Added to Version 3

Command	Description
ATTRIB	Changes the read-only attribute of a file or displays its value.
GRAFTABL	Lets the graphics display card on the IBM PC display the same characters as the text display card.
KEYBxx	Configures the IBM PC keyboard for various country settings.
LABEL	Changes the disk label.
SELECT	Creates an IBM PC system disk with a new keyboard configuration and date/time format.
SHARE	Installs file sharing on IBM PCs.

Common Uses

If you want to prevent a file from being changed or deleted, you can set its read-only attribute. This is useful if you think that you may accidentally erase or harmfully alter an important file. Setting the read-only attribute on a file is similar to covering the write-protect notch on a disk.

The common syntax for the command is

ATTRIB [+R|−R] *filespec*

Including a +R parameter before the *filespec* protects the file from being changed or deleted. The −R parameter changes a read-only file to allow it to be changed or deleted.

For instance, to set the file VNSTALK.TXT to read-only, give the command

```
A>ATTRIB +R VNSTALK.TXT
```

If you don't include either the +R or −R parameter, MS-DOS will tell you if a file is read-only or not by placing an "R" before the file name. For example, if MNGR.COM is read-only but MNGR.TXT is not, entering ATTRIB alone will produce

```
A>ATTRIB MNGR.*
R        A:\MNGR.COM
         A:\MNGR.TXT
```

Thus, if you don't see an "R" in the left column, you know that the file is not protected.

Warnings and Common Errors

If a software manufacturer has protected some files with the read-only attribute, you should probably not change the attribute for these files since the program may check the attribute and report an error if they are not set as the program expects.

The FORMAT command will format a disk even if some of the files on the disk are set to read-only.

Syntax

The syntax for the ATTRIB command is

ATTRIB [+R|−R] *filespec*

You can use the wild-card characters in the file specification. The +R argument tells MS-DOS to protect the file from being changed or deleted, while the −R argument tells MS-DOS to remove any protection from the file.

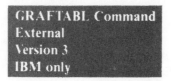

GRAFTABL Command
External
Version 3
IBM only

The GRAFTABL command loads a table of graphics characters for the color display adapter of the IBM PC.

Common Uses

You only use the GRAFTABL command if you want to display the graphics characters of the monochrome display adapter on the color monitor. Its syntax is

GRAFTABL

When you run this program, MS-DOS loads a copy of ASCII characters 128 through 255 into RAM. MS-DOS displays a message indicating that it has loaded the characters:

```
A>GRAFTABL
GRAPHICS CHARACTERS LOADED
```

These characters take up 1200 bytes of memory, and they stay in memory until you reboot your computer. Thus, you shouldn't run the program unless you really need to.

Syntax

The GRAFTABL command takes no arguments:

GRAFTABL

KEYBxx Commands
External
Version 3
IBM only

The KEYBxx commands allow you to specify the type of keyboard you are using.

Common Uses

These commands are only useful if you are using IBM keyboards other than the standard United States version. The commands take no arguments, and the syntaxes are shown in Table B-5.

To switch from a foreign keyboard to the U. S. keyboard, press ALT-CTRL-F1. To switch back to the previously selected foreign keyboard, press ALT-CTRL-F2.

Table B-5. KEYBxx Commands

Command	Country
KEYBFR	France
KEYBGR	Germany
KEYBIT	Italy
KEYBUK	United Kingdom
KEYFSP	Spain

Syntax

The syntaxes of the KEYBxx command are

KEYBGR
KEYBFR
KEYBIT
KEYFSP
KEYBUK

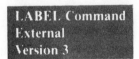

LABEL Command
External
Version 3

The LABEL command allows you to change the disk label (see the DIR command for more information about disk labels).

Common Uses

You can add a label to a disk as a memory aid, or to help differentiate disks that have similar contents. You can see the label on a disk with the DIR command.

The syntax of the LABEL command is

LABEL [*d:*] [*labelname*]

You cannot have a space between the disk letter and the *labelname*. If you do not include a disk letter, MS-DOS will apply the label to the default disk; if you do not give a *labelname*, MS-DOS will prompt you for one.

Labels must have 11 or fewer characters; the allowable characters are the same as those for file names. MS-DOS stores the characters in uppercase.

For example, to give the disk in drive B: the label "WORKFILES", give the command

```
A>LABEL B:WORKFILES
```

To have MS-DOS prompt you for the label, do not include it in the command:

```
A>LABEL B:

Volume label (11 characters, ENTER for none)?WORKFILES
```

Syntax

The syntax of the command is

LABEL [*d:*] [*labelname*]

The *d:* is the drive containing the disk you want to label; if you do not include it, MS-DOS will label the default disk. The *labelname* is the name of the label you want to assign.

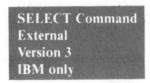

SELECT Command
External
Version 3
IBM only

The SELECT command makes a copy of the current disk and configures the new disk for a new keyboard and date/time format.

Common Uses

SELECT uses the DISKCOPY command (described in Chapter 3) to make an entire copy of a disk. It also creates a file called CONFIG.SYS that contains commands to set up the keyboard (similar to the KEYBxx commands) and the date/time format. Its structure is

SELECT *dtcode kcode*

The *dtcode* is the country code for the date/time format, and the *kcode* is the country code for the keyboard. The values for these codes are shown in Table B-6.

For example, to make a copy of the system disk that is configured for the United Kingdom, give the command

```
A>SELECT 044 UK
```

Warnings and Common Errors

Be sure that the DISKCOPY command is on your disk before you give the SELECT command, since the SELECT command uses the DISKCOPY command to make its copy of the disk.

Table B-6. Codes for the SELECT Command

Country	dtcode	kcode
France	033	FR
Germany	049	GR
Italy	039	IT
Spain	034	SP
United Kingdom	044	UK
United States	001	US

Syntax

The syntax of the command is

SELECT *dtcode kcode*

The *dtcode* is the country code for the date/time format, and the *kcode* is the country code for the keyboard.

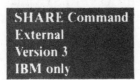

SHARE Command
External
Version 3
IBM only

The SHARE command loads file-sharing information into MS-DOS. It is only available in version 3.1 of PC-DOS. Networking hardware produced by different manufacturers often uses the SHARE command in different ways. Refer to your hardware manual for a description of using the SHARE program on your system.

C

COMPATIBILITY
WITH THE IBM PC

This appendix addresses many of the issues of compatibility with the IBM PC computer. Most manufacturers who make MS-DOS computers advertise them as "IBM compatible." This phrase is overused and often misleading. Since there are many definitions of IBM compatibility, manufacturers can stretch the meaning of the term.

Compatibility is important because most of the application programs designed for MS-DOS are really designed for the IBM PC only. Many non-IBM computers cannot run these programs correctly because they do not have all of the IBM features that the programs expect (such as IBM keys and character display). Some programs use more IBM features than others; some require that the disk drives and graphics display be identical to the IBM PC.

Unfortunately, there are no clearly defined standards for judging compatibility. IBM generally ignores all of the other computer companies and does not support a compatibility standard. Thus, any manufacturer can say that it is "compatible" without it being clear what that means. A computer that runs almost all of the programs that run on the IBM PC is often called a look-alike.

DETERMINING COMPATIBILITY

How can you assess whether a computer is compatible with the IBM PC? You can use the following list to determine your computer's compatibility. None of these features alone makes a computer compatible; in fact, some programs won't run on non-IBM machines even if they have all of the features listed here.

An IBM PC compatible computer must

- Be able to read and write 5 1/4-inch floppy diskettes like the PC.
- Run all versions of MS-DOS with all of IBM's changes.
- Have the internal RAM at the same addresses as in the PC.
- Use the same internal addresses as the input/output system on the PC.
- Allow you to add hardware boards in expansion slots that are identical to the PC's slots.
- Use the same type of monitors and graphics adapters as the PC.
- Have the same keys as the PC's keyboard.
- Use the same internal timing as the PC.
- Communicate with hardware devices like the PC.

Although very few computers meet all of these restrictions, many meet most of them.

It is impossible to quantify the importance of each of these various features. For example, one computer that has several of these features may only run half as many PC-DOS programs as another computer that has a different set of features.

Another method for measuring compatibility involves using standard terms to classify how much PC software a computer can run. Future Computing, a consulting company specializing in the microcomputer market, has developed a four-level scale for judging compatibility. This method for judging compatibility is based on the ability of the computer to run IBM PC software. The categories are *operationally compatible, functionally compatible, data compatible,* and *MS-DOS compatible.*

The two categories that most manufacturers strive for are operationally compatible and functionally compatible. Operationally compatible machines run all of the most popular software; functionally compatible machines run their own versions of the most popular software. The other two levels indicate that there are many popular programs that do not run on the computers because of incompatible disk formats or different hardware and software configurations.

Future Computing offers seminars and published reports on IBM compatibility and a wide variety of other subjects. You can reach them at 900 Canyon Creek Center, Richardson, TX, 75080.

D

COMPUTERS THAT
RUN MS-DOS

This appendix describes many of the computers that run MS-DOS. Most of them come with MS-DOS as a standard feature; on others, it is an option.

THREE IMPORTANT HARDWARE QUALITIES

If you have a computer, you don't really have to know much about the hardware in order to use it, regardless of what "computer experts" may tell you. However, there are three qualities you should know about that affect hardware performance: capacity, speed, and versatility.

- *Capacity.* Capacity refers to the amount of information the computer can save in both internal memory and on disk. There are two ways to measure capacity: the amount of RAM and the amount and type of disk storage.

- *Speed.* How fast does your computer run programs? The speed of your system depends on three main factors: the processing speed of the CPU, the data access time of the disks, and the amount of input/output support provided to the CPU.

  The processing speed of the CPU is measured in megahertz, or MHz. For people who perform numerical calculations with accounting or scientific application programs, the CPU speed is often very important. Each model of CPU can run at different speeds; for example, one brand of computer with an 8088 may have a faster CPU than another.

  The data access time, or the speed of the disks, is often important to people who use word processing and accounting programs, since these programs spend a great deal of time reading and writing information on the disk.

The amount of I/O support given to the CPU is a third factor that affects speed. Some computers use specialized support chips, discussed in Chapter 1, to perform such tasks as displaying graphics on the screen. These chips make the computers run faster by cutting down the number of steps the main CPU performs.

The usefulness of speed in any of these areas may or may not be important, depending on the type of work you do. If speed is important to you, however, you must consider several factors in evaluating it. These technical specifications are often available from your computer dealer.

You may see advertisements in which computer manufacturers claim that their computers run much faster than their competitors'. These claims should be carefully scrutinized because it is easy to manipulate numbers that relate to speed (as in mentioning that the CPU is 10% faster and not mentioning that the disks are 50% slower). In addition, your application programs may or may not be able to use the increased efficiency of your computer. A speedy computer, therefore, is not always the answer.

. *Versatility.* A third quality that affects hardware performance is versatility. How easy is it for you to add new hardware to your computer? The longer you own your computer, the more likely it is that you will want it to perform different tasks. Many manufacturers allow you to increase the versatility of your computer by adding new hardware (often called *upgrading*). For example, you might want to add a hard disk, more RAM, or a different screen. If you can't add any hardware to your computer, then you are limited to the hardware that came with the computer.

There are, of course, many other ways to measure the quality of the hardware in your computer, but capacity, speed, and versatility are three of the most important considerations. The next section describes how these concepts relate to MS-DOS.

GUIDELINES FOR PURCHASING A COMPUTER

Most MS-DOS computers look much alike: a box approximately 25×15×5 inches with a monitor and keyboard (see Figure D-1). In fact, many manufacturers have taken great pains to create products that look as much like an

Figure D-1.   A standard MS-DOS computer (the Eagle PC)

IBM PC as they can. Others, trying to separate themselves from the majority of MS-DOS computers, have designed their computers to be portable. These machines are usually about the size and shape of a sewing machine, resembling the computer shown in Figure D-2. Other portables, such as the one shown in Figure D-3, are much smaller, sometimes small enough to fit into a briefcase.

The three most important things to consider before buying a computer are the support offered by the dealer, the total cost, and the longevity of the computer.

Figure D-2. A portable MS-DOS computer (the Texas Instruments TI Professional)

Figure D-3. A small MS-DOS computer (The Gavilan Mobile)

The support offered by the dealer should be one of your first considerations, not only because your computer may need repair, but also because you may need some guidance on what additional hardware or software to buy for your system.

The amount of help you get in setting up your computer is very important, especially if you have never owned a computer before. Regardless of what dealers may tell you about how easy they are to assemble, there are many small things that will frustrate you in getting your computer set up properly. Surprisingly, even software often needs to be "set up" (or, in computer jargon, *installed*) for your system. You should be sure that your dealer will help you with that too.

The package cost of your whole computer system is a second consideration. You should compare total costs with other dealers' offers before you purchase. The package cost is the total cost of the main hardware, extra added hardware, and all of the software that you need to meet your needs. The following are some important questions to ask:

- Does my package include the monitor, keyboard, or printer in the total cost, or am I required to buy these as accessories?

- Does my computer come with *bundled software* programs (that is, what software is included in the system price), or does it only come with MS-DOS? (Or is MS-DOS even a part of the package?)

- Which software does or does not work with the system? Will it run PC-DOS programs?

- Is there an additional cost for a service agreement? What does the warranty cover?

It is hard to gauge the longevity of a computer (and of its manufacturer), but this factor is also important in determining how happy you will be with your computer. Since a few large microcomputer companies have gone bankrupt in the last few years, computer dealers are especially aware of the fluctuations in the industry. Feel free to ask your computer dealer about the reputation of your computer's manufacturer. If you have a friend who works with microcomputers, you may want to ask his or her opinion about the manufacturer and model you are buying.

The only way to resolve these questions is by visiting a few computer stores to see what they offer. You can also read a few popular computer magazines (such as those discussed in Chapter 7) to get a feeling for the direction the market is heading in, as well as to evaluate some of the capabilities of the computers on the market.

The following section presents computer descriptions that were supplied by the manufacturers. Of course, the details may change as the configurations of their computers change. If you are considering buying a computer, you should ask your dealer for the current specifications. The information presented here is meant only as a general overview of the computers, not as a head-to-head comparison.

MS-DOS COMPUTERS

Table D-1 lists some of the major computers that run MS-DOS; there are literally hundreds of others not included here. The description of each computer includes the following:

- Computer name and model(s).
- CPU.
- Amount of RAM.

Table D-1. Comparison of MS-DOS Computers

Name and Model	CPU	RAM	Disk Drives	Monitor
IBM Personal Computer (PC) and Extended Version (PC/XT)	8088	64K (PC) or 128K (PC/XT)	1 (PC); 1 + 10M hard disk (PC/XT)	None standard
ACT Apricot	8086	256K	Two 3.5-inch (315K each)	M 800×400
Bytec Hyperion	8088	256K	1	M 640×250

- Disk drives. (These are 320K/360K and 5 1/4-inch unless noted otherwise.)
- Monitor. (In the table, M indicates monochrome and C indicates color. Resolution of graphics is listed if available.)
- Serial or parallel ports (denoted by S or P in the table).
- Software included with the computer.
- Special features of the computer.
- Suggested price as of January 1, 1984.

It is important to check with a computer dealer about the features of a computer before you buy. Appendix E lists names and addresses of the hardware manufacturers if you want to write for more information.

Ports	Software Included	Other Features	Price
None standard (PC); 1S (PC/XT)	BASIC	4 slots	$3195
1S, 1P	Concurrent CP/M-86 operating system, interpretive BASIC, SuperCalc, SuperPlanner, communications, graphics, character editor	Portable, conforms to European ergonomics standards	$3190
1S, 1P	BASIC, DBMS, calculator	Portable, clock	$3195

Table D-1. Comparison of MS-DOS Computers *(continued)*

Name and Model	CPU	RAM	Disk Drives	Monitor
Columbia MPC Series (VP, 1600-1, 1600-4)	8088	128K	2 (VP, 1600-1); 1 + 10M hard disk (1600-4)	M 640×200
COMPAQ and COMPAQ Plus	8088	128K	2 (COMPAQ); 1 + 10M hard disk (COMPAQ Plus)	M 640×200
Corona PC	8088	128K	1	M 640×325
DEC Rainbow 100	8088	64K	2	M
Eagle Plus, Eagle Plus XL, Eagle Spirit	8088	128K	2 (Plus and Spirit); 1 + 10M hard disk (Plus XL)	M 640×200
Fujitsu Micro 16	8086	128K	2	C 640×200
Gavilan Mobile	8088	64K	One 3.5-inch (360K)	M 480×128

Ports	Software Included	Other Features	Price
1S, 1P (VP); 2S, 1P (1600-1. 1600-4	BASIC, Perfect Writer, Perfect Speller, Perfect Calc, Perfect Filer, Fast Graphs, Home Accountant Plus, Space Commanders, communications, CP/M-86, Macro Assembler, diagnostics, RAM disk, tutorial	Portable (VP), 8 slots	$2995 (VP); $3620 (1600-1); $5220 (1600-4)
1P	BASIC	Portable, 2 slots	$2995 (COMPAQ); $4995 (COMPAQ Plus)
1S, 1P	BASIC, Multimate word processing, PC-Tutor tutorial	4 slots	$2595
2S	BASIC	Also has Z80 CPU with CP/M-80 and CP/M-86	$3495
2S, 1P	BASIC, CP/M-86	Slots, portable (Spirit)	$2795 (Plus); $4295 (Plus XL); $3295 (Spirit)
1S, 1P	WordStar, SuperCalc, CP/M-86	6 slots, can use other CPUs	$3995
1S	BASIC	Fits in a briefcase, has touch panel (similar in use to a mouse), built-in 300 baud modem, internal battery pack, proprietary operating system and software included	$3995

Table D-1. Comparison of MS-DOS Computers *(continued)*

Name and Model	CPU	RAM	Disk Drives	Monitor
Hewlett-Packard 150	8088	256K	Two 3.5-inch (270K each)	M 512×390
ITT XTRA	8088	128K	1	M 640×200
Leading Edge PC	8088	128K	2	M 640×200
Panasonic Senior Partner	8088	128K	1	M 640×200
Polo	80188	128K	2	C 640×200
Sanyo MBC 550	8088	128K	1 160K	M
Seattle Computer Gazelle II	8086	256K	Two 1.3M 8-inch	Not included (uses terminal)
Seequa Chameleon Plus	8088	256K	2	M 640×200
Tandy TRS-80 Model 2000	80186	128K	2	None included
TeleVideo TS 1605	8088	128K	2	M 640×200
Texas Instruments Professional	8088	64K	1	M 640×200

Ports	Software Included	Other Features	Price
2S, 1 GPIB	BASIC, Personal Applications Manager, tutor	Touch sensitive screen	$3995
1S, 1P	BASIC	Mouse	$3500
1S, 1P	BASIC, Multiplan, word processor	Clock	$2895
1S, 1P	WordStar, Visicalc, PFS File/Report/ Graph	Portable, includes thermal printer	$2495
2S	BASIC, Multiplan, PFS Write/Graph/ File/Report	Includes modem, printer, Z80 CPU with CP/M	$3995
1P	EasyWriter, Wordstar, CalcStar	Game port	$1398
2S, 1P	Editor	S-100 bus	$6995
1S, 1P	BASIC, Perfect Writer, Perfect Calc, Perfect Speller, Condor I, C-Term	Portable, also has Z80 CPU and CP/M	$2895
1S, 1P	BASIC	4 slots	$2750
1S, 1P		1 slot	$2995
1P		4 slots	$2195

E

HARDWARE AND SOFTWARE MANUFACTURERS

Many manufacturers produce MS-DOS computers. Table E-1 provides names and addresses for the manufacturers of the computers listed in Appendix D.

Chapters 5 and 6 describe several software products for MS-DOS computers. Table E-2 provides addresses for the manufacturers that produce those software products.

Table E-1. Names and Addresses of Software Manufacturers

ABW Corporation
P.O. Box M 1047
Ann Arbor, MI 48106

AmeriSoft
345 S. McDowell Blvd., Suite 410
Petaluma, CA 94952

Anderson-Bell
P.O. Box 191
Canon City, CO 81212

Ann Arbor Software
407 N. Main Street
Ann Arbor, MI 48104

Application Executive Corporation
600 Broadway, Suite 4C
New York, NY 10012

Ashton-Tate
10150 W. Jefferson Blvd.
Culver City, CA 90230

ATI Training Company
3770 Highland Avenue, Suite 201
Manhattan Beach, CA 90266

Autodesk, Inc.
150 Shoreline Highway, #B20
Mill Valley, CA 94941

Aware Company
P.O. Box 695
Gualala, CA 95445

Bellesoft, Inc.
2127 Bellevue Way SE
Bellevue, WA 98004

BG Graphics
824 Stetson Avenue
Kent, WA 98031

Blue Chip Software
19824 Ventura Blvd., Suite 125
Woodland Hills, CA 91364

Table E-1. Names and Addresses of Software Manufacturers *(continued)*

Bluebush, Inc.
P.O. Box 3585
Santa Clara, CA 95055

Bourbaki Inc.
P.O. Box 2867
Boise, ID 83701

Broderbund Software
1938 Fourth Street
San Rafael, CA 94901

Bruce and James
4500 Tuller Road
Dublin, OH 43017

Jim Button
P.O. Box 5786
Bellevue, WA 98006

C Ware Corporation
1607 New Brunswick
Sunnyvale, CA 94087

Carousel Microtools, Inc.
609 Kearney Street
El Cerrito, CA 94530

Cdex Corporation
5050 El Camino Real
Los Altos, CA 94022

Central Point Software, Inc.
P.O. Box 19730
Portland, OR 97219

Chang Laboratories, Inc.
5300 Stevens Creek Blvd., #200
San Jose, CA 95129

Comprehensive Software Support
2316 Artesia Blvd., Suite B
Redondo Beach, CA 90278

Computech Group Inc.
Main Line Industrial Park, Lee Blvd.
Frazer, PA 19355

Computer Advanced Ideas
1442A Walnut Street, Suite 341
Berkeley, CA 94709

Computer Aided Design
764 24th Avenue
San Francisco, CA 94121

Computer Innovations
10 Mechanic Street, Suite J
Redbank, NJ 07701

Computer Shack, Inc.
P.O. Box 190
Etobicoke, Ontario, CANADA
  M9C 4V3

Computing!
2519 Greenwich Street
San Francisco, CA 94123

CompuView Products, Inc.
1955 Pauline Blvd., Suite 200
Ann Arbor, MI 48103

Context Management Systems
23868 Hawthorne Blvd.
Torrance, CA 90505

Courseware, Inc.
10075 Carroll Canyon Road
San Diego, CA 92131

c-systems
P.O. Box 3253
Fullerton, CA 92634

Datasoft, Inc.
536 Valley Way
Milpitas, CA 95035

Dayflo Software
2500 Michelson Drive, Building 400
Irvine, CA 92715

Designer Software
3400 Montrose Blvd., Suite 718
Houston, TX 77006

Digital Marketing
2670 Cherry Lane
Walnut Creek, CA 94596

Digital Research
160 Central Avenue
Pacific Grove, CA 93950

Digital Signature
5453 S. Woodlawn
Chicago, IL 60615

Table E-1. Names and Addresses of Software Manufacturers *(continued)*

Duncan-Atwell Computerized
Technologies
924 Worth Avenue #B-2
Linden, NJ 07036

Earth Data Corporation
P.O. Box 13168
Richmond, VA 23225

Ecosoft Inc.
P.O. Box 68602
Indianapolis, IN 46268

Electronic Arts
2755 Campus Drive
San Mateo, CA 94403

Emerging Technology
2031 Broadway
Boulder, CO 80302

Enertronics Research, Inc.
150 N. Meramec, Suite 207
St. Louis, MO 63105

Ensign Software
7337 Northview
Boise, ID 83704

Fox & Geller, Inc.
604 Market Street
Elmwood Park, NJ 07407

FriendlySoft, Inc.
3609 Smith-Barry Road
Arlington, TX 76103

Graphic Software Systems
25117 SW Parkway
Wilsonville, OR 97070

Harvard Associates, Inc.
260 Beacon Street
Somerville, MA 02143

Headlands Press, Inc.
P.O. Box 862
Tiburon, CA 94920

Heritage Group
611 Anton Blvd., Suite 720
Costa Mesa, CA 92626

Heritage Software, Inc.
2130 S. Vermont Avenue
Los Angeles, CA 90007

IBM
P.O. Box 1328
Boca Raton, FL 33432

IMSI
633 Fifth Avenue
San Rafael, CA 94901

Infocom, Inc.
55 Wheeler Street
Cambridge, MA 02138

Information Unlimited Software, Inc.
2401 Marinship Way
Sausalito, CA 94965

Innovative Software
9300 W. 110th Street, Suite 380
Overland Park, KS 66210

International Software Alliance
1835 Mission Ridge Road
Santa Barbara, CA 93103

ITSoftware
P.O. Box 2392
Princeton, NJ 08540

Knoware
301 Vassar Street
Cambridge, MA 02139

Laboratory Microsystems, Inc.
4147 Beethoven Street
Los Angeles, CA 90066

Lifeboat Associates
1651 Third Avenue
New York, NY 10028

Lifetree Software, Inc.
411 Pacific Street, Suite 315
Monterey, CA 93940

Lightning Software
P.O. Box 11725
Palo Alto, CA 94306

Table E-1. Names and Addresses of Software Manufacturers *(continued)*

Living Videotext, Inc.
1000 Elwell Court, Suite 232
Palo Alto, CA 94303

Logical Systems
1355 Sunrise Court
Los Altos, CA 94022.

Logitech
165 University Avenue
Palo Alto, CA 94301

Lotus Corp.
55 Wheeler Street
Cambridge, MA 02138

LXI, Inc.
P.O. Box 3032
West Lafayette, IN 47906

Mansfield Software Group
Box 532
Storrs, CT 06268

Manx Software Systems
P.O. Box 55
Shrewsbury, NJ 07701

Mark of the Unicorn
222 Third Street
Cambridge, MA 02142

Mark Williams Company
1430 West Wrightwood
Chicago, IL 60614

Martin Marietta
P.O. Box 2392
Princeton, NJ 08540

Mathtech, Inc.
P.O. Box 2392
Princeton, NJ 08540

Mattel Electronics
5180 Rosecrans Avenue
Hawthorne, CA 90250

mbp Software
7700 Edgewater Drive, Suite 360
Oakland, CA 94621

Metasoft Corporation
6509 West Frye Road
Chandler, AZ 85224

Micro Data Base Systems, Inc.
P.O. Box 248
Lafayette, IN 47902

MicroBusiness Software, Inc.
Dover Road
Chichester, NH 03263

Microcomputer Taxsystems, Inc.
6203 Variel Avenue, Suite E
Woodland Hills, CA 91367

Micrografx
8526 Vista View
Dallas, TX 75243

MicroPro
33 San Pablo Avenue
San Rafael, CA 94903

MicroRIM
P.O. Box 585
Bellevue, WA 98004

Microsoft, Inc.
10700 Northup Way
Bellevue, WA 98004

Microstuf
1845 The Exchange, Suite 140
Atlanta, GA 30339

Microtaure Inc.
P.O. Box 6039, Station "J"
Ottowa, Ontario CANADA K2A1T1

MicroType
6531 Crown Blvd., #3A
San Jose, CA 95120

MicroWare
P.O. Box 79
Kingston, MA 02364

MLI Microsystems
P.O. Box 825
Framingham, MA 01701

Mountain View Press, Inc.
P.O. Box 4656
Mountain View, CA 94040

MPR/Mathematica
P.O. Box 2393
Princeton, NJ 08540

Table E-1. Names and Addresses of Software Manufacturers *(continued)*

Norell Data Systems
3400 Wilshire Blvd.
P.O. Box 70127
Los Angeles, CA 90010

Omega MicroWare, Inc.
222 S. Riverside Plaza
Chicago, IL 60606

Omnisoft Corporation
9960 Owensmouth Avenue, Suite 32
Chatsworth, CA 91311

Orion Software
P.O. Box 2488
Auburn, AL 36831

Pacific Basin Graphics
1577 Ninth Avenue
San Francisco, CA 94122

PC TechniCorp
40 Grove Street
Wellesley, MA 02181

PCsoftware
9120 Gramercy Drive, Suite 416
San Diego, CA 92123

Peachtree Software
3445 Peachtree Road N.E.
Atlanta, GA 30326

Penguin Software
830 Fourth Avenue, Box 311
Geneva, IL 60134

Perfect Software
702 Harrison Street
Berkeley, CA 94710

Personal CAD Systems, Inc.
15425 Los Gatos Blvd.
Los Gatos, CA 95030

Peter Norton
2210 Wilshire Blvd., #186A
Santa Monica, CA 90403

PFS
422 Aldo
Santa Clara, CA 95050

Phoenix Software Associates, Ltd.
1 Knollwood Street
North Easton, MA 02356

Prentice-Hall, Inc.
200 Old Tappan Road
Old Tappan, NJ 07675

Professional Software, Inc.
51 Fremont Street
Needham, MA 02194

Programmers Shop
908-I Providence Highway
Dedham, MA 02026

Proper Software
2000 Center Street, Suite 1024
Berkeley, CA 94704

Pyramid Data, Ltd.
P.O. Box 10116
Santa Ana, CA 92711

Quarterdeck Software
1918 Main Street, Suite 240
Santa Monica, CA 90405

Quest Research, Inc.
P.O. Box 2553
Huntsville, AL 35804

Quicksoft
219 First N. #224
Seattle, WA 98109

ReadiWare Systems Inc.
Box 107A
Ridgefield, CT 06877

Redding Group
609 Main Street
Ridgefield, CT 06877

Robert J. Brady Co.
Games Division
Bowie, MD 20715

Rocky Mountain Software Systems
1280-C Newell Avenue, Suite 147-J
Walnut Creek, CA 94596

Table E-1. Names and Addresses of Software Manufacturers *(continued)*

RoseSoft, Inc.
4710 University Way, N.E., Suite 601
Seattle, WA 98105

RR Software
P.O. Box 1512
Madison, WI 53701

Ryan-McFarland
609 Deep Valley Drive
Rolling Hills Estates, CA 90274

Satellite Software International
288 West Center
Orem, UT 84057

Schuchardt Software Systems
515 Northgate Drive
San Rafael, CA 94903

Scitor Corporation
710 Lakeway, Suite 290
Sunnyvale, CA 94086

Sierra On-Line, Inc.
36757 Mudge Rance Road
Coarsegold, CA 93614

Soft Lab
P.O. Box 2186
2545 Perry Avenue North
Bremerton, WA 98310

Soft Warehouse
P.O. Box 11174
Honolulu, HI 96828

SoftCorp, Inc.
2340 State Road 580, Suite B244
Clearwater, FL 33575

SoftCraft
P.O. Box 9802
Austin, TX 78766

SofTool Systems
8972 E. Hampden Avenue, #179
Denver, CO 80231

Software 128
363 Walden Street
Concord, MA 01742

Software Arts
27 Mica Lane
Wellesley, MA 02181

Software Link, Inc.
6700 23-B Roswell Road
Atlanta, GA 30328

Software Products International
10240 Sorrento Valley Road
San Diego, CA 92121

Software Technology for Computers
153 California Street
Newton, MA 02158

Softword Systems, Inc.
52 Oakland Avenue N.
East Hartford, CT 06108

Sorcim
2310 Lundy Avenue
San Jose, CA 95131

Spinnaker Software Corp.
215 First Street
Cambridge, MA 02142

Stoneware, Inc.
50 Belvedere Street
San Rafael, CA 94901

Structured Systems Group
5204 Claremont Avenue
Oakland, CA 94618

STSC, Inc.
2115 East Jefferson Street
Rockville, MD 20852

subLogic Corporation
713 Edgebrook Drive
Champaign, IL 61820

SuperSoft
P.O. Box 1628
Champaign, IL 61820

Suttle Enterprises
29844 W. Chicago
Livonia, MI 48150

Table E-1. Names and Addresses of Software Manufacturers *(continued)*

Symmetric Software
1805 Clemson Street
San Bernardino, CA 92407

Telecon Systems
1155 Meridian Avenue, Suite 218
San Jose, CA 95125

Time Arts, Inc.
4425 Cavedale Road
Glen Ellen, CA 95442

Trigram Systems
3 Bayard Road, #66
Pittsburgh, PA 15213

Trillian Computer
P.O. Box 481
Los Gatos, CA 95031

Ultragraphics Systems
1100 South Main
Racine, WI 53403

Vandata
17544 Midvale Avenue N., Suite 107
Seattle, WA 98133

VisiCorp
2895 Zanker Road
San Jose, CA 95134

Visual Age
642 N. Larchmont Blvd.
Los Angeles, CA 90004

Wadsworth Electronic Publishing
   Company
Statler Office Building, 20 Park Plaza
Boston, MA 02116

Washington Computer Services
3028 Silvern Lane
Bellingham, WA 98226

Waterloo Microsystems Inc.
175 Columbia Street West
Waterloo, Ontario, CANADA N2L 3B6

WATSOFT Products, Inc.
158 University Avenue
Waterloo, Ontario, CANADA N2L 3E9

Windmill Software, Inc.
2209 Leominster Drive
Burlington, Ontario, CANADA
   L7P 3W8

Word Associates
55 Sutter Street, #361
San Francisco, CA 94104

XOR Corporation
5421 Opportunity Court
Minnetonka, MN 55343

XyQuest Inc.
P.O. Box 372
Bedford, MA 01730

Table E-2. Names and Addresses of Hardware Manufacturers

ACT North America, Inc.
3375 Scott Blvd., Suite 336
Santa Clara, CA 95051

Bytec Corporation
8 Colonnade Road
Ottawa, Ontario, CANADA K2E 7M6

Columbia Data Products, Inc.
9150 Rumsey Road
Columbia, MD 21045

Compaq Computer Corporation
12330 Perry Road
Houston, TX 77070

Corona Data Systems
31324 Via Colinas, Suite 110
Westlake Village, CA 91362

Digital Equipment Corporation
2 Mt. Royal Avenue
Marlboro, MA 01752

Eagle Computer, Inc.
983 University Avenue
Los Gatos, CA 95030

Fujitsu Professional Microsystems
3320 Scott Blvd.
Santa Clara, CA 95051

Gavilan Computer Corporation
240 Hacienda Avenue
Campbell, CA 95008

Hewlett-Packard
974 E. Arques Avenue
Sunnyvale, CA 94086

International Business Machines
Armonk, NY 10504

ITT
1515 West 14th Street
Tempe, AZ 85281

Leading Edge
225 Turnpike Street
Canton, MA 02021

Panasonic
1 Panasonic Way
Secaucus, NJ 07094

Polo Microsystems, Inc.
2570 El Camino Real
Mountain View, CA 94040

Sanyo
51 Joseph Street
Moonachie, NJ 07074

Seattle Computer Products
1114 Industry Drive
Seattle, WA 98188

Seequa Computer Corporation
8305 Telegraph Road
Odenton, MD 21113

Tandy Corporation/Radio Shack
1800 One Tandy Center
Fort Worth, TX 76102

TeleVideo
1170 Morse Avenue
Sunnyvale, CA 94086

Texas Instruments
P.O. Box 402430
Dallas, TX 75240

F

GLOSSARY

Absolute path name.   A path name that shows how a sub-directory is linked to the root directory.

Adapter card.   An expansion board that allows you to add monochrome or color monitors to your computer (generally, this is only used on the IBM PC and look-alikes).

Address.   A number that represents an exact location in RAM.

Application program.   A program that performs a task. Word processing or data base management are examples of application programs.

Archiving.   Making copies of files or disks. See also *backup.*

Argument.   A modifier that gives more information to a command. For example, the TYPE command takes as an argument the name of the file that is to be displayed.

Argument substitution.   The method that allows you to substitute arguments into commands when you run a batch file.

Artificial intelligence (AI).   The field of computer science involved in developing more human-like features for computers, such as deductive reasoning, vision, and learning.

ASCII.   The standard sequence used to match numbers with characters. Since computers only think in terms of numbers, each character has to have a number associated with it (for instance, A is 65 and B is 66). ASCII is an acronym for the group who developed the standard, the American Standard Code for Information Interchange.

Assembly language.   A programming language used to control the CPU directly.

Asterisk.   A symbol (*) used in a file specifier as a wild-card character. The asterisk can substitute for any number of characters at the position in which it appears. The question mark is another wild-card character.

Auto-dialing. The capability of a modem to call other computers without the user dialing the phone.

AUTOEXEC.BAT. The batch file that is automatically executed when you boot your computer.

Backup. A copy of a file or disk that can be used in case the original is damaged. Backing up your data and programs is necessary to prevent loss from accidental damage.

Bad sector. A sector on a disk that MS-DOS cannot read. This is usually caused by a physical error on the disk, such as a fingerprint.

Bank. A 64K set of RAM chips. Additional memory is usually added to a computer in banks.

Batch commands. MS-DOS commands that are only used in a batch file. These commands are ECHO, FOR, GOTO, IF, PAUSE, REM, and SHIFT.

Batch file. A text file that contains MS-DOS commands. MS-DOS executes the commands in a batch file as it would a program. Batch files always have the extension BAT.

Baud. A measure of how fast data is transferred between a computer and a device. One baud is equivalent to 1 bit per second; 300 baud is approximately 30 characters per second.

Binary file. A file that contains special nontext characters. These files are usually programs and data bases.

Bit. The smallest unit of memory; it consists of one on/off switch. A bit is one eighth of a byte.

Boot. To load the operating system into RAM (also called booting up). You boot the operating system each time you start your computer or press the RESET button.

Boot tracks. The area of a disk that keeps the information on how the computer should load the operating system.

Break key. A key that stops a program after it is running (on the IBM PC, this is the CONTROL-SCROLL LOCK key).

Bundled software. Software that is included in the purchase price of a computer. This is often business software like word processing and communications.

Byte. The standard measure of memory for both RAM and mass storage. A byte is a group of 8 bits that represent a number or character. A byte can have one of 256 values and can hold one alphanumeric character.

Cell. A specific location in the grid of a spreadsheet program. A cell holds information for the program to process.

Central processing unit (CPU). The primary "brains" in a computer. The

CPU is the chip that processes the computer's data and performs the instructions in a program.

Child sub-directory. A sub-directory that is under another sub-directory in the directory tree. See also *parent sub-directory.*

Circuit board. A board with wires and chips on it.

Command. An instruction given to MS-DOS. See also *internal command* and *external command.*

Command interpreter. The part of MS-DOS that reads commands, finds where the command programs are, and starts the command programs.

Communications protocol. The means by which two hardware devices communicate with each other.

Compiler. A program that turns text written in a programming language into machine instructions. The resulting program can be run like an application program. See also *interpreter.*

Concatenate. To connect files end to end.

Concurrent processing. The ability to run two programs at the same time.

Console. The combination of the keyboard and the screen. You use the console to give commands to MS-DOS and to see the results.

Contiguous file. A file whose data blocks are all next to each other on disk.

Copy protection. A procedure that some software manufacturers use to prevent users from copying the program diskette. It prevents normal MS-DOS commands from copying a diskette.

Crash. To stop completely. If your computer crashes, you must reboot it.

Cursor. The box or underline on your screen that the computer uses to show where the next character you enter will appear.

Data base. A structured collection of related information stored on disk.

Data base management system (DBMS). A program that lets you put information into and get information out of a data base.

Data bits. A protocol that tells how many bits of information in the communications stream are data.

Debug. To correct a program's errors.

Decrypt. To convert a coded file to one that is readable. See *encrypt.*

Default. Something that is assumed unless you specify otherwise.

Default disk. The disk that MS-DOS looks on for programs and data unless you tell it to look elsewhere.

Default sub-directory. The sub-directory that MS-DOS looks on for programs and data unless you tell it to look elsewhere.

Device. A piece of hardware used for input or output.

Directory.   An area on each disk that contains a list of all the files on that disk.

Disk.   A storage medium made of metal or plastic covered with magnetic material. The disk spins at high speed in a disk drive, and the information is read by a magnetic head (similar to the head in a tape recorder). See also *floppy disk* and *hard disk.*

Disk drive.   A device that allows you to read from and write to a disk. The drive consists of a motor that spins the disk and a movable magnetic head that reads and writes information.

Disk label.   See *volume label.*

Diskette.   A low-cost disk made of flexible material (also called a floppy disk). Diskettes are usually 5 1/4 inches, although some computers use 8-inch diskettes; they can be removed from the disk drive and stored separately.

Distribution diskette.   A diskette that you receive when you buy software. The distribution diskette holds the application program.

Dot-matrix printer.   A printer that forms characters on paper by pressing a series of pins against an inked ribbon.

Double-dot.   A symbol (..) used in a path to represent the parent of the default sub-directory.

Echo.   To repeat information on the screen. For instance, the ECHO command displays its arguments on the screen.

Edit.   To change a text file with a program.

Encrypt.   To convert a readable file into an unreadable form with a code. Encrypting a file prevents unauthorized people from understanding the contents of a file.

End-of-file marker.   A character that specifies the end of a text file.

Environment.   An area of RAM that MS-DOS uses to store variables. It is altered and viewed with the SET command. For example, the prompt string is kept as an environment variable.

Error level.   A number set by a program that indicates if a program was completed successfully or what prevented the successful completion of the program. The IF command allows you to look at the error level.

Error message.   A message printed on your screen that indicates that a program is not able to be completed normally.

Expansion slot.   A plug into which you can add circuit boards. Some computers have expansion slots that permit you to add RAM and special hardware (such as additional graphics capabilities).

Extension.   The second part of a file specifier that appears to the right of the dot. The extension usually describes the type of the file and can be three characters long. It is also called the file type.

External command.   A command that is stored on disk rather than in RAM. Each time you enter an external command, MS-DOS must read it from the disk in order to execute it. In MS-DOS, external commands have the extension COM or EXE. See also *internal command.*

Field.   A subsection of a record in a data base that contains one type of information. See also *record.*

File.   A collection of information that is stored on disk and accessed using a unique file specifier.

Filespec.   See *file specifier.*

File allocation table.   The area on each disk that MS-DOS uses to determine which data on disk belongs in which file.

File name.   The part of a file specifier to the left of the dot. A file name may be up to eight characters long.

File specifier.   The complete identification of a file. The full specifier includes the file name and the extension. It may also include the disk name and the path name.

File type.   See *extension.*

Filter.   A program that takes the output of another program as its input.

Fixed hard disk.   A hard disk with nonremovable storage media.

Floppy disk.   See *diskette.*

Font.   A print style. Some common fonts are Roman, italic, and bold.

Formatting.   The process of placing magnetic markers on a disk so that it can be read from and written to by a disk drive. The FORMAT command is used to do this before you use a new disk.

Formatting commands.   In word processing, commands that you use to change the appearance of your text on the printed page.

Fragmented.   Split into pieces. A fragmented file is one whose parts are on many places on a disk. MS-DOS accesses a disk with many fragmented files more slowly than it accesses contiguous (nonfragmented) files.

Generic argument.   An argument in a command syntax that can take many values. A generic argument is used for illustrative purposes only.

Hard disk.   A rigid, magnetically coated disk. Hard disks hold more information than floppy disks, and the data on them is accessed more rapidly. They are more expensive than most other forms of mass storage.

Hardware.   The physical part of a computer system, such as the CPU, disk drives, or monitor.

Hidden file.   A file that is not seen in the disk directory listing. Hidden files have a special flag in their directory entry that prevents MS-DOS commands from acting on them.

IBM PC work-alike.   A computer that runs most of the software that runs on the IBM PC.

Input.   Information that is used by a program. As a verb, input means to give information to a program when requested.

Integrated software.   A software package that combines many programs (such as spreadsheets, graphics, and data base management) into one package, which can use information generated by each of its component programs.

Interactive.   Able to ask questions and respond to answers. An interactive program asks you for information as it runs.

Internal command.   A command that is kept in RAM once MS-DOS is booted. Unlike external commands, MS-DOS does not need to read internal commands from disk each time they are invoked.

Interpreter.   A program that reads and executes a computer program step by step. Interpreted programs cannot be run from MS-DOS: they must be run from within the interpreter.

I/O.   Input and output.

K (kilobyte).   1024 bytes. Memory and disk capacity are usually measured in K bytes (thus, 64K is 65536 bytes).

Keyed field.   A field that a data base management system keeps special information about. Finding values in keyed fields is much faster than finding values in normal fields.

Language.   A program that is used to write other computer programs.

Line editor.   A text-editing program that only displays one line of a file as you edit it. In contrast, see *screen-oriented editor.*

Loading.   Moving a program from mass storage into RAM.

Mass storage.   Devices that keep information after your computer is shut off. The most common mass storage media are disks or tape.

Master.   The original disk on which software is distributed.

Megabyte.   A unit of measure equal to 1024 kilobytes, or 1,048,576 bytes.

Memory.   Parts of the computer or associated devices that can store information or programs. See also *random-access memory* and *disk.*

Menu.   A list of choices that a program gives you on the screen. You select an option by pressing a key or typing a word. Since menus show you all of your choices, they are easier to use than prompts.

Modem.   A device that allows you to communicate with other computers over normal telephone lines.

Monitor. The screen of your computer used for displaying text and graphics.

Monochrome. One color. Monochrome screens are most often black and green, black and white, or black and amber.

Mouse. A hand-held hardware device used for moving the cursor around on the screen.

Multitasking. The ability to run several programs at the same time on one computer.

Multiuser. The ability for many people to run programs simultaneously on one computer.

Operating system. The program that controls your computer and allows you to run other programs.

Output. Information that is generated by a program. As a verb, output means to generate information. Also called writing.

Parallel port. A printer port that uses a protocol that sends and receives information at the same time. See also *serial port.*

Parent sub-directory. A sub-directory that is hierarchically above another sub-directory in the directory tree. See also *child sub-directory.*

Parity. A protocol used when two hardware devices communicate. Parity is used to increase the chance that each byte sent is correct.

Path. A description of how one sub-directory is linked to another directory or sub-directory.

Path name. The name MS-DOS uses to describe the connection between a sub-directory and the root.

PC-DOS. A variation of the MS-DOS operating system used on the IBM PC.

Percent sign. A symbol (%) used in batch files to indicate a replaceable argument.

Peripheral. A piece of hardware that you add to a computer. Some common peripherals are printers and modems.

Pipe. A connection between two programs in which the output of the first program is used as the input of a second program.

Plotter. A device, similar to a printer, that draws graphics images with a pen.

Pop-up window. A "mini-screen" that appears temporarily on your screen. Pop-up windows usually contain menus of choices.

Port. A plug on your computer to which you can connect a device like a printer or modem.

Programmable key.   A key on the keyboard whose function you can change. For instance, you can change a programmable key to type out the word PRINT when it is pressed.

Prompt.   A message printed out when MS-DOS or a program is waiting for you to type in a command. MS-DOS's default prompt is A>.

Protocol.   A standard method used by hardware devices to communicate.

Public domain software.   Software that is not copyrighted and is available for free.

Question mark.   A symbol (?) used in a file specifier as a wild-card character. The question mark can substitute for any one character at the position at which it appears. The asterisk is another wild-card character.

Queue.   A list of files waiting to be printed.

RAM disk.   A method for making MS-DOS treat part of your RAM as a disk drive.

Random-access memory (RAM).   The memory chips that hold the information your computer uses.

Read only memory (ROM).   Memory that you can only read from, but not change. ROM is used to hold small programs that never change.

Record.   A single collection of information in a data base. A record is made up of fields.

Redirected input.   Data that are normally typed on the keyboard but that are retrieved from a file instead. A program that uses redirected input reads the file instead of the keyboard for its input.

Redirected output.   Characters that are normally displayed on the screen but are stored in a file instead. A program that uses redirected output writes characters to a file instead of displaying them on the screen.

Relational DBMS.   A data base management system that can relate the information in one file with the information in different files.

Relative path name.   A path name that shows how a sub-directory is linked to the default sub-directory.

Removable hard disk.   A hard disk that has removable magnetic media.

RESET button.   A button or switch on your computer that causes the hardware to act as if the computer were turned off and on again.

Resident program.   A program that remains in RAM after it is loaded.

Root directory.   The base directory of a tree. When MS-DOS is first booted, the root directory is the default sub-directory.

Screen-oriented editor.   A text editing program that uses most of the lines of the screen to display a file as you edit it. In contrast, see *line editor.*

Scroll.   To move through a text file line by line.

Search order.   The order in which MS-DOS looks for command files. The search order is set and displayed with the PATH command.

Sector.   A portion of a track on a disk. There are a fixed number of sectors per track. See also *track*.

Serial port.   A port that uses a protocol to send and receive information at different times. See also *parallel port*.

Shareware.   Software that is available for free and can be given away to other people. The authors of shareware programs request a donation from people who use them.

Shell.   A program that acts as an intermediary between the user and the operating system.

Software.   Computer programs that perform tasks like word processing and accounting.

Spreadsheet program.   A program that calculates numbers on a grid similar to an accountant's spreadsheet. When a part of the grid is changed, other parts of the grid that are related to the changed part are automatically updated.

Stop bits.   A protocol that tells how many bits of information in the communications stream follow the data bits.

Streaming tape drive.   A tape drive used to copy data from and to disks.

String.   A sequence of characters. Strings are used in some MS-DOS commands to give the command a piece of text.

Structure.   The overall organization description of a data base.

Sub-directory.   A directory that is hierarchically below another directory (see also *tree-shaped directory*). Version 2 of MS-DOS permits you to subdivide the directory on your disk into sub-directories.

Sub-program.   A small part of a larger program. Sub-programs have individual functions that are used by other programs.

Support chip.   A chip that helps the CPU do less processing, thus making the computer run faster.

Syntax.   The standard order in which the arguments of a command must be given.

System disk.   A disk that is used to boot MS-DOS. The distribution diskette for an application program may also be called a system diskette.

System files.   Files that are used only by MS-DOS.

System settings.   Characteristics of MS-DOS that you set with MS-DOS commands (such as VERIFY).

Template.   A generic copy of an application into which information can be placed like a fill-in-the-blanks form.

Terminal emulator.   A program that mimics the actions of a terminal.

Text editor.   A program that allows you to create and change the contents of a text file.

Time-out error.   An error that occurs when MS-DOS tries to send information to a port, but does not receive confirmation that the port is ready.

Track.   A concentric ring on a disk, similar to a groove on a record.

Tree-shaped directory.   A system for organizing files on a disk. A tree-shaped directory has sub-directories branching off of the root directory.

Upgrading.   Adding hardware to your computer to increase its versatility or capacity.

Utility program.   A specialized program that helps you work with other programs (for example, a debugging program). Utilities are similar to tools in a tool set.

Version.   The number assigned to the current revision of a piece of software.

Volume label.   An area on a disk that holds the name of the disk.

What-if calculation.   A calculation in which you can change some of the assumptions. After computing the answer to an equation, you can change the value of one of the variables and rerun the calculation.

Wild-card character.   A symbol used in a file specifier to match any character at the position where it appears. See also *question mark* and *asterisk*.

Word processor.   A program that lets you edit and format text.

Write-protect.   A procedure that prevents a disk from being written on. This is usually done by covering the write-protect notch of a diskette.

Write-protect notch.   The notch on the upper right side of a 5 1/4-inch disk. When the notch is covered, no information can be written on the disk.

TRADEMARKS

The italicized names are trademarked products of the corresponding companies, with registered trademarks noted with an ®.

1-2-3	Lotus Development Corp.
1 Dir	Bourbaki, Inc.
87 BASIC	MicroWare
ABSTAT	Anderson-Bell
APL*Plus®/PC	STSC
Apple®	Apple Computer, Inc.
ASCOM	Dynamic Microprocessor Associates, Inc.
Atari	Warner Communications
AutoCAD	Autodesk, Inc.
Benchmark®	Metasoft
C86	Computer Innovations, Inc.
CADPLAN	Personal CAD Systems
CalcStar	MicroPro International Corp.
CBASIC-86	Digital Research
CBASIC Compiler	Digital Research
Commodore	Commodore Business Machines, Inc.
Context MBA	Context Management Systems
CP/M®	Digital Research
Crosstalk XVI	Microstuf, Inc.
C-window	C-Systems
Data Design	Insoft
dBASE II	Ashton-Tate
Delta Drawing	Spinnaker Software Corp.
Desktop Accountant	Rocky Mountain Software Systems
Disk Mechanic	MLI Microsystems
EasyWriter	Information Unlimited Software
EnerGraphics	EnerTronics Research, Inc.
FriendlyWare	FriendlySoft, Inc.
Global Thermonuclear War	Omnisoft Corp.
Hyperion	Bytec-Comterm, Inc.
IBM®	International Business Machines, Inc.
IBM® PC/XT	International Business Machines, Inc.
InfoScope	Microstuf, Inc.
InfoStar	MicroPro International Corp.
Janus/Ada®	RR Software
KnowledgeMan	Micro Data Base Systems
Micro 16	Fujitsu
MicroStat®	ECOsoft
Microsoft® Word	Microsoft Corp.
Millionaire	Blue Chip Software
Mousekattack	Sierra On-Line, Inc.
MS-DOS®	Microsoft Corp.
Multiplan	Microsoft Corp.
Number Cruncher	Pyramid Data
PC Logo	Harvard Associates, Inc.
PC/FORTH	Laboratory Microsystems, Inc.
PeachText 5000	Peachtree Software
Perfect Filer	Perfect Software
Perfect Writer	Perfect Software
PFS:® File	Software Publishing Corp.
PFS:® Graph	Software Publishing Corp.
PFS:® Report	Software Publishing Corp.
PFS:® Write	Software Publishing Corp.
Planetfall	Infocom
Project Scheduler	Scitor Corp.
ProKey	RoseSoft, Inc.
Radio Shack®	Radio Shack, A Division of the Tandy Corp.
Model 2000	
Rainbow 100	DEC
ReadiWriter	ReadiWare Systems
RealWorld	MicroBusiness Software
Savior	Omega MicroWare, Inc.
Starcross	Infocom
SuperCalc® 3	Sorcim Corp.
SuperWriter	Sorcim Corp.
Symphony	Lotus® Development Corp.
Textra	Ann Arbor Software
The Final Word	Mark of the Unicorn
Think Tank	Living Videotext, Inc.
T.I.M.®	Innovative Software
TK!Solver	Software Arts, Inc.
TRS-80	Radio Shack, A Division of the Tandy Corp.
UNIX	AT&T Technologies
VisiCalc®	VisiCorp
VisiWord	VisiCorp
Volkswriter®	Lifetree Software
WordPlus	Professional Software, Inc.
WordStar®	MicroPro International Corp.
WordVision	Bruce & James Program Publishers, Inc.
Zork®	Infocom

INDEX